Pilot John G. Hamilton on the wing of the bridge of the *Peter Stuyvesant* berthed at the Delaware, Lackawana, and Western Railroad terminal at Hoboken, New Jersey to receive two trainloads of guests from the Scranton-Wilkes Barre area for a spring trip up the Hudson in June 1945. (Author's collection)

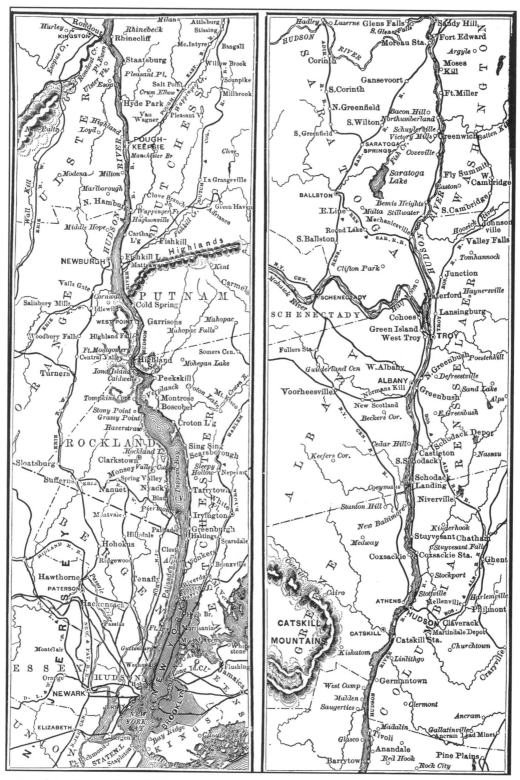

Map of the Hudson River 1875.

Hudson River Pilot

From Steamboats to Super Tankers

By Captain John G. Hamilton

Black Dome Press Corp.
1011 Route 296
Hensonville, New York 12439
Tel: (518) 734-6357
Fax: (518) 734-5802
www.blackdomepress.com

Published by

Black Dome Press Corp.
1011 Route 296
Hensonville, New York 12439
Tel: (518) 734-6357
Fax: (518) 734-5802
www.blackdomepress.com

ISBN 1-883789-29-X

Library of Congress Cataloging-in-Publication Data:

Hamilton, John G., 1913-
      Hudson River pilot : from steamboats to super tankers / by John G. Hamilton.
         p. cm.
      ISBN 1-883789-29-X (trade paper)
      1. Hamilton, John G., 1913- 2. Pilots and pilotage—Hudson River (N.Y. and
N.J.)—Biography. 3. Pilots and pilotage—Hudson River (N.Y. and N.J.)—History—20th
century. 4. Hudson River (N.Y. and N.J.)—Navigation—History—20th century. 5. River
boats—Hudson River (N.Y. and N.J.)—History—20th century. I. Title.

VK140.H244 A3 2001
386'.35—dc21
[B]
                                                                    2001043123

Cover: *Alexander Hamilton* running as a daily round-trip excursion steamer between New York and
Poughkeepsie following the demise of the Hudson River Day Line. The *Hamilton* is on a southbound approach
to the Bear Mountain Park pier, having just passed under the Bear Mountain Bridge. (Oil painting by William
G. Muller)

Design by Carol Clement, Artemisia, Inc.
Printed in the USA

Dedication

I dedicate this book to my extended family: my parents; Captain Melvin Eckerd Hamilton and Catherine Barton Hamilton; my wife, Norma Frances Hamilton; our children; John Gerard, Patricia Ann, Melanie Frances, Charles Richard, and Terry Maria; and to our fourteen grandchildren and (as of this date) fifteen great-grandchildren.

Day Line steamer *Robert Fulton* southbound and nearing Indian Point in 1940. (Oil painting by William G. Muller)

Acknowledgments

I wish to express my sincere thanks and give special credit to the great Hudson River steamboat historian, the late Donald C. Ringwald, whose three books, *Mary Powell—Queen of the Hudson*, *Hudson River Day Line—The Story of a Great American Steamboat Company*, and *Steamboats for Rondout* gave me many hours of enjoyable reading and greatly increased my knowledge of events that occurred prior to my birth.

I thank author Arthur G. Adams, whose excellent book, *The Hudson Through the Years*, is, in my mind, outstanding in its wide coverage of Hudson River Valley history. In addition, his advice and guidance to me, a novice in the field of writing, was invaluable as I sailed the unfamiliar waters leading toward publication.

My friend and fellow Cornellian, the late Captain Bill Benson's articles in the *Kingston Daily Freeman* and his "Heard on the Fantail" column in the quarterly Steamboat Bill Journal published by the Steamboat Historical Society of America, dealt with a lot of the information that I have incorporated into this book. However, I must add that much of the same historical information has come to me from many of the same sources that Bill used. But as a year-round working boatman for over 50 years, I never intended to publish this knowledge until I was urged to do so at this late date, at age 87, by my son John.

I am grateful to the Steamship Historical Society for permission to reprint portions of two articles: "Saugerties Evening Line," by John S. Overbagh & Donald C. Ringwald (#145, Spring, 1978), and "Heard on the Fantail," by William O. Benson (#157, Spring, 1981).

Pertinent information in my book has been gained through over a half century of active service as a Hudson River master and pilot and through almost 300 years of direct family association with Hudson River water transportation.

This book contains anecdotes from many personal conversations that I have had with my employer, Alfred Van Santvoord Olcott (past president and owner of the Hudson River Day Line, and later a member of the New York State Board of Commissioners of Pilots while I was president of the Hudson River State Pilot Association); with Fred Coykendall, my employer and friend, president of the Cornell Steamboat Company; and with the late Mr. Carl Crosby, my employer and superintendent of the Trailerships, Inc., who also once served in the same capacity for the Hudson River Night Line.

This work includes information from my dad, Captain Mel Hamilton, my grand uncle, Captain Harvey Hamilton, and many other uncles, cousins, and other relatives, all river boatmen from both my father's and mother's families.

Conversations with the following Hudson River captains, pilots and engineers were also productive: Carl Barnes, John Barton, Bill Burlingham, Frank Briggs, George Carroll, Thomas Brennan, Sr., John Cullen, Ira Cooper, John Dearstyne, Jr., John Hickey, Aaron Relyea, George Reitnauer, Maurice Howard, Clarence Plank, Francis Chapman, Harry Kellerman, Charles Holliday, Richard Howard, Howard Palmatier, DeForrest Rainey, Melvin Van Woert, Fred Parslow, Alexander Hamilton, Alfred Walker, William Barnett, George McCabe, Harold Dederick,

Barney McGooey, Nat Dunn, Jerry Brennan, Charles Barton, Ned Bishop, William Whitmore, and my brother, Melvin Francis Hamilton.

I would also like to acknowledge the information I received in conversation with Frank Dunham, manager of the Port of Albany; Roger W. Mabie, grandson of William H. Mabie, 1st pilot of the *City of Kingston*; Mary Elizabeth Hamilton, my grandmother; and Margaret Hamilton, my aunt. Additional information was found in the writings of Edward J. Reilly of the *Marine News;* Ruth Boyce, the Monroe bureau chief of the *Times Herald Record*; and Wayne Hall, the Newburgh bureau chief of the *Times Herald Record.*

I owe a further debt of gratitude to Roger Mabie for providing some of the photographs included in this book and graciously agreeing to proofread a manuscript copy. I also wish to thank the proofreaders at Black Dome Press—Matina Billias, Larry Bauer, John Poelker, the late Patricia H. Davis, and copyeditor Steve Hoare—for their diligent work.

I wish to especially thank my eldest son, John G. Hamilton, Jr., who, after his recent move to Florida upon retirement, urged me to write this book and helped in its composition.

I thank my dad, Captain Melvin E. Hamilton, from whom I learned steamboating from the bottom up, which was so useful as I climbed the steamboat ladder of life.

As I finish writing this book I wish to thank all those who gave me the opportunity to advance in my chosen profession (one in which I was never out of work for even one day), where I was able to take care of my family—daughters Patricia Ann, Melanie Frances, and Terry Maria, sons John Gerard Jr. and Charles Richard, and my loving wife, Norma—both spiritually and financially.

Hudson River steamboat *Mary Powell* rounding Dunderberg Mountain on her morning run to New York City in 1885. The towing steamer *Norwich* with a tow of canal barges is on the right. (Oil painting by William G. Muller)

Chronology of the Life of Captain John G. Hamilton

1913   1 October. Born at Union Hill, New Jersey, to Melvin Eckerd and Catherine Barton Hamilton.

1919-1928   On vacations from grammar and high school, made many trips with his dad, Captain Melvin Hamilton, on Cornell vessels, giving him the opportunity to discuss Hudson River history with many old-time river boatmen. Spent summer vacations with his Grandma Hamilton in Port Ewen, New York.

1928   Completed sophomore year at Ridgefield Park High School, New Jersey.

1929-1931   At age 16, went to work full time on Cornell Steamboat Company tugs. Served as a deckhand for his dad aboard *Jumbo* and *Hercules*, and on *Perseverance* where he served as deckmate.

1932   At age 19, received Second Class Pilot's license for the Hudson River, New York Harbor, East River, Kill Van Kull and Newark Bay. Was assigned as pilot of Cornell #41, but shortly thereafter became pilot of the tug *Jumbo*.

1934-1942   At age 21, received First Class Pilot's license; at age 25, obtained Master's (Captain's) license for all lakes, bays, sounds and rivers within the United States, which was later upgraded to vessels of any tonnage and unlimited draft. During this period, served as pilot and/or captain of the Cornell tugs *Jumbo*, *Pocahontas*, *Lion*, *Perseverance*, *Stirling Tompkins*, and *Geo. W. Washburn*.

1938   23 January. Married Norma Frances Sowa. At this time, there were three crews assigned to each vessel. Crewmembers worked aboard the vessel around the clock, six hours on and six hours off, for two weeks, then had one week off. Because of a shortage of licensed personnel, however, this did not always work well. Hamilton and his new bride returned from their honeymoon on February 5th. Mrs. Hamilton left for her job at the *Hudson Dispatch* newspaper the next morning, and Captain Hamilton got an emergency call from Cornell to return to work that afternoon. They did not see each other again for six weeks.

1938-1944 During this period, three of the Hamiltons' five children were born: John on November 22, 1938; Patricia on July 27, 1942; and Melanie on April 28, 1944. They built their first house in Teaneck, New Jersey, in 1940.

1944-1948 Joined the Hudson River Day Line and served as Second Pilot on the *Peter Stuyvesant* under Captain Frank Briggs, with First Pilot De Forest Rainey. Rainey became ill the second day of the second season Hamilton was on board, and never returned. Briggs and Hamilton agreed that Hamilton would be the only pilot on board in Rainey's absence so that Rainey would receive his full salary for the remainder of the year. The Hamiltons' second son, Charles, was born on April 29, 1947.

1948 Left the Day Line to become captain of the trailership *Albany*.

1950 Hamilton was chosen and approved for membership in the Hudson River Pilots Association. These pilots were engaged in navigating large, deep-draft ocean vessels from the Narrows to the Port of Albany.

1950-1976 As a Hudson River Pilot, Hamilton handled an average of over 75 ships a year.

1956 1 May. The Hamiltons' youngest daughter, Terry, was born.

1957-1969 Served 12 years on the Executive Committee of the Hudson River Pilots Association, and as president. He was most influential in convincing the membership to become New York State licensed pilots, supervised by the Board of Commissioners of the State of New York, and he worked with the New York State Legislature to formulate a state pilot bill. Governor Nelson Rockefeller signed the bill into law on April 22, 1959. At Hamilton's suggestion, two-way walkie-talkie bridge radios were carried aboard ship by pilots to add to navigational safety. He convinced the Board of Commissioners to shorten the length of the piloting voyage of the Hudson River State Pilots by moving the beginning point of their responsibility from Staten Island to Yonkers. Sandy Hook pilots agreed to lengthen their jurisdiction to Yonkers. Hamilton also spearheaded the building of a new pilot launch for the Yonkers Pilot Station. He drafted and won approval for an excellent pension plan for all Hudson River State Pilots. Declined nomination for president in 1970.

1976 1 November. Captain John Hamilton and his wife retired to Florida.

1979 1 February. Melvin F. Hamilton, Captain John Hamilton's brother, retired as a Hudson River State Pilot, thus ending more than 240 years of Hamilton family members making their livelihood on the Hudson River.

2001 Publication of first book, *Hudson River Pilot* (Black Dome Press).

Preface

While many writers seek material for their books through long tedious hours of research and expensive travel, I have had the material for my book available in my memory. Circumstances brought me in close touch with the river and the men who worked upon it. I have had conversations with men whose lives on the river began in the 19th century. As a young schoolboy on vacation sailing with my dad aboard his vessel, I had the opportunity to speak to many oldtimers on various types of river vessels who were eager to tell "Captain Mel's" son stories about the river and its changing moods. Records kept by my family documenting almost 300 years of association with Hudson River vessels further strengthened my undertaking.

No book previously published about the Hudson River has been written by a pilot and master holding a federal license (issued originally by the U. S. Department of Commerce, and now by the U. S. Coast Guard) and a New York State Pilot License issued by the Pilot Commission of the State of New York.

The term *pilot* on the Hudson River includes two categories of trained individuals. First, there are the pilots aboard a vessel who are part of the regular crew of officers. These include the pilots who were aboard the large night boats like the *Berkshire, Fort Orange, Trojan, Rensselaer, Benjamin B. Odell, Clermont,* etc. These boats carried a captain and 1st and 2nd pilots. The 2nd pilot navigated the first watch after leaving the pier and brought the ship half way to its destination. The 1st pilot served the second or graveyard watch, so-called because this watch was often subject to bad weather and fog. These officers lived aboard the vessel they served.

The Day Line steamers like the *Washington Irving, Hendrick Hudson, Robert Fulton, Alexander Hamilton, DeWitt Clinton,* etc., also carried a captain and a 1st and 2nd pilot as members of the crew of officers. Both pilots, however, were always in the pilothouse alternating at the helm, although the 1st pilot usually guided the vessel to and from the docks en route. The pilots lived aboard, with the exception of a few like me who went home at night when the vessel was berthed in New York.

The towboats and tugs carried a captain and a pilot. Both worked two six-hour watches in a twenty-four-hour period. The captain worked from 6:00 AM to 12:00 noon, and again from 6:00 PM to midnight, while the pilot worked from 12:00 noon till 6:00 PM, and again from midnight till 6:00 AM. These officers lived aboard their vessel.

The second category of pilot to be mentioned is the *ship pilot*. Unlike the first category, who hold only a Coast Guard Federal License, the ship pilot holds two licenses, a Federal License issued by the U. S. Coast Guard, and a State License issued by the Board of Commissioners of Pilots of the State of New York.

When navigating a vessel flying the American flag between two United States cities (say, from Houston, Texas, to Albany, New York), the Hudson River State Pilot navigates the vessel, documented as being under "enrollment," under his federal license, the same license as the first type of pilot mentioned, although the tonnage on the license may vary. For the ship pilot, tonnage is unlimited. Should the same vessel sail foreign (say,

Pilot De Forest Rainey in the pilothouse of the *Peter Stuyvesant* approaching the Poughkeepsie railroad bridge in September 1944. (Author's collection)

son trying to guide a vessel without local knowledge could ground a vessel and block the channel for days or weeks, thereby disturbing American commerce. These rules remain in effect to this day.

The flag of the country that is the homeport for the ship flies from the stern. The *H* flag (half-white and half-red vertical), signifying that a pilot is aboard, flies from the forward mast.

When I was a very young boy visiting my Hamilton and Barton grandparents, both of whom had homes along the Hudson in Port Ewen, New York, or when I was swimming at the foot of the hill at Tony's Beach, I would see in the distance one of the Day Line's steamers landing at Kingston Point. The vessel would be disembarking passengers from upriver towns, who, after picnicking at the park, would return home on the upbound Albany boat later that day. In addition, the vessel would be loading passengers for down-river landings. As the beautiful, white, paddle-wheel steamboat passed speedily downstream sending large breakers on the beach, much to the delight of the swimmers, my hope was that one day I would serve as an officer on one of these vessels. I guess this was not an unusual thought for young boys in the Hamilton family. My dad, grandfather, great-grandfather, etc., all the way back to 1712, had all followed the river.

My dream came true in my early 30s when I became pilot of the Day Liner *Peter Stuyvesant*, the first screw propeller boat built for the line. Captain Frank Briggs, a very fine native of Coxsackie, New York, and a true shipmate, was her master. I spent one of the happiest periods of my life on the river with him and the *Stuyvesant's* crew. Even after I left to become master of the trailership *Albany*, and then was chosen to be a member of the Hudson River State Pilot Association, the friendships I made on the *Stuyvesant* remained strong.

When I first began working full time on the river in 1928, it was bustling with activity as a main

from Albany, New York, to Naples, Italy), the vessel is now documented under "registry," and the ship pilot uses his New York State Pilot License. When a ship pilot boards a ship flying the flag of any foreign country in the world, he again is piloting the vessel under his New York State Pilot License, regardless of the Hudson River port from which the ship sails or its destination anywhere in the world.

These marine rules were brought about by the Second Congress of the United States to protect the safety of navigation in harbors and on certain inland rivers of the United States. An inexperienced per-

Original sketch circa 1959 of the Hudson River State Pilot Association emblem. (Courtesy of Jim Sherman, son of Captain Dick Sherman)

highway of transportation to the north and west. Long luxurious night boats carried passengers and freight between New York City, Albany, and Troy. Smaller vessels served Coxsackie, Hudson, Catskill, Hyde Park, Highland, Poughkeepsie, Milton, Marlboro, New Hamburgh, Beacon, Newburgh, Haverstraw, Ossining, and Yonkers.

The great White Flyers of the Hudson River Day Line sped daily during their season between New York City and Albany, stopping at Yonkers, Indian Point, Bear Mountain, West Point, Newburgh, Poughkeepsie, Kingston Point, Catskill, and Hudson.

The gigantic fleet of tugs and towboats of the Cornell Steamboat Company, the largest towboat company in the world, plied the river daily with large flotilla tows. Towboats used rope hawsers or flexible cables to tow an average of 50 or 60 units or more made up of scows and barges carrying coal, grain, bricks, crushed stone, cement, ice, hay, sand, etc. At night, with the required lights on all units,

the tows looked like small cities moving up and down the river.

Numerous cross-river ferries connected villages and cities on the opposite banks, and many small commuter lines operated in the lower river.

This is now all in the past. Travel on the river is now limited to a few tugs and barges, large deep-draft ocean vessels, and recreational craft.

In my years of service, the topography of the Hudson Valley has changed little. Sure, there has been some disturbance of the terrain by quarries, power plants, and some ugly bridges; and I will always miss the magnificent steamboats. Through all these changes, the river of today still remains beautiful and majestic.

I am grateful and proud that I had the opportunity to earn my livelihood on this great river, doing a job I wanted to do since I daydreamed it as a young boy. The friendships that I made and kept for so many years among my peers remain treasured memories.

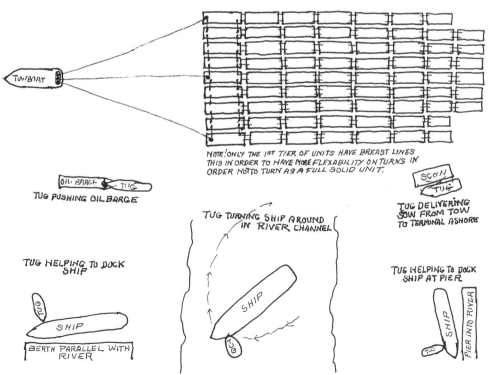

Sketches related to the duties of towboats and tugs on the Hudson River. (By the author)

Have you seen ...
by Captain John G. Hamilton

Have you seen ...

... moon beams on the smooth water of Newburgh Bay on a still night?

I have.

... the bright sun rising over the towers of New York after an overnight trip from Albany, or the evening sun looking like a ball of fire sitting over Storm King Mountain?

I have.

... the reflection of a brightly lit church shining out upon the river during evening services?

I have.

... the bright lights of New York Central's *Twentieth Century Limited* streak by, winding along the river's banks?

I have.

... a familiar sight during a break in the fog assuring you of your location, that you are right on the proper course?

I have.

... a smile in the pilothouse as your whistle's echo bounces off an object just at the right moment in the fog?

I have.

... the bow of a ship under your command sailing through a snowstorm on a crisp winter day?

I have.

... crowds of happy people disembark at Kingston Point and Catskill, heading for their mountain vacations?

I have.

... bathers frolicking on the beach awaiting the vessel's wake ("rollers," as they called them), shouting " Make them big!"

I have.

... a waving white towel or a flashing light in response to a whistle salute as you pass a family home?

I have.

... a brightly lit steamboat as you pass it on a dark night?

I have.

... a couple kissing on the bow of the deck below, perhaps honeymooners?

I have.

... a deer swimming across the river just ahead?

I have.

Have you ever ...

     ... listened to the conversations in the pilothouse and marveled at the stories told?

           I have.

     ... felt the loss of a fellow boatman with whom you have spent many hours in the pilothouse on dark nights when it seemed the two of you were the only people on God's earth?

           I have.

     ... heard the bells ringing loudly calling the monks to prayer at the Capuchin monastery near Garrison?

           I have.

     ... been angered by the folly of a speedboat operator towing a skier round and round a moving vessel?

           I have.

     ... watched deer run on the ice begging for food alongside a ship?

           I have.

     ... smelled the fragrance in the mid-river reaches during fruit season?

           I have.

     ... experienced the breathtaking beauty of the fall colors on the hillsides from the deck of a moving vessel?

           I have.

     ... seen the man of the mountain in deep slumber atop the Catskills?

           I have.

     ... remembered your father teaching you all the ins and outs of Hudson River navigation and the handling of different types of vessels?

           I have.

     ... waved at your father, captain aboard the tug *Jumbo*, while passing Esopus light as the pilot of the *Peter Stuyvesant,* and learned upon arrival at New York that he had passed away from a heart attack two hours later?

           I have.

Table of Contents

PART I

The View from the Pilothouse

Esopus Meadow Light as seen from the *Peter Stuyvesant* in July 1945. (Author's collection)

Cunard liner *Queen Elizabeth* docking at Hudson River ocean liner passenger terminals. Already docked are the *Constitution, America, United States*, an aircraft carrier, and the *Mauretania*. (1952 Hudson River State Pilot Association Christmas card, author's collection)

CHAPTER ONE

The River

Henry Hudson, an Englishman sailing for Holland's East India Company, is credited with discovering the Hudson River in 1609. However, Giovanni de Verrazzano, a Florentine in the service of France, explored the entire Atlantic Coast from Maine to North Carolina in 1524 and was probably the first European to venture into the river's mouth, entering lower New York Bay at Sandy Hook. The next visitor was a Portuguese, Esteban Gomez, sailing for Spain in 1525. Circa 1598, several Dutch captains visited New York Bay. The first well-documented visit, however, was by Henry Hudson. He explored the coastline from Nova Scotia to Chesapeake Bay and entered New York Bay on September 3, 1609.

Most historians agree that Henry Hudson and a crew of twenty on his vessel, *Half Moon*, were the first explorers to venture into the depths of the Hudson River Valley. After many anchorages en route, they reached as far north as Overslaugh Bar, located near what is now the city of Albany, one hundred forty-five miles from the Atlantic Ocean. The river was too shallow at that point to proceed further. Hudson anchored, and on September 22nd he sent a party in a small boat further north. The small party continued on to where the Mohawk River, the Hudson's largest tributary, empties into the main stream at what is now Waterford. Henry Hudson realized at that point that he had failed in his original mission to discover a short route to the Orient. He returned down the river and sailed back to the Atlantic on October 3rd.

The Hudson was not always "the Hudson," of course. It has been known by many names. Verrazzano called it the "River of Steep Hills." Gomez named it varyingly "Rio De Gumas" and "Rio San Antonio." Henry Hudson himself called it the "Great River" and "Manhattes," after the Indians who roamed its lower banks. In 1610, the river received its first official name from the Dutch Government "Prince Maurice" or the "Mauritius," after Prince Maurice of Orange. Traders who came to the area in the years following referred to it as the "Groote," "Manhatten," "Nassau," "Noordt" or "Montaigne". We find the first referral to its present name on a chart in 1621, where it is called "Hudson's River."

The Hudson River is considered by many world travelers and ship masters to be one of the most beautiful rivers in the world, rivaled only by the River Platte in Argentina. It is actually a fjord, with a bed of rock along its entire navigable length. Much of the rock is covered by silt from thousands of years of the movement of waters to the sea.

This rock bed is deeper than the existing bottom of the Atlantic Ocean off the North American continent. It is a generally accepted theory that when the last of the great glaciers melted, a great river gushed to the sea cutting deep into the sediment of the ocean floor. This bored a great gorge into the ocean bottom. The gorge, known to this day on charts as the Hudson Trough, extends almost halfway to Bermuda. Geologists call this extension into the sea a "drowned river." Outside

Gee's Point and Magazine Point as seen from the trailership *Albany* southbound during the winter of 1948. (Author's collection)

Storm King Mountain from the stern of the northbound trailership *Albany* entering Newburgh Bay, January 1948. (Author's collection)

the entrance to New York Harbor, this five-and-a-half-mile-wide canyon reaches an amazing depth of 3,600 feet below the bottom of the ocean floor. It is 1,000 feet deeper than the Royal Gorge of Colorado.

The Hudson has its source in Lake Tear of the Clouds at an elevation of 4,293 feet on the Adirondack Mountains' highest peak, Mount Marcy, once called "Tahawas" (the cloud-splitter) by the Indians. The incipient river continues down the mountainside, joining up with the splashing Schroon, Sacandaga, North, and Mohawk Rivers until it reaches the head of tidewater at the Government Dam at Troy, 150 miles from its source. From this point, it flows an additional 160 miles to the sea.

The river becomes a tidal stream at Troy; that is, it flows downstream toward the sea at "ebb tide"and upstream from the sea at "flood tide." The short interval between ebb and flood tides is known as "slack water." The depth of water in the river varies because of the conflicting currents of the tides. The extremes of each are known as "low water" and "high water," and the nautical measurement between each is called "range of tide." In the Hudson River, the range is between three and five feet, depending on location. The range is higher in the narrower areas and lower in the wider areas. In springtime when heavy winter snows are melting, the current coming in from the sea is curtailed and the river may flow mostly toward the sea.

Because the Hudson's currents normally flow both ways (unlike the Mississippi, for example, where currents flow only toward the sea) it is an estuary of the Atlantic Ocean and not a river as we normally know one. As an estuary, the water is salty as far as Poughkeepsie, and fresh from there to its source. However, as the snow melts in the spring, it is possible for the water to be fresh as far south as the George Washington Bridge.

The present Hudson River is not broad for a tidal stream of its length, but it is extraordinarily deep in some places for a river of its width. It reaches its greatest depth, 216 feet, seventy miles from the sea, between West Point (Gees Point) and Magazine Point (Constitution Island). This section is called World's End. However, many shallow areas also exist. In order to accommodate deep draft ocean ships, it was necessary for the U. S. Army Corps of Engineers to dredge a channel 32 feet deep at low water and 600 feet wide through Haverstraw Bay from Long Cove to Grassey Point. Another channel 32 feet deep and 400 feet wide was dredged from Kingston to Albany, a distance of forty-five miles. Much of the area dredged was solid rock, so extensive drilling was required to reach the desired depth. At Albany, a turning basin of the same depth and 1,000 feet wide including the river's width was dug out of the east bank to allow pilots sufficient room to turn large vessels for their voyages back downstream. Vessels measuring over 900 feet long can be turned here.

One of the distinguishing characteristics of the Hudson River is its beautiful and varied natural scenery. There are steep cliffs (the Palisades), followed by the Hudson Highlands from Peekskill to Newburgh. Rolling hills from Newburgh to Kingston lead to the mountain ranges of the

Catskills and Adirondacks and the fertile valleys of the river's upper reaches. It is a river forever different, always beautiful. Its twisting channel gives the impression that it is a continuous chain of lakes and, indeed, it has been nicknamed the "River of Lakes." It always seems to end within eyesight, then another bend reveals another section of this magical river.

HUDSON RIVER ISLANDS

There are 84 islands in the Hudson River totaling 20,453 acres, or slightly less than 32 square miles. Because of their strategic importance, several played important roles in the development of America and its earlier wars; yet, as the automobile came to transform American culture, the islands were bypassed by expressways and super highways. In spite of their obvious recreational potential, they have been virtually ignored.

These islands range in size from Westchester County's Fisk Island, a scant 1/4-acre, to Rensselaer County's Papscanee Island, 672 acres (more than one square mile), formed when several small islands were joined together during the dredging of the channel. The majority of these islands are located between Kingston and Troy, although some of the most important are located south of there-Staten Island, Bedloe's, Ellis, Governor's, Manhattan, Iona, Con's Hook, Constitution, Pollepel (also known as Bannerman) and Esopus. From Kingston to the Government Dam at North Troy, the following islands will be passed: Goose, Rogers, Hudson Middleground, Stockport Middleground, Coxsackie, Rattlesnake, Lighthouse, Bronks, Houghtaling, Mills, Lower Schodack, Shad, Schmerhorn, Poplar, Middle Cow, Upper Campbell, Bear, Beacon, Parrs, Marsh, Pixtaway, Papscanee, Cabbage, Westerlo, Van Rensselaer and Green Island.

The quality and size of the islands changed as American development progressed. In the mid-19th century, Cornelius Vanderbilt's Hudson River Railroad on the east bank and General Horance Porter's and George Mortimer Pullman's (the parlor and sleeping car manufacturer) West Shore Railroad on the west bank helped to turn many islands into peninsulas and marshes. Similarly,

Jumbo at the Poughkeepsie highway bridge, 1947. (Author's collection)

when the United States Army Corps of Engineers dredged the upper river for the deepwater channel, millions of cubic yards of sand joined islands together.

During the Revolutionary War, George Washington became convinced that the defense of the Hudson Highlands was crucial for an American victory. In 1777, British redcoats attacked Stony Point, then an island, and Iona Island. They were badly beaten by the Americans. In an attempt to block British ships from penetrating further upriver, the Americans strung an iron chain across the river between Constitution Island and West Point.

Doctor C. W. Grant began one of the country's earliest experiments in grape growing on Iona Island's rich soil. According to *The Hudson Through the Years* by Arthur G. Adams, "he produced more grape and fruit plants than all other establishments in the United States combined." Iona Island later played an important role in World War Two by serving as a major ammunition depot. A total of 2,300 Navy and U. S. Merchant Marine ships received their ammunition from Iona. Seventy-seven military bases and many foreign flag naval vessels were also served.

Other islands have served a variety of roles. Governor's Island housed America's largest Coast Guard station until recently. The station is now closed. The Statue of Liberty stands on Bedloe's and Ellis Island served as the main point of entry for millions of immigrants from 1892 to 1924. Esopus, Crugers, Constitution, and Cow have navigational aid lights. Bear Island, near Castleton, was the birthplace of the first white child born in the Hudson Valley. Parr's Island, near Glenmont, was known for its motorcycle races. Goat Island is owned by the Boy Scouts of America, and Goose Island near Barrytown claimed Gore Vidal as its owner. The New York State Office of Parks and Recreation has preliminary plans to acquire some islands for recreational uses such as boating and swimming.

NAVIGATION

The maximum draft through the New York-to-Albany dredged channel is thirty-two feet, although various depths in the natural river areas reach much deeper. Unlike many navigable American rivers, the Hudson has a variable bottom made up of sand, clay, mud, and rock. The most notable area of solid rock, encountered when the deep-water channel was being dredged, was the New Baltimore Reach, where they had to drill 32 feet of solid rock 400 feet wide, extending over 1/8 of a mile. The Van Wies Point area, four miles south of the Albany Port, also required substantial drilling through rock.

There are many rock pinnacles rising from the river's bottom but hidden below the surface of the water. There are reefs between Jefferies Point and Spuyten Duyvil Creek, between Iona Island and Bear Mountain, Con's Hook reef (the only ship to hit this rock and sink was a Coast Guard cutter), a reef on the north side of Constitution Island, Diamond reef in mid-river off New Hamburgh, an 18-foot midstream reef off Barnegat, another 18-foot reef midstream off Blue Point, and finally a reef extending south from Esopus Island.

There are two primary things to keep in mind when piloting deep-draft vessels on the Hudson River. A ship with a draft of 32 ft. when entering the Hudson from the salt water sea will increase its draft by 1/4 inch per foot of draft when it sails into the river's fresh water areas. Thus, a ship with a draft of 32 ft. in salt water will draw 32 ft. 8 in. navigating the upper Hudson. Secondly, a ship underway in the confined waters of the Hudson will show little added depth to its stern when sailing at 8 knots or less. However, for every knot of increased speed, the draft of the stern of the vessel increases substantially.

These two factors combined mean that to safely navigate upriver to Albany requires a rising tide and reduced speed in the dredged area north of Kingston. Southbound vessels with 32 ft. of draft must leave Albany between one and two hours after low water at reduced speed, navigating the river's upper reaches on rising tide and passing below Kingston before the next low water.

The average range of tide (the vertical difference between low and high water) at selected Hudson River points is:

	Summer	Winter
Battery, New York City	4.24 ft.	4.37 ft.
Haverstraw Bay	2.88 ft.	2.71 ft.
Kingston	3.46 ft.	3.37 ft.
Hudson	3.91 ft.	3.82 ft.
Albany	4.38 ft.	4.30 ft.

The duration of rise and fall of tide is:

	Rise	Fall
Battery, New York City	6.80 hrs.	6.34 hrs.
Haverstraw Bay	5.51 hrs.	6.91 hrs.
Kingston	5.76 hrs.	6.66 hrs.
Hudson	5.80 hrs.	6.62 hrs.
Albany	5.47 hrs.	6.95 hrs.

Normal velocity of Hudson River tides at midstream is:

	Flood tide (Knots)	Ebb tide (Knots)
Battery, New York	1.5	2.3
Haverstraw Bay	0.8	1.3
Kingston	1.3	1.6
Hudson	1.6	2.0
Albany	0.3	0.8

CANALS

In the 19th century, four major canals poured their commerce into the Hudson River—the Champlain, Erie, Delaware and Hudson, and Morris. The Champlain and Erie handled general cargo, while the Delaware and Hudson and Morris specialized in coal and iron ore. The Delaware and Hudson and Morris canals remained important as long as coal continued to be used as a heating fuel and until railroads reached their full potential. The importance of the Erie and Champlain Canals, now known as the New York State Barge Canal System, to the development of New York City cannot be overemphasized.

Work began on the Erie Canal with the full support of Governor DeWitt Clinton and the New York State Legislature on July 4, 1817. President Thomas Jefferson said, "Talk of building a canal over 350 miles long through a wilderness is little short of madness." The project took eight years to complete. Wild "bog trotters," imported from western Ireland, began the job of digging what became known as "Clinton's Big Ditch." The 363 miles from the Hudson River to the city of Buffalo were dug with conventional hand tools of the time. The depth of the original diggings was 4 feet. It was 28 feet wide at the bottom and 40 feet wide at water level. It contained 83 locks built of massive stone. The chambers were 90 feet by 15 feet. (In 1903, the canal was deepened to 12 feet with a width of 100 feet. Locks are now 310 feet long and electronically operated.)

Upon completion of the Erie Canal, a great celebration was held. It began in Buffalo on October 26, 1825, and continued along the canal through what are now the cities of Rochester, Syracuse, Utica, Rome, Schenectady, Troy and Albany, and on to New York Harbor where Governor Clinton poured a keg of Lake Erie water into the Atlantic Ocean, calling it the "Marriage of the Waters."

The financial success of the Erie Canal was immediate. Tolls paid exceeded New York's debt even before the full completion of the canal.

The principal commercial route of the nation, helping to settle and develop New York State and the midwest, was now the Hudson River, Erie Canal and Great Lakes. By 1883, 28,000 men and boys, and 16,000 horses and mules worked on the canal. During an average day, 150 boats reached Albany from the west. From there, they were towed downriver to New York by towboats in large flotilla tows.

In the first quarter of the 20th century, the canal lost a significant portion of its traffic to a modern railroad system that moved 300 freight and passenger trains daily along a route adjacent to the canal, but the canal is still in operation today, moving about 5,000,000 tons of freight on a yearly basis plus numerous pleasure craft. Today, three different modes of transportation parallel each other—canal, railroad, and the New York State Thruway.

Perhaps, the second most active canal in New York State was the Delaware and Hudson Canal that ran from Honesdale, Pennsylvania, to Kingston, New York, a distance of 108 miles. This canal, completed in 1828, was constructed to transport large barges loaded with anthracite coal from the mines of Pennsylvania to the deep waters of the Hudson at Kingston. From there, it was loaded into larger vessels for shipment locally or worldwide. It was 4 feet deep (expanded to 6 feet at a later date), 20 feet wide at the bottom and 36 feet wide at water level. It had 109 locks, 15 aqueducts, and 14 boat basins. It crossed the Delaware River by way of an aqueduct.

The canal bed was lined with clay to prevent seepage and special care was taken to ensure that it would not be undermined by otters, beavers, muskrats, moles, or other aquatic animals. It was considered an engineering marvel of the time and was paralleled by a new telegraph line to be used for dispatching. Philip Hone, a future mayor of New York City, was the first president of the canal company in 1825. Famous engineers such as John Bloomfield Jervis, Horatio Allen, America's first locomotive engineer, Benjamin Wright, a famous surveyor, and John Roebling, the developer of the suspension bridge, worked on the Delaware and Hudson.

The village of Honesdale, named after Philip Hone, was connected to the coal mine by a gravity railroad. The loaded cars rolled to the canal for boat loading. Empties were hauled up to the mine by a combination of cables and winches on inclined planes in steep sections, and by one of the first steam locomotives used in the United States, the *Stourbridge Lion*, in less steep sections.

Manville B. Wakefield in *Coal Boats to Tidewater* reported that on January 6, 1870, 300 boats with cargoes aggregating 37,000 tons were frozen en route in the canal. Rondout (Kingston) docks had 9,000 additional tons stored, and boats there had 4,500 tons more aboard. When the freshet came the following spring, the canal and several bridges completely disappeared. Eight full breaks occurred between Ellenville and High Falls. The towpath was torn away and the surrounding area was severely flooded. Five tenement houses, five private dwellings, two stores, the post office, two hotels, and twenty barns were swept away.

The canal operated successfully until 1898 when parallel railroads put it out of business. It was sold to Samuel D. Coykendall of Kingston, sole owner of the Cornell Steamboat Company, who operated the section between Ellenville and Kingston in order to transport Rosendale cement and general merchandise until 1904, when it was abandoned.

The 107-mile-long Morris Canal between Phillipsburg on the Delaware River and Jersey City on the Hudson River was completed in 1836 in an attempt to invigorate the iron industry. The canal succeeded in restoring prosperity to the industry and so stimulated the growth of Newark, New Jersey, that it doubled its population in five years. This canal was also put out of business by the railroads, in 1924.

The other segment of the New York State Canal System is the Champlain Canal, which connects Troy on the Hudson River to Whitehall on Lake Champlain, a distance of 66 miles. From Whitehall by way of Lake Champlain and the Richelieu River, one has a through waterway to Sorel on the Saint Lawrence River and on to Ottawa and Montreal. This canal is still in operation, used largely to transport petroleum and paper, and for recreational boating by pleasure craft.

BRIDGES

Between the Narrows at Staten Island and the Government Dam at Troy, there are eighteen bridges across the Hudson River's channel.

The Rensselaer and Saratoga Railroad built the first bridge across the Hudson River between Troy and Green Island. It opened on October 5, 1835. On May 10, 1862, this wooden bridge caught fire from the sparks of a locomotive. Whipped by high winds, the fire destroyed 507 major buildings in Troy and killed many people. A new bridge to Troy was built in 1884, and rebuilt in 1925. The most luxurious train between New York and Montreal, the Montreal Limited, operated over this bridge. Rail operations over the bridge ceased in 1963, and it became a highway bridge.

In 1871, a charter was granted to build a railroad bridge across the Hudson River at Poughkeepsie. It took seventeen years to complete because of political and economic factors and because it required the construction of four bridge piers in the navigable Hudson River channel. In 1873, the Pennsylvania Railroad, through its representative, J. Edgar Thompson, bought one million dollars worth of stock in the company tasked with the project, about half of the projected cost. Completion seemed assured; however, with the financial crises of 1873 and the death of Thompson, the scheme collapsed. In 1876, the American Bridge Company of Chicago took over the contract and construction began. Within a year, financing failed. The charter was kept alive, and in 1886 the Manhattan Bridge Company was organized to finance construction. Union Bridge Company built the bridge under a subcontract.

John Flank Winslow, a specialist in steel construction who was also president of the Poughkeepsie and Eastern Railroad, was one of the structural engineers. Winslow had introduced Bessemer process steel to the United States, which he supplied for the Civil War battleship *Monitor*, built in 1862. The new Bessemer process steel was used entirely in the construction of the bridge. Dawson, Symmes, and Usher did the concrete work; Atlantic Dredging and Union Lumber did the falsework (temporary forms and structures). In addition to overcoming the already mentioned hurdles, the engineers had to devise solutions to such physical obstacles as a deep, wide, tidal river, the great depth to the bearing rock, the height of the banks on both sides, and the great length (6,767 feet) of the structure. This length was a record for steel construction at the time. Bridge construction was finished on August 29, 1888. The approaches were ready later that year. The first train proceeded across on December 29, 1888, on tracks 212 feet above the water.

De Witt Clinton passing the George Washington Bridge in the early 1930s. The *Clinton* was laid up and did not run from 1933 through 1938 because of the Great Depression. It was again operated for one season in 1939 because of the New York World's Fair. (Hudson River Day Line postcard, author's collection)

For several years after its opening, the bridge was under the control of the Philadelphia, Reading and New England Railroad. By 1906 the New York, New Haven and Hartford had gained control, and it was used as a fast freight route to Boston to bypass the use of car floats in New York Harbor. For a brief time, it served as a passenger route from Washington, D.C. to Boston via the famous "Federal Express." The completion of the Hell's Gate Bridge across the East River, the building of Pennsylvania Station, and the tunnel from New Jersey helped the Poughkeepsie Bridge lose its value as a passenger train bypass. The bridge remained operational as a freight route until May 8, 1974, when fire damaged the eastern approaches, which were never repaired. Trains were re-routed to the Castleton Bridge, nine miles south of Albany.

For years, the bridge was used by an electric trolley car service that connected the village of New Paltz with the city of Poughkeepsie. The trolley was pushed across the bridge by a steam locomotive, then connected onto the Poughkeepsie City trolley tracks.

My dad had an opportunity to assist in the construction of the Poughkeepsie Highway Bridge, just as years before he had assisted in running the cables for the George Washington Bridge. One of the new abutments had tipped during construction. The *Perseverance* was called in to assist. Dad was the captain of the "Percy" at that time. He put steel towing cables around the abutment, and the "Percy" straightened it right up. Then, they finished filling cement under the abutment, which was surrounded by a steel cofferdam.

When I first came to work on the river, there were only two railroad bridges across the Hudson, at Castleton and Poughkeepsie. During my lifetime, I have seen nine new bridges constructed over the Hudson's waters and two vehicular tunnels underneath.

Steamer *Newburgh* of the Central Hudson Line off Breakneck Mountain, the northern gateway of the Hudson Highlands, showing the Catskill pumping station, part of the water supply system from the Catskill Mountains to New York City, circa 1908. (Roger Mabie collection)

Bear Mountain Bridge, connecting Bear Mountain with Anthony's Nose on the east bank, came first in 1924. This beautiful structure was privately built. At the time, it was the world's largest suspension bridge. The State of New York acquired it in 1940.

The first vehicular tunnel, the Holland Tunnel, named after its chief construction engineer, Clifford M. Holland, was built under the river for the New York-New Jersey Port Authority. It opened in 1927 and connected Canal Street in Manhattan with Jersey City, New Jersey.

The George Washington Bridge opened in 1931, connecting West 178th Street, Manhattan, and Fort Lee, New Jersey. At completion, it was the largest suspension bridge in the world, with a main span of 3,500 feet and 4,760 feet between the anchorages.

The Rip Van Winkle bridge, just above Catskill, is a cantilevered bridge that opened in 1935. It does nothing for the beauty of the area.

The Lincoln Tunnel, connecting Weehawken, New Jersey, with West 40th Street in Manhattan, opened for vehicular traffic in December 1937. This 8,216 foot tunnel was of similar construction and design as the Holland Tunnel. The addition of two additional tubes, one in 1945 and the other in 1957, made it the only three-tube tunnel in the world.

The Tappan Zee Bridge, which connects Tarrytown on the east with South Nyack on the west, is a part of the New York State Thruway. This three-mile-long bridge over water was first opened for traffic in 1955. While it is considered an engineering marvel, I think it destroyed the beauty of the area.

Another ugly bridge opened in 1957 between Kingston and Rhinecliff. It is built of continuous deck design, with several abutments in the river. I suspect it is considered an eyesore by the residents of the beautiful estates on the east bank of the river.

The Castleton-on-Hudson Bridge was built in 1959. It is part of the Berkshire Extension of the New York State Thruway that connects the Thruway with the Massachusetts Turnpike to Boston.

Newburgh and Beacon were connected by a bridge in 1963. The designers do not seem to have given much consideration to the preservation of the scenic panorama of Newburgh Bay.

The Verrazano Narrows Bridge, connecting Staten Island with the Bay Ridge section of Brooklyn, opened in November of 1964. This massive and beautiful structure was built at a natural site for a suspension bridge. In no way does it adversely affect the beauty of the surrounding area. When it was built, its superstructure surpassed the George Washington Bridge as the longest suspension bridge in the world. The center span is 4,260 feet long, with a total length of 13,700 feet.

Needless to say, the building of all these bridges led to the downfall of all cross-ferry traffic on the river.

NAVIGATIONAL AIDS

During my several terms as President of the Pilots Association, I worked closely with the United States Corps of Army Engineers who were in charge of the new thirty-two-foot dredged channels in Haverstraw Bay and from Kingston to Albany. The rest of the navigable river channel has various depths in excess of thirty-two feet, to a maximum of 216 feet between Gees Point and Magazine Point near the West Point Military Academy.

I also worked with the United States Coast Guard in marking the new channels' aids. The lighted aids, floating on water but anchored, are removed during the winter because the ice would move them from their proper location, as happens with the buoys that remain on station. Piloting is

then done by using personal ranges and markings gathered through years of experience.

There were nine lighthouses on the river. Keepers actually lived in them during my time on the river. The first, the Jeffrey Hook Light in New York City under the George Washington Bridge, was built in 1899. Further north are lighthouses at Tarrytown and Stony Point, built in 1883; Esopus Meadow, built in 1891 and rebuilt in 1911; Rondout Creek, at the mouth of the creek at Kingston, built in 1880 and rebuilt in 1913; Saugerties Light, at the mouth of Esopus Creek, built in 1838 and rebuilt in 1934; Hudson, built in 1874; Old Maids Light at Coxsackie Island, originally built in 1820 and replaced in 1939; and Kinderhook Light, built in 1829. These lights had bells to aid a vessel during fog. In addition to these lights, the Coast Guard had numerous steel towers with lights on rock bases, lighted buoys, etc. along the navigable river all the way to the Government Dam and Lock at Troy. The river north of Troy is part of the New York State Canal System.

Many of the lighthouse structures have been abandoned by the United States Coast Guard and taken over by various clubs and societies. Rondout Light at Kingston still maintains its place as an active navigational aid, but it is also a museum telling the story of the lighthouses along the river. The restoration of this building is being accomplished by the Hudson River Maritime Museum and the State of New York.

Hudson-Athens, the other still-active light, is now automated. It is leased to the Hudson-Athens Lighthouse Preservation Society.

The Coast Guard retains a functional light mounted on a small steel tower on the south side of the Esopus Creek across from where Saugerties Light is positioned on the north side. The two-story, stuccoed, red brick Saugerties Lighthouse, with its glass cupola on top, is being restored.

The Old Maids and Kinderhook lighthouses have been removed, and steel towers have replaced them.

Looking upriver from West Point circa 1936. *Hendrick Hudson* southbound. Bannerman's Island and Newburgh Bay in the distance. (Postcard, author's collection)

CHAPTER TWO

A Trip Up River Aboard the *Peter Stuyvesant*

Most of the pilothouse officers of the Day Line fleet lived in upriver towns and stayed overnight aboard the vessels when docked at the New York terminal. They were only able to go home on their one day a week off. There were a few exceptions. Frank Brown the *Hendrick Hudson*'s captain lived on Long Island. George Reitnauer, captain of the *Robert Fulton* had his home in Fort Lee, New Jersey. Frank Briggs, the *Peter Stuyvesant*'s captain, lived in White Plains, New York. And I resided in Teaneck, New Jersey.

One July Sunday in the mid-1940s, my day began with a trip to Bogota, New Jersey's railway station where my wife Norma and I boarded a West Shore Railroad commuter train bound for Weehawken, New Jersey. Norma was making one of her infrequent trips with me. After a twenty-minute train ride, we boarded the railroad's ferryboat, *Niagara*. It was but a short walk from the 42nd Street ferryboat terminal to the Day Line pier at West 41st Street.

It is 8:30 AM. The *Robert Fulton* is just leaving her berth with a capacity load of excursion passengers headed for the Day Line's park at Indian Point. She will deadhead back to New York for another trip north at 1:45 PM bound for Newburgh and return, with a stop at Indian Point to help pick up the excursion passengers. The steamer *Alexander Hamilton*, the 10:00 AM boat to Poughkeepsie with all way stops and return, and my vessel, the *Peter Stuyvesant*, remain at our pier. We are to leave at 9:20 AM for Albany, our usual Sunday trip.

As Norma and I board the vessel's gangway, we meet 2nd mate, John Susic, who is busy with the passenger tally clock, counting heads so that we do not exceed the vessel's capacity of 3,750 passengers. I had previously arranged with the office for Norma to make the trip in one of the vessel's private parlors. It was the Day Line's policy that no women guests were allowed in the pilothouse of a vessel underway, not even officers' wives and Captain Briggs of the *Peter Stuyvesant* certainly adhered to that rule.

We will be sailing on this day with 3,055 passengers on board. Captain Briggs is in the pilothouse at the wheel, while I am stationed on the main deck at the gangway entrance. We are ready to sail promptly at 9:20 AM. I oversee the gangway being taken ashore and check that the lines are taken and stowed onboard. After this is completed, I signal the pilothouse by a bell pull system that we are ready to sail. It was Day Line policy that the master take the vessel into the stream from its New York pier. During all other landings, the roles are reversed; the pilot remains in the pilothouse, and the captain lines up the gangplank at the various piers along the route.

There is a noteworthy difference between maneuvering a large side-wheel paddle steamer and a large single screw propeller vessel when leaving or arriving at a river dock. Leaving New York, a vessel sails from its pier into a cross ebb or flood tidal current. A screw vessel, like the *Peter Stuyvesant*, has steerage immediately because the propeller

Author and wife, Norma, on the bridge of the *Peter Stuyvesant* in 1946. (Author's collection)

thrashes water right against the rudder. This is not so with the large side-wheelers. The pushed water has to go from the paddles mid-ship aft to the rudder before steerage is obtained. Consequently, a side-wheeler leaving its New York berth falls one way or another with the existing tidal current until the actual full steerage maneuverability is reached.

All landings at river ports are made broadside with the vessel's length. Day Line vessels landed in the direction they were headed in either ebb or flood tide. That saved substantial time en route. This procedure is far simpler for a side paddle wheeler than a single screw propeller vessel. The *De Witt Clinton*, a twin screw vessel, could move its propellers back or forward, giving greater maneuverability when docking or leaving.

Although some small side-wheel paddle vessels can move their paddles individually, the large Day Liners could not. When approaching a dock on fair current, the pilot would stop the paddles close to the designated landing. The buckets on the wheels served as brakes. You could actually feel the vessel slow down. Then, the pilot would angle the vessel's bow away from the pier and, at just the right time, back the vessel so that the stern headed at an angle toward the dock. A line was thrown ashore and the bow would fall toward the dock. A quick landing

was accomplished using the experience of the pilot, the ability of the crew, and the natural tendencies of the vessel. When the current was against the vessel, the pilot had to be careful not to angle the vessel's bow too much and let the current get between the vessel and the dock. If it did, the vessel's bow might not line up appropriately or the current could cause the bow to fall away from the dock, making a landing impossible.

The procedure with a large, single screw vessel like the *Peter Stuyvesant* is far different. Most vessels will round up to be against the current to dock. However, this loses valuable time en route. Rounding up at seven way stops would add a lot of additional time to the trip. On a fair current, the pilot must slow and stop the vessel a good distance from the dock and drift with sufficient steerage. If the landing is to be made on the port side, the vessel, when put in reverse, will back toward the pier. When landing on the starboard side, however, it is necessary to skim close to the dock and allow a line to be put ashore before the propeller is put in reverse, because the vessel's stern will now be backing away from the dock. This becomes a precise maneuver accomplished by the pilot on the bridge and the captain at the gangway. We frequently would make the entire trip with only one back at each landing, properly lining up the ship's gangway with the one on the landing.

After we clear our mooring on this beautiful July day, I proceed up to the pilothouse and relieve Captain Briggs of the navigational duties. All Day Line vessels had two pilots as part of the crew. They relieved each other at the steering wheel intermittently. Both were always on duty in the pilothouse except when one was relieved by the captain to go to dinner, etc. During this particular season, DeForest Rainey, the other pilot, became seriously ill and went home on the 2nd day of the season. From that time until mid-September when the *Hendrick Hudson* will lay up and Tom Brennan, one of her pilots will come aboard to help, I am the *Stuyvesant's* lone pilot (with the aid of a quartermaster). Cadet James Maloney, who had been our dining room cashier, was chosen to assist me. DeForest Rainey never returned to duty. He died shortly thereafter.

We are now headed upstream, passing the site at the top of the Palisades where Alexander Hamilton and Aaron Burr fought their tragic duel in 1804. The vessel is proceeding at reduced speed to ease the swells as we pass the yachts moored at the 79th Street Yacht Basin.

We sail along Riverside Park where beautiful slopes covered with grass and trees stretch from Riverside Drive to the riverbank. The Park begins at 72nd Street and its top is lined with beautiful homes, apartment buildings, and monuments. The first residence is owned by Charles M. Schwab. It is one of the finest homes in the United States, an excellent example of the chateau style of architecture. We increase our speed as we pass the Soldiers and Sailors Monument at 86th Street. At 110th Street, we get a glimpse of the giant Cathedral of Saint John the Divine, an imposing Episcopal edifice. A little north of this point, the Riverside Church and some of the buildings of Columbia University come into view. Columbia was originally chartered as Kings College during the time of George II. We pass the tomb of President Ulysses S. Grant at the north end of Riverside Park. This great square structure of white granite cost $600,000 when it was built.

It is now time to reduce speed and make ready for additional passengers at the 129th Street landing. Here, a ferry once crossed the river to Edgewater, New Jersey. This line was abandoned sometime after the George Washington Bridge was built.

Palisades Amusement Park is high up on the Palisades. This park has the usual rides and entertainment, but is most famous for its immense swimming pool. It has its own sandy beach and features a machine that throws swells toward the beach. Had we been on the port side of the vessel, we would have seen the giant Ford Assembly Plant and the Jack Frost Sugar House.

The Day Line steamers operated from mid-May through early October, then went out of service until the following spring. The officers were paid all year. This was a company policy that insured the return of the same experienced officers every season. I always went to work for some other company, however, usually the Cornell Steamboat Company, to supplement my income as we were seven, Norma and I and our five children, and, of course, our Shetland sheep dog, Skipper, who made eight.

One year, Norma and I decided it would be nice if I took a job where I would be able to come home part of every day and night, so I applied for a job with the Public Service Gas and Electric Company of New Jersey, which owned buses and trolley cars throughout New Jersey. In addition to being a utility supplier and a surface transportation giant, the company owned a fleet of ferryboats that ran between 125th Street, New York City, and Edgewater, New Jersey, serving Palisades Amusement Park as well as the northern New Jersey suburbs. They also owned the trolley line that ran from the ferry terminal through Bergen County to Paterson, New Jersey. This job represented a substantial loss of income when compared to Cornell, but I would be home with the family. When the job was offered, I took it.

One evening, about 5:30 PM, I was piloting the ferryboat *Fort Lee* from 125th street to Edgewater. As I approached the ferry slip at Edgewater, I slowed down and entered between the wooden ferry racks. The bow walkways on both sides of the cars and trucks were jammed with commuters waiting to get off. At the appropriate time, I signaled for full reverse of the engine. No response! I then turned to the emergency backup bells. Again, no response. *Fort Lee* was continuing toward the ferry bridge. This apparatus was maneuvered up and down by shore personnel to meet the ferry's level according to the tide. *Fort Lee* continued until it hit the bridge, which, in turn, lifted the terminal's wooden planks into the shape of a pyramid. After the first solid hit, it bounced back, but because the propeller was still revolving forward, it hit it again, and did so several more times until it remained firm against the bridge.

The bow was so packed with people that no one fell or appeared to be hurt. The cars, which were blocked, had not moved sufficiently to damage each other. As was usual in any accident, several claims were made by passengers against the ferry's owners, but none of the claimants prevailed.

The investigation revealed that the engine was caught on center, and the engineer could not reverse it to the backing movement. We were very lucky that the shore personnel had the bridge at the proper tide levels; this could have been a tragic accident had the ferry's bow gone under the bridge. As people went ashore that day, I received many dirty looks, as if the accident had been my fault and not a mechanical problem over which I had no control.

We could unload the passengers, but because of the damage to the bridge and the terminal's roadway planking, we could not unload the vehicles. After a short period of time during which the engine was repaired, we moved to another slip and unloaded the cars and trucks.

We leave 129th Street promptly at 9:40 AM and proceed at full speed. We soon pass the former home of John J. Audubon, the great ornithologist, and a little later, Trinity Cemetery where he is buried. At the same time, we see the buildings of Columbia Presbyterian Medical Center.

Washington Heights runs for a mile or so. On the hill's summit, behind Fort Washington Point (Jefferson Hook), are the remains of a fortification known as Fort Washington. This was the site of one of the bitterest battles of the Revolutionary War. This fort, and Fort Lee on the New Jersey side were built to prevent British vessels from moving upriver.

We are now passing under the George Washington Bridge. When the towers for the bridge had been completed on both the New York and New Jersey shores, the Cornell Steamboat Company tug *Jumbo* (my dad, Captain Mel Hamilton, was her captain at the time) and the tug *Shamrock* ran the cables between the towers that hold the roadway section. This was done by loading the cable drums aboard a scow and pushing it across the river. Patrick McGuire, who owned *Shamrock*, was very active politically in Tammany Hall, so he was extended the honor of participating in the event.

Directly under the bridge is Jefferies Hook Lighthouse, featured in the children's storybook *The Little Red Lighthouse and the Great Grey Bridge* by Hildegarde Swift and Lynd Ward. This structure was the first of many on the river where the keeper and his family actually lived.

On the west side, we see the Palisades which extend 16 miles to Piermont, New York. They form a splendid continuous solid wall featuring some of the river's finest scenery. The wall consists of dark red rock crystallized in columnar forms showing vertical chasms and projections whose upright lines add to the apparent height of its facade. Its highest point is 500 feet above the river, and it is believed to have greater depth below the water line. The narrow space between the Palisades and the river is a park owned by the states of New Jersey and New York.

As we return our glance to the east side of the river, we see plainly some of the buildings of New York University situated some distance back from the river. We also pass a castle-like, large structure at Fort Tryon Park, the Cloisters.

We are approaching Spuyten Duyvil on the right. This stream, known as the Harlem River, connects to the East River at Hell Gate, and together with the Hudson surrounds the island of Manhattan. On the bold promontory just north of Spuyten Duyvil, on Tibbets Hill, stands the monument to Henry Hudson. It was here at the foot of this hill that Hudson had his first fight with local Indians who tried to board his vessel.

The high ground above on the right is Riverdale, the northern end of the Bronx. Here stands the Roman Catholic Convent, Girl's School, and Hospital of Mount Saint Vincent. One residence, known as Font Hill, was built by the American tragedian, Edwin Forrest. It is now part of the convent and headquarters in America of the order of Sisters of Charity of Saint Vincent. The large yellow building nearby is the Leake and Watts Asylum.

We are now approaching Yonkers, the first landing after leaving New York City. Several hundred more passengers are waiting for our arrival. They should fill the vessel to capacity. A close check will have to be kept on the tally clock.

Yonkers derived its name from the Dutch words *Jonk Heers* meaning Young Lords. Yonkers is a thriving city with a population over one hundred thousand. Its commercial establishments include Otis Elevator, hat factories, a sugar refinery, and one of the largest carpet factories in the world, Alexander Smith's. Philipse Manor in Yonkers is one of the last remaining Hudson Valley manor houses and is a museum today. The first American golf course was built at St. Andrews in Yonkers. (The second was Dinsmore's in Staatsburg, New York.)

Across the river from Yonkers is Alpine Landing, which can be reached by the ferry from Yonkers or a road built down the Palisades from Englewood Cliffs, New Jersey. The British General Cornwallis had his headquarters at the Landing during the Revolutionary War.

We are leaving Yonkers ten minutes late because of a delay in loading passengers. We will easily make the time up with a strong flood tide on the long run to Newburgh, our next landing point.

The country north of Yonkers is very beautiful. Many wealthy men established fine estates over-

Norma Hamilton and son, John, in June 1940 atop the Palisades in Weehawken Heights, New Jersey, at the park where Aaron Burr killed Alexander Hamilton in a duel. (Author's collection)

looking the river. Conspicuous among them is the lofty tower of Greystone, formerly the residence of Samuel J. Tilden, once governor of New York State and a candidate for president.

Hastings, the next village we approach, is directly across from Indian Head, the highest point of the Palisades, near which stands a stone called Boundary Monument. It marks the beginning of the boundary between New York and New Jersey. The determination of this boundary came close to causing an interstate war.

Dobbs Ferry's involvement in the struggle for independence is well known. As we cruise by, we see the Washington-Rochambeau Monument, unveiled in 1894, standing before the Livingston Manor House. Here, Washington planned the Yorktown campaign, and it was here he met Sir Guy Carleton of the British Army on May 3, 1783, and arranged for its evacuation from America's shores. Offshore from here, on May 8, 1783, a British war vessel fired a salute in honor of George Washington, the first salute of Great Britain to the sovereignty of our great nation.

I have to slow the *Stuyvesant* down because we are approaching and about to pass the large, powerful, Cornell two-smokestack towboat *Perseverance,* which is southbound with a tremendous flotilla tow of 53 scows and barges. I give my dad, her captain, a salute, and he returns my gesture.

After we clear the tow with little wake, we enter the Tappan Zee (*zee* is Dutch for "sea"), where the river reaches a width of three miles. The Palisades terminate here, and we can see the opening between them and the next elevation where the Sparkill comes down from the western hills to the Hudson. This deep valley gave an outlet to the Erie Railroad and is the place where the first railroad reached tidewater. A long wharf, Piermont Pier, was built over the marshes and extended out to the channel. This pier was used as an embarkation point for U. S. troops during World War I.

Opposite Piermont Pier is Irvington, named after Washington Irving, whose gabled home, Sunnyside is just north of the village. Lyndhurst, the former residence of Jay Gould, the financier, is half a mile further north. It is modeled after the historic Newstead Abbey, the home of Lord Byron.

Many other handsome residences capture the interest of our passengers as we pass. In a matter of minutes, we are abreast of Tarrytown. Our view of this picturesque village is blocked somewhat by the giant Chevrolet assembly plant. Tarrytown is famous for its many old landmarks, elegant modern residences and schools. The best known school is Marymount, a private, Catholic women's college. My granddaughter, Deanna Esposito, is a graduate of this college. The second lighthouse along the Hudson is here, also.

On September 23, 1780, the British officer and spy Major John Andre was captured here by three townsmen. He had hidden in his boots the incriminating documents he had received from the traitor Benedict Arnold regarding the proposed surrender of West Point. A few days later, he was taken across the river and executed at Tappan.

Just above Tarrytown, we cruise by the valley of Pocantico Creek, the mouth of which is marked by Kingsland Point. A glimpse up the valley shows the site of the ancient Philipse house, its antiquated mill, and a famous old bridge. This area is known as Sleepy Hollow and is identified with the Washington Irving legend. The remains of this early American writer rest in the cemetery just beyond and beside an ancient Dutch church built in 1699, the oldest church edifice still in use in New York State. We see it for a brief moment as we sail past. Above Washington Irving's grave, the land rises into a knoll topped by the Delavan family memorial, a tall shaft plainly seen from the river with six marble statues arranged around the pedestal of the column. Near the shore just above Kingsland Point, the splendid home of William Rockefeller comes into view near the riverbank. The estate of his more famous brother, John D. Rockefeller, is among the trees beyond it.

Nyack is the town on the west bank across from Tarrytown. A steam ferry connects the two towns. When Al Walker, once the ferry captain, served with me as pilot of the towboat *Geo. W. Washburn,* he told me that when John D. Rockefeller crossed the ferry in his car, he always tipped the deckhand one shiny new dime.

The high hill that rises abruptly some distance north of Nyack is called Hook Mountain. The devastating hand of the trap rock manufacturer well-

Peter Stuyvesant at the Bear Mountain pier in 1947. Note Iona Island and Dunderberg Mountain in the background. (Author's collection)

nigh destroyed the beauty of this mountain before it was stayed. It was from here that the ice cut from Rockland Lake just over the hill was first shipped by barge to New York City.

We pass Ossining (formerly called Sing Sing, founded in 1826) on our right. We note the grim structure of this state prison with its surrounding walls in plain view at the water's edge. The main line tracks of the New York Central Railroad pass through a tunnel underneath.

A short distance beyond, the Croton River joins the Hudson, and just here Tellers Point projects into the river. The mainland of this cape is Croton Point, and the water between it and the riverbank is called Croton Bay. At this point, the New York Central trains change from electricity to steam, and visa versa. Croton Point separates the Tappan Zee from Haverstraw Bay, a three-and-a-half-mile-wide and six-mile-long expansion of the river.

On September 22, 1780, the British man-of-war *Vulture* lay at anchor in the waters off Tellers Point, waiting for Major John Andre to return from his fatal conference with Benedict Arnold on the opposite side of the river. A party of Americans brought a cannon from Verplanck's Point, which is several miles north, and with it forced the British

vessel to flee downstream. This prevented Andre from returning to his ship. He was captured after crossing the river at Verplanck.

Across the river from Croton Point, the foothills on the western shore rise abruptly to a height of 505 feet in High Tor's prominent peak. Our passengers may be surprised to see a train appear suddenly from its face and race along the ledge. It runs on the tracks of the West Shore Railroad, which has emerged from a tunnel and will follow the river's bank to West Park, New York, where it turns inland to pass over the Rondout Creek Bridge. Major Andre landed just beneath this tunnel. From there, he walked to a house beyond the village of Haverstraw to meet Benedict Arnold.

The slight breeze has died down. We are now sailing through still waters on Haverstraw Bay and passing the village of Haverstraw. This village was once considered the brick making capital of the United States. James Woods discovered the modern way to bake bricks here in Haverstraw. At its peak production, there were 42 brickyards producing 326,000,000 bricks a year. The finished product was shipped daily to the metropolitan areas as part of a Cornell Steamboat Company flotilla tow.

This might be a good time to tell you about the vessel that we are sailing on today, the Hudson River Day Liner *Peter Stuyvesant*, the fleet of which it is a part, and the duties of the crew. The *Stuyvesant*, the first screw vessel actually built for the Day Line, was constructed at the Pusey and Jones Corp. shipyard at Wilmington, Delaware, in 1927. She is 269 ft. 6 in. in length overall, with a 60 ft. beam, and 13 ft. 5 1/2 in. draft. The engine is a triple expansion engine with cylinders 25 in., 40 in., 47 in., and 47 in. by 3 ft., and 4 boilers. The engine develops 2,700 horsepower. The hull is of steel and the deckhouse is made of steel and wood. During this season, Frank Briggs is captain and I am the pilot.

When you come aboard through the main deck gangway, you immediately notice the purser's office situated in the center of the entrance lobby. The dining room is aft, across the full width of the vessel. Just forward of the purser's office, you find the baggage room where trunks and excess baggage checked on the pier and carried aboard by the deckhands are stored. Further forward, at mid-ship, we see the glass-enclosed engine room, which was designed so passengers could view the operation of the propulsion system. Past this point, we enter the forward viewing area, where the main staircase to the upper decks is located. The men's and women's restrooms are located on this deck.

This brings to mind an embarrassing situation that happened to me on one of our voyages. After leaving Newburgh, I had been relieved in the pilothouse by Captain Briggs so that I could go to dinner. My usual practice was to stop in the men's room on the main deck and wash my hands before entering the dining room. On this particular day, a woman passenger stopped me just before I entered the men's room to ask me a question. After answering her, I proceeded to the bathroom. The doors were adjoining, and I mistakenly entered the ladies' quarters. I was in full uniform, and I am sure I was also in full blush. What could I do? Thinking quickly, I pulled a small note pad from the inside pocket of my uniform jacket and walked by several closed stalls, writing on the pad as if I was con-

ducting an inspection. I quickly headed for the door. I don't know if the two ladies who were washing their hands were shocked or not. I never looked back, and I never heard any report of a ship's officer entering the ladies' room.

A walk up the staircase brings you to the second deck. This is called the parlor deck. Its forward area is fully carpeted and lined with plush chairs. The walls are decorated with beautiful paintings. An unobstructed glass-enclosed viewing area with large wooden chairs completely surrounds this deck. A fully stocked souvenir counter is always available. There is an orchestra pit and dance floor aft of mid-ship, centered within the width of the vessel.

The next deck up features another enclosed viewing area forward, with several private parlors lining both sides of the vessel behind it. The pilothouse is on the top deck. Quarters for the captain, pilots, purser, and chief engineers are found aft of the pilothouse. Behind the ship's stack there is a large open deck with folding chairs available.

When the *Stuyvesant* first entered service in May 1927, her theater of operations was the lower Hudson Valley. Folks in the upper valley didn't get a chance to know her until the changing times later resulted in her being used in Albany service. This vessel did not gain whole-hearted, enthusiastic favor when she entered upriver service. She was not designed for through service to Albany, but for lower river, one-day excursion service and for large chartered parties. This screw propeller vessel was something of a shock to passengers who were used to traveling on the side-wheelers with their broad open decks and beautifully decorated roomy interiors.

The deck crew consists of the chief purser and two assistants (the first and second mates), twelve deckhands (sailors whose duties consisted of handling the vessel's lines at terminals, moving the baggage trunks aboard and ashore, and handling the boat's maintenance), a night watchman, two baggage men, and several Day Line cadets. These cadets were usually college students on summer vacation who staffed the souvenir counter and the ship's cafeteria. The cafeteria, located below the main deck, provided guests not wanting a full meal with the opportunity to secure something to eat. Tables and booths were provided. The main dining room staff included a head chef and two assistants, a maitre d' and waiters in mandatory tuxedos. The engine room department consisted of the chief engineer, two assistant engineers, two oilers, and two wipers.

We are now abreast of Stony Point, where one of the most famous battles of the War for Independence took place. On the night of July 5, 1779, the daring soldier "Mad" Anthony Wayne successfully stormed a fortress that had been deemed impregnable by the British. They boasted that it was "a little Gibraltar." Here, too, we can see the third of the Hudson River lighthouses, erected on the site of the battle and built from the stone of the old fortress that was so gallantly captured.

Across from Stony Point, on the eastern shore, we find the historical village of Verplanck Point. In colonial times, the boats of King's Ferry ran across the Hudson between these two points as part of the main highway between New England and the west. This also was where, in 1778, American soldiers trained under Baron von Steuben (later Major General), the German nobleman who offered his services to General Washington. I have to reduce the *Stuyvesant's* speed so that we do not throw too large a wake to the barges tied up awaiting loading at both the Tomkins Cove and Verplanck plants of the New York Traprock Corp.

The two landing piers at Indian Point Park, which is owned and operated by the Day Line, now come into view. The steamer *Robert Fulton* has just left and is deadheading southbound to make the 1:45 PM sailing from New York. As is the practice, the northbound vessel makes the long one-whistle salute, and Pilot Grant Lazatte of the *Robert Fulton* reciprocates.

Abreast of us on the port side between Tomkins Cove and Jones Point is the gigantic fleet of United States government mothballed ships. Later in my career, as a member of the Hudson River Pilot Association, I piloted many foreign flag tugs down the river with one or two of these ships in tow bound for foreign interests, mostly for scrap.

Abreast of us on the starboard side is the village of Peekskill. In 1777, the British landed here and attacked a small American contingent forcing them to retreat. Annsville Creek enters the Hudson here. We can see the grounds of the New York State Military Camp, which is occupied in the summer by different regiments of the National Guard. The mother house of the Sisters of St. Francis, and the giant Fleischmann's plant can also be viewed from the river. Peekskill Military Academy, founded in 1833, is also here. Henry Ward Beecher had a summer home here, and ex-Senator Chauncey M. Depew was born here. Present Governor George Pataki is a native of Peekskill.

We are passing 1,100-foot-high Dunderberg Mountain on the left. Kidds Point is at the foot of the mountain. Legend has it that the notorious pirate Captain Kidd buried some of his treasure here.

After making a sharp turn to the left, we enter the Hudson Highlands. This area presents some of the most beautiful scenery to be found on the whole river. Years later, I heard many masters of foreign flag vessels, after making their voyage to Albany, praise the Hudson as the most beautiful river they had ever sailed on. South of the Highlands, the river's average depth is in the 40-foot range. Now, we cruise into waters of markedly increased depth—91 feet off Dunderburg Mountain, 165 feet off Iona Island, 127 feet off Bear Mountain. The Hudson reaches its greatest depth, 216 feet, at Worlds End in the 450-yard-wide area between West Point and Constitution Island.

We are entering the narrow area between Iona Island and the eastern shore that is called "The Race." The island is occupied by the U. S. government as a naval arsenal and supply depot. The neat workshops and storehouses dominated by a fine tower and the officers' quarters, surrounded by beautiful cultivated grounds, form a charming scene.

Bear Mountain Park is now on the west shore. It has all the vacation facilities—a hotel, restaurant, cafeteria, picnic area, swimming pool, boat livery, anchorage, fishing, hiking, skiing in the winter, etc. There are two landing piers at the water's edge. One was built by the State of New York for use by their excursion steamers, the *Clermont* and *Onteora*, which left Pier 1, the Battery, New York, daily for Bear Mountain. The larger pier was built by the Day Line for the sole use of its steamers. About one and a half hours from now, the *Alexander Hamilton* will drop off thousands of day excursionists. Just behind the flat plateau and lake, Bear Mountain rises to a height of 1,350 feet.

As we approach Anthony's Nose, a sharp blind cove, I blow one long blast of the whistle to signal any southbound vessel that we are approaching. We make a sharp turn to the right, rounding Anthony's Nose, a high promontory (1,228 feet) on the eastern bank. The name is said to have been given by Governor Stuyvesant because Anthony Van Corlear, who accompanied the governor on a sloop voyage to Albany, stood on the deck next to him as they passed the promontory. Anthony had a rubicund nose of unusual size.

We pass under the Bear Mountain Bridge, which was opened to traffic in 1924. It is a 2,257-foot-long suspension bridge with no abutments in the river to hinder navigation. The roadbed, 155 feet above the water, is the lowest point of the Appalachian Trail between Maine and Georgia.

Slightly beyond Bear Mountain and the bridge, Popolopen Creek flows down to the river through a deep ravine. The Popolopen Valley was an early source of iron ore. In colonial times, Fort Montgomery stood on the north side and Fort Clinton on the south. The British under Sir Henry Clinton took both forts in 1777.

We pass Pellwood, the residences of William Pell and John Bigelow, and Cragstone, the residence of J. Pierpont Morgan. Cragstone is partly hidden from view by trees, but its gabled roof and flagpole may be seen. We are now passing Con's Hook Reef and Island. The Coast Guard cutter *Sassafras* ran aground on this reef in January 1969. Mount Sugarloaf is on the east shore.

Comparison is often made between the Hudson River and Germany's Rhine River. The Rhine, above Cologne, is similar, although it has nothing like the Palisades. The mountains that hem the Rhine at Rudesheim and Bingen are just like the Highlands, which are now closing about us. The Hudson does lack the many vineyards seen along the Rhine. (Later in the twentieth century, Hudson Valley wineries became more prominent.) I have sailed both rivers, making the full Rhine voyage by

steamer. Perhaps I am biased, but to me the ever-changing scenery of the Hudson ranks our river superior.

High above the river on the west bank is Ladycliff College, a superior girls' institute staffed by the Sisters of Saint Francis, whose mother house we passed at Peekskill. My children attended the elementary school staffed by the Sisters of Saint Francis in Bogota, New Jersey.

I owned a thirty-six-foot cabin cruiser built by Whalen, an excellent boat builder located on the Harlem River. We named the vessel *Pilot Hi*. The boat slept six and had a nice galley, lounge, and head. We flew a blue pennant flag forward, Old Glory aft, and a red and white "H" flag topside meaning " we have a pilot on board," (something I would venture to say was rarely seen on a small cruiser).

We took trips on *Pilot Hi* up the Hudson River and into the New York State Canal System to Lake Champlain, and down through New York Harbor and the upper and lower bays. One summer vacation, we invited the nuns from our children's school for a sail up the Hudson. On the chosen day, Norma, I, and eight good sisters set sail from the Alpine Boat Basin up the Hudson. We stocked the boat with an abundance of food, beverages, and all sorts of goodies. However, because we had Catholic nuns onboard, we did not bring any beer or liquor. In fact, we usually tried to keep the boat completely free of alcohol.

We traveled as far upriver as West Point, and then turned back down, passing Ladycliff Academy. Much shouting and waving took place from the boat and shore as we stopped our cruiser and lay at full stop in the river for a short period of time just off the site of the Academy. We then sailed downstream to Bear Mountain Park, where the nuns went ashore for a few hours.

We returned to our boat basin at about 9:00 PM. The sisters were very grateful and could not thank us enough. Norma and I felt good that we had the opportunity to show them a good time. Some time later, one of our neighbors mentioned that he had heard how great the nuns were treated by the Hamiltons on the boat outing, with the exception that we had failed to offer them a beer or a cocktail.

As we approach Garrison, we pass the Capuchin Fathers Monastery, while inland on Route 9W may be found Graymoor, the Monastery of the Franciscan Friars of the Atonement. The homes of many prominent families surround Garrison. Near here on Route 9D is Boscobel, a castle-like chateau built between 1806 and 1808 and completely restored in the style of Robert Adam, the famous Scottish architect. This home of States and Elizabeth Dyckman is open to the public. Governor Nelson Rockefeller called Boscobel "one of the most beautiful homes ever built in America."

The U. S. Military Academy is across the river from Garrison at West Point. Buttermilk Falls plummets down to the river on the north side of Ladycliff, and just beyond we find the Thayer Hotel on the south end of the grounds of the Academy.

The Academy, established in 1802, is considered to be the foremost officers' training school in the world. As we approach, we see a terraced mass of buildings, that, in my opinion, are greater and more picturesque than anything along Germany's Rhine. The nearest and lowest is the power house, beyond which the riding school presents a fort-like front. Above that, is the parade ground. The administration building and the beautiful white memorial hall are also on this level. Other buildings, including residences of the post's officers, form a lovely scene as they circle the parade grounds. On the heights beyond is the striking fortress-like chapel and the remains of the Revolutionary War's Fort Putnam, which was a key to the control of the Hudson River. Flirtation Walk is a wooded path running from Kosciuszko's Gardens northward to Gee's Point (the lighthouse point), near which the great chain stretched across the river in Revolutionary days as a barrier to British ships attempting to move upriver.

No river in the entire United States provides a grander vista than the northward view upriver from Victory Monument. The same view is seen by the steamboat passenger as we round Magazine Point. I now slow down the vessel to half speed and blow one long blast of the whistle in preparation for the very sharp turn at Gee's Point. As we complete this turn, we enter Worlds End Reach, where the Hudson River is at its deepest at 216 feet. In a matter of minutes, we round Magazine Point and turn sharply to the right. The point is part of Constitution Island, where the ineffective great chain was laid across the river during the Revolutionary War. For many years, the island was the home of Susan and Ann Warner, authors of *The Wide Wide World.*

Old Crow's Nest, a picturesque elevation (1,396 feet), is just north of the Military Academy, and the village of Cold Spring is on the other side of the river. The West Point Foundry was located in Cold Spring. In 1830 this foundry cast the first American steam locomotive, *Best Friend*, which set the world speed record in 1832. In 1838, the foundry made the biggest power-driven hammer, weighing in at four tons. This operation also produced a flour mill for Austria and many cotton presses for the American South. By 1865, the foundry was casting 2500 cannon a week for the Union Army. In 1908, its expanded works were being used to forge parts for a railroad tunnel between New York City and Jersey City. The Astor dining room above the foundry is noteworthy. The first Catholic church in the Hudson Valley north of Manhattan was built here along the shore as a place of worship for the foundry workers.

After we pass Cold Spring and 1,425-foot Mount Taurus (also called Bull Hill), our admiration is divided between the two attractions before us—1,365-foot Breakneck Mountain on the east and 1,340-foot Storm King Mountain (also called Butter Hill) on the west. They stand as gatekeepers of the Hudson Highlands' northern gate.

Storm King Highway (Route 208) leaves Route 9W after passing Fort Montgomery, and continues through Highland Falls and the Military Academy. Then, it climbs along the west bank, rounding Storm King Mountain well up its side. There is a small, pull-off parking area at its highest point along the river. From there the traveler may see beautiful views of Newburgh Bay to the north and West Point to the south.

Newburgh ferry house and bus station in 1944. (Author's collection)

At the Highlands' northern gate, the tunnel of the great Catskill Aqueduct passes under the Hudson at a depth of 1,100 feet. A tunnel of this depth was required because of the extreme depth of the bedrock in the channel of the prehistoric Hudson.

As we continue northward, we see Cornwall on the west bank. The estate of E. P. Rose, the writer, and Idlewild, the former home of Nathaniel Parker Willis, the poet and editor, are nearby. The coal terminal of the New York, Ontario and Western Railroad extends into the river north of the village. Bannerman Island arsenal is opposite Cornwall on the east bank. The owner, Francis Bannerman, purchased a large supply of obsolete material sold by the U. S. government. He established his storehouses here on Pollopel Island. The complex was constructed to look like a castle surrounded by a moat. Worn building blocks taken from New York City streets were used as building materials. The business continued after his death in 1918. Later, arsenal operation was abandoned, but the structure still stands.

We now enter the wide stretch of the river known as Newburgh Bay. We sight a group of mountains dead ahead. Passengers often ask if these are the Catskills, but they are not. They are the Shawangunk range. Beacon Mountain (1,635 feet) is on the eastern shore. It is on this mountain that beacon fires were lighted as signals of British troop movements during the War for Independence. Today, the summit is easily reached by means of a cable railway that is said to be the steepest of its kind in the world.

The strong flood current has brought us to Newburgh, our next landing point, ahead of schedule. We signal our arrival to the dockhands with one long, one short, and another long blast of the *Stuyvesant's* whistle. We dock, unload passengers, and take on a few passengers. Most of the new arrivals will sail with us to Poughkeepsie and return back home on the southbound steamer from Albany. It is approximately a two-hour round-trip sail.

Newburgh was settled in the early part of the 18th century by Palatine Germans. They were followed by the Dutch, English, Irish, Scots, and French Huguenots. The town served as George Washington's Headquarters during the years 1782 and 1783. Early manufactured goods included window and bottle glass, gunpowder, gunflints, spittoon heads, bayonets, knives, soaps, and candles. Later, Caldwell lawn mowers were manufactured here. Thomas Caldwell became the "father of the lawnmower" in 1878, when he produced the successful Excelsior side-wheel lawnmower.

Andrew J. Downing, the well-known horticulturist who designed the grounds of many of the valley's estates, as well as the grounds of the White House and the Capitol in Washington, D.C., was a native of Newburgh. The Day Liner *Hendrick Hudson*, J. P. Morgan's yacht *Corsair* and many other vessels were built at the Thomas S. Marvel shipyard here.

What is said to be the oldest winery in the United States (1839) still makes wine on its original premises at nearby Washingtonville, New York. The Balmville Tree, a seedling in 1699, is still alive 300 years later as I write.

The Orange County area was dairy country. Every evening, the Central Hudson Steamboat Company steamer, *Homer Ramsdell*, sailed from Newburgh for New York City loaded with fresh milk.

Here at Newburgh is located another fine Hudson Valley educational institution, Mount Saint Mary College. Two Dominican nuns who purchased the McAlpine mansion and seven acres founded it in 1882. It progressed from an elementary school, high school, and normal school to a junior college offering an associate degree in nursing. On October 30, 1956, "the Mount" became a four-year college, and became coeducational in 1968. This college was among the first to create a wireless academic network that linked its student body to the Internet.

After a pleasant stop at Newburgh, we get underway at 12:30 PM so as to maintain the schedule. Our next port is Poughkeepsie. Captain Briggs makes his way to the bridge to relieve me for dinner. I have 45 minutes to eat and return to the pilothouse to make the landing at Poughkeepsie. I meet Norma at the parlor where she has been enjoying the voyage, and we head for the dining room aft on the main deck. The ship's officers have a reserved table with a waiter at the ready, because time is of the essence. The always-efficient service allows me to enjoy a fine meal with my wife. The dining room is surrounded by glass so that passengers do not miss any of the scenery or points of interest along the river while they are eating.

Beacon, formerly Fishkill-on-the-Hudson, is across from Newburgh. The original crown patent was issued in 1685. This was the largest military depot in New York State during the Revolutionary War. Although no battles were fought in the area, the sufferings of the Continental soldiers here rivaled those of Valley Forge. The ferry that connects Beacon and Newburgh opened to traffic in 1743 on a grant from King George II of England. (It was in service until 1963, when the new bridge rendered it obsolete.)

A short distance north of here, we pass the Verplanck House where the Society of Cincinnati was established by the officers of the American Army in 1783. Its purpose was "to perpetuate friendships and to raise money for relieving the widows and orphans of those who fell in the war." Baron von Steuben had his headquarters in this house, and the state legislature held its session here before moving to Kingston. Here, too, General Lafayette lay ill with fever. Emock Crosby, the hero of Cooper's novel *Spy*, is said to have been confined in a nearby church. We can see also the large building that is the state asylum for the criminally insane.

We sail past the village of Chelsea, where Moses Collyer built many Hudson River sloops in bygone days. In dry seasons, the City of New York takes fresh water from the river here to supplement its reservoir water supply. The town of Roseton, where two major brickyards are in operation, is on the west bank.

Just north of here, at a turn in the river, is Danskammer Point. Henry Hudson had the privilege of viewing an Indian pow-wow at a clearing among a grove of cedar trees on the point. The crag was henceforth known as Devil's Danskammer (Devil's Dance Hall), because the dancing of the Indians around the campfire seemed to the Dutch to be nothing less than the dance of fiends.

Wappinger's Creek, named after the Wappinger Indians, once a powerful tribe, flows into the river on the right. It is navigable for small craft for about one and a half miles to the town of Wappinger Falls. The old German settlement of New Hamburg, where the Central Hudson steamers landed to receive passengers and goods from both towns, is at the mouth of the creek. Hampton Bluff, where we observe beautiful white cedar trees, the finest along the river, is on the opposite shore. Diamond Reef, a rock about the size of a scow, is between the two under only five feet of water. When the ice season requires removal of the lighted buoy marker on the reef, the reef has been hit by unsuspecting diesel tug boats whose officers are not required to have a Hudson River pilot's license.

The spires and housetops of the summer homes of many men of wealth come into view at Marlboro high on the west bank. The mid-Hudson fruit belt stretches along the west bank from here at Marlboro all the way to Catskill. Apples, pears, peaches, berries, and cherries grow in abundance.

The vessel has slowed because we are approaching the New York Traprock Corporation's giant Clinton Point, where stone is mined, crushed, and shipped by scow to New York City. The *Stuyvesant* picks up speed again as we approach Milton, an old town settled by Quakers. There are many vineyards here where wine is produced. Just above, on the east bank, is Locust Grove, the residence of Samuel F. B. Morse, the inventor of the telegraph. Not far below Locust Grove was the Milton horse-boat ferry that plied across the river to Camelot for many years.

We are now approaching Blue Point, and I must return to the pilothouse to prepare for our landing at Poughkeepsie. I leave Norma in one of the plush chairs in the carpeted front saloon, which is now available because many of the passengers are disembarking here to return to New York or Yonkers on the down boat.

I can see the southbound Day Line steamer *Hendrick Hudson* in the distance as I reach the pilothouse to relieve Captain Briggs. Shortly, we will pass under the Mid-Hudson suspension bridge, built in 1930, which my dad assisted in constructing while captain of the Cornell Steamboat Company towboat *Perseverance*.

We land on schedule at Poughkeepsie at 1:30 PM. Many passengers disembark. Only those bound for Albany or Catskill Mountain resorts remain. Poughkeepsie is a modified Indian name that means "reed-covered lodge by the little water place." The first recorded white settlers purchased land from the Indians in 1683. Following the burning of Kingston by the British in 1778, Poughkeepsie was the temporary capital of New York, and Governor Clinton lived here.

Poughkeepsie was the site of the modern intercollegiate rowing regatta, which was first held here

Boys diving for coins thrown by passengers aboard *Peter Stuyvesant* berthed at the Poughkeepsie dock, 1944. (Author's collection)

in 1895. Huge college letters, blocked out with rocks along the riverbank by visiting crewmen remain today. The colleges taking part included Cornell, Syracuse, the United States Naval Academy, Princeton, Pennsylvania, Wisconsin, Washington, California, and Columbia. All of these universities had boathouses in the vicinity along the river. They came to the area about a month before the race and trained with their shells for the big day. The races started in the vicinity of Hyde Park near President Franklin Delano Roosevelt's estate and ended a mile below the Poughkeepsie Railway Bridge. There were three main races—the freshman race (a two-mile event), the junior varsity race (a three-mile event), and the varsity race (a four-mile race).

The riverbanks were loaded with spectators who had come from all over the country, and the river was full of pleasure craft. The Hudson River Day Liner *De Witt Clinton* with its 5,000 passenger capacity booked weeks ahead, would be anchored near the finish line. The West Shore Division tracks of the New York Central Railroad ran along the water's edge, and the line had a train of specially-built cars with stadium-type seats about four rows high facing the river. This train followed the race from the start to the finish and was always filled to capacity. The tug *Jumbo* from the Cornell Steamboat Company owned by Mr. Fred Coykendall, who was also President of the Board of Trustees of Columbia University, had the distinction every year of transporting the shells and other equipment from the Columbia University boathouse in the Harlem River to their boathouse just north of Poughkeepsie, and then returning after the races. My dad and I had this assignment for several years.

After many years, the races on the Hudson were discontinued there and moved to Lake Onondaga at Syracuse. When the races were held on the Hudson, the main race was started during tidal slack water. When a good breeze blows against the current, there can be a substantial swell and, at times, shells would be swamped. This may have been a factor in the decision to move the races to Lake Onondaga.

Several educational institutions are located in Poughkeepsie. Chief among them is Vassar College,

one of America's outstanding academies for women. Matthew Vassar, whose grave is marked by the ancient symbol of fertility and strength, the acorn, had a desire to leave something permanent behind him. Vassar had amassed his fortune brewing ale and beer, but he had no formal education. In 1861, he decided that "woman, having received from her creator the same intellectual attainments as man, has the same right as man to intellectual development." Educating women was a new idea at the time. He provided the land and the money for an institution called Vassar Female Seminary. At first, it was the butt of many jokes and was referred to as "Vassar's Folly." Today, the undergraduates are said to sing:

Matthew Vassar's generous heart
Found a brain in every lass,
So he made his beer and the college here
For the good of the freshman class.

Another famed school in Poughkeepsie is Marist College, which opened in 1905 to train future brothers for this Roman Catholic teaching order. They purchased two parcels of land, the Bech and MacPherson estates. In 1946, the New York State educational system granted Marist College a charter. In the 1980s, Marist College formed a partnership with IBM so that technology could enhance the teaching and learning process.

The city is also active commercially. The DeLaval plant is just south of the city, and Dutton's lumberyard lies just north. As a state pilot after leaving the Day Line, I piloted numerous lumber ships coming from Oregon and Washington ports to this facility. Here too, William and Andrew Smith became cough drop tycoons with their recipe for candy syrup in 1866.

The *Poughkeepsie Journal* is the oldest newspaper in the State of New York. It began publication as a weekly on August 11, 1785, and soon became a daily. The *Journal* (which changed its name 13 times during its history) is the third oldest newspaper in the United States. Two Connecticut papers, one in Hartford and the other in New Haven, are older.

Across the stream is New Paltz Landing, a dock that is actually part of the village of Highland, which is located on the plateau at the top of the bank. This is an area of farms and wineries. High on the banks, the Bolognesi family make Hudson River wines. One of their best is made from Iona grapes, which are named from the island where they were discovered and developed.

New Paltz, the site of New Paltz State College, lies several miles inland. Our son Charles and his family live there today. New Paltz was settled by 11 French Huguenot families who purchased 40,000 acres from the Esopus Indians in 1677. Huguenot Street's first stone house was built by Pierre Deyo in 1692, and homes built by other families quickly followed, several of which still stand today. This street is known as the "oldest street in America."

Near New Paltz, at the top of a mountain, stands the famous Lake Mohonk Mountain House, built in 1870. It has been owned by the same family ever since. (On our last visit, Norma and I had dinner with Roger and Grace Smiley, the current owners.)

At one time, an electric trolley line ran from New Paltz to Highland, where it then shifted onto the railroad tracks. It was pushed across the railroad bridge by a steam locomotive. Upon its arrival at Poughkeepsie, the trolley shifted onto the city's electrified system and proceeded to its destination at the city's center.

We are now letting go the lines of the *Stuyvesant* from the Poughkeepsie mooring. Kingston Point Landing is our next destination. We soon pass under the Poughkeepsie railroad bridge. In 1871, a charter was granted to build this bridge across the Hudson River at Poughkeepsie. It took seventeen years to complete because of political and economic factors, and the fact that it required the construction of four bridge piers in the navigable Hudson River channel.

Just north of the bridge, we meet the southbound *Hendrick Hudson*. I blow one long blast on the steam whistle in salute, and Pilot Clarence Plank returns the gesture. Clarence, born in Catskill, New York, now lives with his wife Runa and their family in Bogota, New Jersey, about a mile from my home. The *Hudson* had let ashore at Kingston Point Park many one-day excursion passengers from Albany who will return home with us.

Frequently on Sundays or holidays, the *Hudson* had to make unscheduled stops at Bear Mountain Park and Indian Point Park to help handle the overflow crowds from the other vessels.

High on the east bank, we can see the red brick buildings of the Hudson River State Hospital and, a little further north, the imposing structure that is the Jesuit College of Saint Andrews. (Later this building became the Culinary Institute of America, famous for training gourmet chefs.) Today, it has three popular restaurants open to the public.

We turn left into what is known as Crum Elbow. Here, on the top of the hill to the east, is the Franklin D. Roosevelt home, a National Historical Site. Our thirty-second president was born here at Hyde Park on January 30, 1882. His ancestral home is now a public shrine. The president's books, ship models, photographs, gifts, and other personal belongings are on display in the library. The president and his wife Eleanor are buried in the rose garden. Almost abreast is one of the homes and dock of the black evangelist, Father Devine.

Leaving Crum Elbow reach, we turn north just as a New York Central passenger express train flies along the east bank. The engineer signals on the whistle with one long and one short blast. This is a hello greeting that I return with one long and two short blasts from the *Stuyvesant's* whistle.

We are now approaching Hyde Park Village, the center of a beautiful residential district filled with elegant dwelling places and fine parks. The great estate beyond the railway station is that of Frederick W. Vanderbilt. It is a magnificent mansion with Corinthian columns of white marble.

Mother Cabrini, America's first saint, founded the orphanage managed by the Sisters of the White Cross that we now see on the west bank. It was here that Mother Cabrini discovered water for a well in the rocky soil. We also see among the vineyards the Irish Christian Brothers Institute; the dwelling of John Burroughs, the well-loved naturalist and writer; and the Episcopal Monastery of the Brothers of the Holy Cross.

Two miles beyond, we sail past the ancient town of Esopus and Esopus Island, a favorite area for campers and fishermen. Rosemont, the home of the Honorable Alton B. Parker, once a Democratic candidate for president, stands on the hill near the water to the left of the island. To the right of the island is Norrie State Park and Yacht Club. The large edifice of grey stone just north of Rosemont is a seminary of the Redemptorist Order of Catholic priests. The seminarians from this school were a familiar sight on the river as they rowed their large rowboat to Esopus Island to picnic and swim. It is said that, at one time, the Catholic Church was the largest property owner in the Hudson Valley.

While I was serving as a deckhand in the late 1920s for my dad aboard the Cornell tugboat *Jumbo*, the boat's main cylinders in the diesel engine gave way and it became necessary to seek a safe berth so that the engine could be shut down and the engineers could make the necessary repairs. The nearest dock available was at Mount St. Alphonsus Seminary. There were many such small docks along the river's banks in those days because the schools, convents, and large estates burned coal for heating purposes, and the coal was delivered by boat. The *Jumbo* limped to the dock. The engineers shut her down and began repairs.

There were no telephone communications to shore at that time, so it was necessary to find a shore phone to call the towboat dispatcher to let them know that we would be out of service. Dad and I, dressed in our usual working clothes, climbed up the steep hill to the seminary building. When we entered the main lobby, we found several men sitting around. We did not see a priest or abbot among them. We suspected that the men were hoboes because of the way that they were dressed. We were proven right. When my dad approached one of the doors to knock and try to draw the attention of one of the resident priests, almost in unison the men jumped up and shouted, "Sit down! Don't spoil it! When they are ready, they will call us for breakfast."

On the east bank, we see two fine estates. The first is the home of Odgen Mills, and just above it is that of the late W. B. Dinsmore, former president of the Adams Express Company. The fourth lighthouse that we have seen on our trip stands in the center of the river, guarding the Esopus Meadow shoal from which it gets its name.

As we sail along, we see the beautiful country homes of Levi P. Morton, ex-vice president of the United States and one-time governor of the State of New York, and Jacob Ruppert, the beer baron and former owner of the New York Yankees.

We are approaching the village of Port Ewen on the west bank. My parents were both born in Port Ewen. This village of approximately 2,500 souls has given a substantial number of its citizens to service on river vessels over the years. Port Ewen was named after John Ewen, president of the Pennsylvania Coal Company whose large coal terminal at the village received coal from their mines in Honesdale, Pennsylvania via canal boats through the Delaware and Hudson Canal (opened in 1828). The coal was stored here and later shipped out on larger vessels.

Great sheds for storing ice are still to be seen in this area. Using plows, horses, rakes, and saws, ice was farmed out of the river to be stored in more than one hundred gigantic ice sheds constructed along the river's banks between Hyde Park and Albany for summer shipment to New York and beyond, even as far away as the Orient. Sawdust was packed between the ice blocks to keep them from melting. In the late 1800s, over 1800 workers and 1000 horses were involved in the ice trade. Wages ranged from $1.00 to $1.50 a day.

Development of mechanical ice-making equipment and refrigeration took the profit out of the river ice business, and all operations were discontinued. For years, the great ice sheds sat empty. Then, in 1920, someone discovered that they were excellent structures to be used in growing mushrooms. Several still survive and continue to be used for that purpose.

Halfway up the hill, we can make out the Catholic church where stands the beautiful Ulster County blue stone monument dedicated to all those who worked on river vessels. Two other churches serviced the town, the Methodist church and the Dutch Reformed church, where my dad's family worshipped.

A short distance beyond, on the west bank, we find Kingston Lighthouse on the dike marking the entrance to Rondout Creek and Kingston Harbor. Rondout is by far the most active creek along the river. It was the eastern terminal of the Delaware

Scenes of Kingston Point circa 1920s in a souvenir book published by L. C. Nelson Co., Portland, Maine. (Author's collection)

and Hudson Canal, a busy place when coal was the principal fuel.

My family's sloops sailed from the Hamilton Dock here from the mid-1700s to the early 1800s. On the south side of the creek above the village of South Rondout (now Connelly) stands the Hamilton family homestead overlooking Rondout Creek and Kingston. My grandfather, Captain John Hamilton, was born here.

Shipbuilding was an active business along the creek. This was the homeport of the Cornell Steamboat Company's fleet of towboats and tugs that numbered 112 in their years of existence. Cornell's fleet of night boats sailed from here to New York City until Cornell gave up the passenger business for the more lucrative towing business.

The well-known and popular steamboat *Mary Powell* served Kingston on the daytime route to New York City and return. The vessel was built for

Absalom Lent Anderson of Port Ewen at the shipyard of Michael S. Allison. Fletcher, Harrison and Company built the engine. Anderson had two partners, Captain John Ketcham and John L. Hasbrouck. The vessel was named after the widow of Thomas Powell. Mary Ludlow Powell had a firm marine background. All four of her brothers—Charles, Robert, Augustus, and Lawrence—served as officers in the U.S. Navy. In the battle between *Chesapeake* and *HMS Shannon* off Boston, the mortally wounded Lawrence gave his famous command, "Don't give up the ship."

The *Mary Powell*, although ready for service in October 1861, ran briefly till October 30th, when she was placed in winter layup at Port Ewen. In the spring of 1862, when the river was ice-free, *Mary Powell* went to New York to have her wooden hull bottom coppered and to receive furniture and such finishing touches as Captain Anderson's wife felt she needed. Regular service between Kingston and

Scenes of Kingston Point circa 1920s in a souvenir book published by L. C. Nelson Co., Portland, Maine. (Author's collection)

New York roundtrip, with Captain Anderson in command, began on May 5, 1862, and continued through 1917. The vessel was very fast for a steamboat of her time, although many of the Hudson River Day Line boats exceeded her speed by two or three miles per hour. Her reputation for cleanliness, service, and speed earned her the title "Queen of the Hudson."

Kingston, settled in 1653 by a group of Dutch colonists from Albany, is one of New York State's oldest towns. In 1661, Governor Peter Stuyvesant gave the original charter. At first, it was called Wiltwyck; but later, after being burned by the British in 1777, it was named Kingston by its British governor.

We are preparing to land at Kingston Point as we pass the Kingston lighthouse. After we are tied up, Norma watches the deckhands perform the "human chain" maneuver for putting steamer trunks ashore. This fast and proven procedure is always a hit with the passengers.

I used to see Ulster and Delaware passenger trains almost parallel to the passenger building as the train crews were preparing to load passengers for the trip to various Catskill Mountain vacation resorts. On Saturdays during the summer months, extra steamers and several trains were required to handle the volume of vacationers bound for the Catskills.

It is a short walk through the park to board trolley cars bound for the city of Kingston and surrounding areas. The first meeting of the state legislature took place in September of 1777 at the old Senate House uptown. The state's first constitution was adopted in this building on Sunday, April 20, 1777. George Clinton, afterward a vice president of the United States, was inaugurated here on July 30, 1777, as the first governor of New York. On September 9th of the same year, Chief Justice Jay opened the first state court.

On September 16, 1924, the oldest military organization in the state became Kingston's 1st Battalion 156th Artillery, New York Army National Guard. This service is the successor to the militia of citizen-soldiers who banded together in 1658 as the "Trainband of Wiltwycke" to be better prepared to preserve themselves and theirs from an onslaught of Indians.

The Dutch Reformed congregation was organized in 1659 and is the oldest ecclesiastical body in the state of New York. It has been in continuous worship on the same piece of ground since that time. Its current house of worship was built in 1852.

This city, with a population of less than 30,000, has much industry, which drafts its workers from the surrounding areas. IBM, Rosendale Cement Works, and a number of brickyards and dress factories employ many people. The New York State Trolley Museum is found here.

The city's first newspaper, the weekly *Ulster County Gazette*, began publishing in 1866. The present-day daily, *The Kingston Daily Freeman*, began publishing in 1871.

Hurley, a town a few miles away, is called the summertime sweet corn capital of the world. Every day, 20 trailer trucks, each carrying crates containing 45,000 ears of corn covered with ice to keep them fresh (a total of 900,000 ears a day), leave this town for sale.

Kingston is a great sports city. Its semi-pro team baseball team, the Colonials, was ranked with the Brooklyn Bushwicks and the Paterson Silksox, and its professional basketball team once beat New York's Original Celtics in a three game series for the World Championship.

After we unload the vacationers bound for the Catskills and the local passengers from New York, we board about 1,000 passengers who came down from Albany via the *Hendrick Hudson* on a one-day excursion and are now returning home. Perhaps, some of the passengers who left us at Kingston are bound for the Beekman Arms in Rhinebeck, New York. This is the oldest continuously operating hotel in America. Its doors opened for the first time in 1700.

Such large numbers of passengers leave and board the *Stuyvesant* that we are ten minutes behind our 2:30 PM departure time as we cast off from Kingston. We take the east channel north of Rhinebeck to allow the middle ground shoal to break up the swells that might otherwise damage the scows loading at the many brickyards along the ship channel to the west. Once clear of the yards, I signal for top speed. We sail past Vincent Astor's estate and Annandale, the former home of Revolutionary War General Richard Montgomery who was killed on December 31, 1777, while conducting the attack on Quebec. In 1818, his remains were brought down the Hudson with great pomp aboard the steamer *Richmond*. He was interred in St. Paul's Church cemetery on lower Broadway in New York City.

Nearby is Bard College, founded as St. Stephen's College in 1860 by John Bard with the New York City leadership of the Episcopal Church. He gave the college the Chapel of the Holy Innocents and part of his estate, Annandale. In recent years, the college's educational facilities have been expanded greatly.

At Barrytown, we slow down momentarily to cross the 18-foot shoal bar between the Middleground Flats and Hog's Back to reach the main ship channel at Turkey Point. Soon, we are abreast of Cruger Island, with Magdalen Island just to the north. In the early 1840s, John Church Cruger hired the explorer John Lloyd Stevens to bring an ancient Mayan village from the Yucatan to Crugers Island by ship. This brought to the Hudson Valley ruins older than those along the Rhine or the Thames.

The village of Glasco, located on the bank opposite the islands, is separated from the main channel by a wide flat. The Glasco docks are usually reached by taking a channel from Turkey Point close to the west bank. However, there is also a northern entrance that can be used by lining up the corner of a shed with a large maple tree as your range. Glasco has many brickyards and a glass factory. At one time, the road known as the Glasco Turnpike reached the river here from the Catskill Mountains.

Shortly after sailing by the Pines, Chateau de Tivoli, and the Callender home, we pass the Saugerties Long Dock where a ferry ran across to the village of Tivoli on the east bank. At the mouth of Esopus Creek, considered one of the best trout streams in the state as it wanders down through the Catskills, we see the Saugerties Lighthouse, built in 1869. The creek is navigable for river steamers to the village dock, where the Saugerties Evening Line night boats in the 1800s and early 1900s loaded their freight and passengers bound for New York City. They operated the *Robert A. Snyder* and *Ida*, serving several landings between Saugerties and Hyde Park on their trip to New York.

Saugerties was settled in 1710 by 3,000 Palatine Germans. Its factories in the 1800s shipped iron, glass, and paper to New York City and beyond.

Near Tivoli are: Blithewood, the Donaldson estate; Rosehill, the estate of General J. W. DePeyster; and just to the north, Clermont, the family mansion of the once powerful Livingstons whose lands stretched as far east as Connecticut. Robert Fulton named his famous steamboat after this chateau.

We can see Malden and West Camp on the west bank. As we approach Alsen-Cementon, we find two large cement manufacturing plants on the hillside. Their product is shipped by both barge and large ship.

Abreast of here is Germantown, where we can see the mother house of a group of Carmelite nuns on the hillside. Germantown was the former home of the Burden Iron Mine, which produced 450,000 tons of ore annually in the late 1800s. Its caves became a mushroom farm in the 1930s.

At Linlithgo, the Roeliff Jansen Kill flows into the Hudson, while to the west for over two hours our passengers' eyes will rest on the summits of the Catskill Mountains, a breathtaking sight. The Catskills cover over 2,400 square miles, and they loom close at times to the river.

As we pass above Linlithgo, Catskill Landing comes into view, with Greendale opposite on the east shore. Before we reach this point, we pass the mouth of Catskill Creek. About a mile west of here, the creek receives a lively tributary called the Kaaterskill Creek, which flows down from the great ravine of Kaaterskill Clove. The deep clove, or gorge, separates South Mountain from High Peak, the loftiest point of the front range as seen from the river. Its natural beauty sustains the legendary interest of old Indian tradition and the

imagination of Washington Irving. This is the scene of the story of Rip Van Winkle.

The outline of the mountains against the sky as seen from here bears a fanciful resemblance to a giant human figure lying on its back. The peak to the south is the knee, the next to the north is the breast, and three projections north represent the chin, the nose and forehead.

When we land at Catskill, we will disembark several hundred passengers who are bound for the many Catskill Mountain hotels in the Palenville, Tannersville, Hunter, and Haines Falls areas. This old town was the only point of entrance to the Catskills before the completion of the Ulster and Delaware Railroad into the mountains from Kingston. In 1678, the first Robert Livingston bought this site from the Indians. Many relics of the early Dutch days are seen still in the village, although it now has a modern and, in summer, lively appearance.

We approach the dock. Lines are fastened, the gangways put in place, and most of our disembarking passengers seem anxious to begin their summer vacations in the mountains.

In the old days, stage lines ran from the village and slowly made their way to where the Catskill Mountain House stood. In 1882, a railroad was built from the boat landing to the foot of the mountain, and ten years later, Otis Elevator built an inclined cable railway up to the plateau, which was formerly reached only by a round-about stage route.

Early tavern keepers in Catskill were known as "retailers of liquid damnation." Catskill Mountain-brewed applejack was a staple during prohibition. The moonshine trade attracted the leaders of New York City gangsters because of the inaccessibility of the surrounding hills. "Legs" Diamond was tried in Catskill at the Greene County Courthouse.

Tanning, using the bark of the hemlock trees, was an important Catskill Mountain industry. In 1836 alone, 250,000 sides of shoe sole leather were shipped downriver.

The Catskill Evening Line night boats also served the village. The vessels started at Coxsackie and stopped at Hudson before continuing to New York. The Beach family, who also owned the Catskill Mountain House and a network of narrow gauge railroads, owned the line. Many vessels were used on this route, the *Kaaterskill, Catskill, Reserve, Storm King, Onteora,* and *Clermont* most recently.

A ferry operated from Catskill to Greendale, serving a station of the New York Central Railroad system. Naturally, the ferry was named *A. F. Beach.* Olana castle, the home of the 19th-century artist, Frederic E. Church, sits high on a hill above Greendale.

We leave Catskill slightly behind our 3:35 PM scheduled departure time. We will not be able to make up any time on our short 20-minute run to Hudson.

We sail under the Rip Van Winkle Bridge, which opened to traffic in 1935. The main channel of this 5,041-ft. bridge is crossed by an 800-ft. cantilevered structure with a clearance above water of 145 feet. Passing Hamburg on the left and Rogers Island on the right, we approach Mount Merino, so-called because in the first decade of the last century the area was given over to grazing merino sheep.

We sail past Hudson lighthouse, built in 1870, located on the south end of Hudson middleground, which extends almost four miles to Four Mile Point. We prepare to land at Hudson and reduce speed as we pass the docks of two giant cement works.

Hudson is not an easy landing to make when traveling with a strong flood tide because the dock next to the Day Line pier on the south side was built to fit the Catskill Evening Line's *Clermont,* and it extends out beyond the Day Line landing. I have to skin the *Stuyvesant* close to that dock, giving our boat a short thrust forward with a hard left rudder before backing, because, as I mentioned before, a single screw vessel will back away from this landing. This procedure is successfully performed, and we are now docked at Hudson.

Hudson was the third city chartered in the United States (1785) after the signing of the Declaration of Independence. Although land was purchased from the Indians in 1663, the first settlers didn't arrive until a hundred and twenty years later in 1783. They were mostly New England Quakers from Nantucket and Martha's Vineyard whose fishing and whaling activities had suffered during the

Revolution. The location had been called Claverack, Dutch for "Clover Reach Landing" because of its fields of fragrant clover, but the new settlers renamed it Hudson. By 1790, twenty-five schooners in the whaling, seal, and West Indies trade registered Hudson, New York, as their homeport.

In the 1920s and 1930s, Hudson's Columbia Street had 15 brothels with up to 75 prostitutes. It was infamous throughout the northeastern United States and even in Europe during the war.

The American Museum of Fire Fighting, owned and operated by the Firemen's Association of New York State is located in Hudson. It has one of the oldest and most complete collections of firefighting equipment in America.

A ferry, with a channel dredged for its use in the middleground, connects Hudson with the village of Athens, the fourth incorporated village in the state (1803). The Dutch settled it in 1680. This town was famous for brick making, shipbuilding, and ice harvesting. I knew many men from this village who served on Hudson River vessels.

There is a channel along the west shore that meets with the ship channel at Four Mile Point and will safely pass vessels up to 16 feet draft. Even though we are leaving Hudson ten minutes late, with no unforeseen delays we should reach Albany on time. In a short time, we will be passing Coxsackie. The town derives its name from an Indian name meaning "hoot of the owl." The Dutch settled it in the late 17th century. The community preserved its pure Dutch origins until migrations from Europe and New England between 1790-1830. On January 27, 1775, two hundred twenty-five residents of the village signed a declaration of independence calling for opposition to the oppressive acts of the British Parliament. This document preceded by a year the Declaration of Independence that was signed by the 13 colonies. Our captain, Frank Briggs, is a native of Coxsackie. His brother also captained Day Line steamers. Newton Hook, which lies across the river, was connected to the village by ferry for years, but this ferry service has been discontinued.

The river from Coxsackie to Albany was only 12 feet deep until it was dredged first to 27 feet, and then to 32 feet. We will be passing a number of islands on what remains of our voyage to Albany: Coxsackie, Rattlesnake, Bronx, Houghtaling, Lower Schodack, Mulls, Schermerhorn, Barren, Poplar, Cow, Campbell, Bear, Beacon, Parr, and Bogart.

Above Coxsackie, at Rattlesnake Island, we pass the Coxsackie lighthouse, built in 1820, better known by boatmen as Old Maids Light. Two unmarried women were the keepers of the light.

U. S. Coast Guard cutter *West Wind* berthed at the Port of Albany in January 1960. (Author's collection)

We see the site of the Odd Fellows home, a large grey building on a hill, as we pass the next town, Stuyvesant. A short distance beyond, we see the Upper Kinderhook lighthouse, built in 1829, the ninth and last of the original, occupied lighthouses. Old Maids (in 1939) and Upper Kinderhook (in 1933) have been dismantled and replaced by automatic lights on a steel tower.

One summer Sunday, with a capacity crowd of about 3,700 aboard *Peter Stuyvesant*, we were northbound for Albany when a severe thunderstorm hit. It was one of my worst experiences as a pilot because of the real danger to the lives of so many passengers. The storm hit us in the vicinity of Old Maids Lighthouse about a mile north of the village of Coxsackie. This was possibly the worst storm I had seen in my fifty-one years on the river. I later learned that it was a tornado. The wind blew very hard across the channel and the driving rain caused us to lose all visibility. The wind threatened to blow us off course.

The *Stuyvesant's* four decks stood very high out of the water, and she had only fifteen feet of draft. There was a sharp turn ahead requiring a major course change just north of the lighthouse. This was not a problem in clear weather, or even in fog. Now, however, with the wind blowing so strong broadside against the vessel and no visibility to keep her in the narrow 300 feet of dredged channel, it was a major problem. I could not slow the vessel, because then she would surely blow out of the channel, fetch up against the dredged channel edge, and possibly blow over. I had to keep maximum speed, take an

educated guess when to turn into the new channel heading at an angle, and hope my knowledge and experience would pay off for all onboard.

Thank God, it took us only ten minutes to pass through the storm. It cleared almost as fast as it came, and I saw Bronk Island light abreast of us as the sun came out. The passengers, who had all crowded inside the vessel, causing her to lean to the starboard, now started to return to the outside deck. The *Stuyvesant* straightened up and the remaining trip to Albany was uneventful.

Kinderhook is the birthplace of the 8th president of the United States, Martin Van Buren. He was born on December 5, 1782, six years after the Declaration of Independence was signed, and he was the first president born a United States citizen.

As we pass the Upper Kinderhook light and the Schodack dike, we are entering New Baltimore reach, where almost three-fourths of a mile of solid rock 400 feet wide and 32 feet deep was drilled and removed from the river to complete the present ship channel. At the northern end of this rock cut is the village of New Baltimore, where a large icehouse and shipyard once supplied employment to the villagers.

Almost two miles upstream on the left bank we see the village of Coeymans, where another large icehouse and two brickyards are located. Inland about a mile, at Ravena, is the huge Selkirk freight yards of the New York Central Railroad system. Here, freight connections between the Boston and Albany Railroad and the West Shore Railroad take place.

We see the village of Castleton on the right after we have passed under a railroad bridge and an adjoining highway bridge. This is the farthest point north (nine miles below Albany) that Henry Hudson reached with his vessel *Half Moon*. His crew explored beyond this point as far as the falls at what is now Troy, New York, but it was done by longboat.

After proceeding past Cedar Hill on the left and Staats on the right, we enter another rock cut, but it is considerably shorter than the New Baltimore cut. Once we have navigated the cut, we pass the first of Albany's deepwater oil terminals, Esso and Sears. Across the river, almost opposite, is the Atlantic Refining Company terminal.

We have reduced speed while passing these facilities. Next on the left is Texaco. On the right are Gulf Oil, City Service, and Tidewater. Just below the Port of Albany is the Cerillo terminal. This company supplies the Albany school system with heating fuel. As we pass the port docks, we find the Cargill grain elevator, the largest such facility east of Buffalo. We see a Dutch ship loading, Spaniard and Italian vessels waiting to load, a British vessel unloading molasses, and a Finnish ship unloading wood pulp. The Mobil Oil terminal is just to the north of the port docks. Across the river at Rensselaer, we find an American vessel from our northwest Pacific Coast unloading lumber. On the east side of the river, just south of the lumber dock, we find a deep cut in the shore bank for the turning basin. This cut, plus the river allows 1000 feet of turning area minus the breadth of any ship at the Albany port dock. Just north of the Mobil terminal and the lumber dock, the deepwater channel ends and we are into natural river depth.

As we approach the Dunn Memorial Bridge, I blow three long blasts of the whistle, a signal to the bridge tender to raise the bridge so that we may pass under. We can hear him ring the bell to stop vehicular traffic. In minutes, he starts to raise the bridge and blows his horn, indicating it is all clear for us to pass.

As we prepare to land, I turn the *Stuyvesant* around and we back into the berth so that the boat is headed down river for our 9:20 AM departure tomorrow. The gangplanks are put ashore, passengers and baggage unloaded, and all is well.

I usually have supper at this time, go ashore to bowl or catch a movie, and then sleep aboard in my stateroom. On this trip, because Norma is with me, we change clothes and head for Jack's Oyster House, a well-known and established restaurant on Albany's State Street. After dinner, we will spend the night at the Ten Eyck Hotel.

Although I have finished my duties for the day, I will add some facts about Albany. In addition, since I have sailed the river to the Government Dam at Troy, I will continue a scenic tour to there.

The Dutch settled Albany, the capital of the Empire State, when they established a trading post there in 1614. In 1624, several families arrived here from Holland. The settlement was first called Beverwyck, then Fort Orange. The British took possession in 1664 and renamed it Albany for the Duke of York and Albany, who later became James II. It was incorporated as a city in 1686, and was made the state capital in 1797.

It was the meeting place of the Continental Congress of 1754, in which all the colonies north of Virginia convened delegates to discuss the proposal of a federal union. The plan, proposed by Benjamin Franklin, was agreed to, but none of the colonies would ratify the document because it delegated too much power to the federal government, while the King refused to approve it because it did not go far enough in that direction. A few years later, it did serve as a starting point for the stable union to come.

After climbing wide State Street from Broadway along the river to the heights on which the city sits, you can see several buildings of architectural interest—the State Education Building, the 31-floor Governor Alfred E. Smith Office Building, North Dutch Church, and Saint Peters Episcopal Church. Saint Peters, built in 1715, was refurbished in 1859. It has been called one of the richest specimens of French Gothic in the United States. You can also see the Roman Catholic Cathedral of the Immaculate Conception with its twin lofty spires, and the Episcopal Cathedral of All Saints.

A few years ago the state appropriated funds for the preservation of the city's chief historical relic, the Philip Schuyler mansion. Built in 1671-1672, this building was the home of the courteous and chivalric general who contributed so much to the success of the American Revolutionary Army that captured Burgoyne at Saratoga. In this house, Alexander Hamilton married Elizabeth Schuyler. After the battle of Saratoga, Burgoyne, Baron and Baroness Riedesel, and British Major Ackland and his wife were hospitably sheltered beneath its roof.

Albany is the key point in the state's transportation system. Nearby is the terminus of the Erie and Champlain canals, and here the Boston and Albany, Delaware and Hudson, and West Shore meet the New York Central System railroads. Day Line and Night Line steamboats connect with New York and other river ports.

As we continue our scenic trip up the Hudson, we will pass through two drawbridges: the New York Central, and Boston and Albany railroad bridges. (In May 1978, at a cost of $985 million, sixteen years after the start of construction, the Governor Nelson A. Rockefeller Plaza on "the Mall" opened in Albany, as did a new network of highways, which included a new bridge over the Hudson.)

Across from Albany is Rensselaer, an amalgam of the villages of East Albany, Greenbush, and Bath. On the grounds of Rensselaerwyck, one of the most successful of the early patroonships, stands Fort Crailo, a Dutch manor house built about 1704. "Yankee Doodle," the Revolutionary War marching song, is said to have been written here by Richard Shuckburgh, a British army surgeon. The large red structure on the hillside is a monastery.

Four miles upstream, we pass under Menands Vehicle Lift Bridge. Just above it on the east is a giant iron and steel works. In a few minutes, we begin passing Troy, the furthest point Henry Hudson's longboat reached. By that time, he realized he had not discovered the northwest passage to the Orient.

For 120 years, Troy was a meadowland for Dutch farmers. The town began to grow in the early 19th century, and in 1816 a city charter was granted by the state legislature. Three people who came to Troy in the 1820s created this city's "golden age." Amos Eaton spurred interest in mechanical and scientific development. Emma Willard pioneered liberal education for women by opening Troy Female Seminary in 1821, the first girls' high school in the United States. And Henry Burden stimulated the city's iron industry by his inventions. He was the one who developed the Bessemer process for making steel. Troy steel making prospered until Andrew Carnegie opened his plant in Pittsburgh, Pennsylvania. Troy is the site of Rensselaer Polytechnic Institute, one of the leading schools of its type in the country.

In 1825, a Troy housewife developed a detachable collar for men's shirts. She started the city on its road to fame as a collar and shirt-manufacturing center. Troy's Cluett Peabody Plant was the largest shirt factory in the world.

Troy's "Uncle Sam" Wilson, a local meat packer, supplied beef to the Army and Navy during the war of 1812. Soldiers stationed near Troy interpreted the government meat stamp, "U. S. Beef," to mean "Uncle Sam's Beef." From that point on, government property stamped "U. S." was referred to as "Uncle Sam's." Later, a caricature of Sam Wilson came to personify the United States.

We are now passing the night boat *Trojan*, ready to leave its berth for a 7:00 AM arrival in New York City. Across the river on the west bank, we see Waterford, where a large United States arsenal is located. Just above is Cohoes, an important manufacturer of cotton goods. The water power furnished by the Cohoes Falls in the Mohawk River, together with the Hudson River, have had a marked influence on the immense growth of industry in the area.

We are now arriving at the Troy dam and lock at the end of the tidal estuary of the navigable Hudson River, 180 miles from the sea. North of here is the New York State Barge Canal system which winds its way west to Buffalo with 12 feet of draft, and the Champlain Canal and Lake Champlain with 12 feet of draft to Rouses Point, then 6 feet of draft through the Richelieu River and Canal to Sorel on the Saint Lawrence River.

The natural river continues past Glens Falls to its source at Lake Tear of the Clouds on Mount Marcy in the Adirondacks.

PART II

From Steamboats to Super Tankers: A History of Hudson River Navigation

Chain ferry *Riverside* crossing Rondout Creek circa 1920. Locals called it the *Otherside* or *Skillypot*. (Postcard, author's collection)

Cornell towboat/icebreaker *Hercules* in the upper Hudson during the winter of 1897-1898. My grandfather, Captain John Hamilton, is standing on the left in front of the pilothouse; my father, pilot Mel Hamilton, is on the right. On the bow forward, left to right are uncles John, Jerry, and Harve Hamilton. (Roger Mabie collection)

CHAPTER ONE

The Hamilton Family on the Hudson, 1712-1979

In 1712 James Hamilton arrived in America from his birthplace in Scotland. He married Hannah Whitaker on May 9, 1723. A son, James, was born in July 1729. James Sr., opened up a chandler's store in South Rondout, New York on Rondout Creek. Some time later, he realized there was more profit in transporting goods than in selling them. He built a Hudson River sloop, and then two more. One of his sons captained one of the sloops, while he maintained the store. From then on, the family engaged in the transportation of goods and passengers by sloop until the coming of the steamboat.

The Hudson River sloops, of which Pete Seeger's *Clearwater* is a copy, were sturdy sailing ships that handled most of the Hudson Valley's commerce into the middle of the nineteenth century. They were equipped with a centerboard that extended down below the vessel's hull. The centerboard would rise higher on deck as the vessel approached shallow water. The method used of tacking upstream against wind and current made these voyages slow, uncertain operations with respect to time schedules. Most sloop captains owned the vessel. They were important and respected people in their home communities. Often, they were charged with the care of children, elderly, or infirm passengers. They were commissioned to make purchases in the city or to sell the produce of upriver shippers in the city. They held positions of great trust and responsibility.

James Hamilton Jr. married Maria Schoonmaker on November 21, 1761. Their son, James, was born in 1774 and married Maria Van Kuren on June 4, 1801. A son, Alexander, was born in 1805. Alexander Hamilton married Margaret Felter in 1840. A son, John, my grandfather, was born in 1846. They had another son, Harvey, born in 1849. As a boy, I remember visiting Granduncle Harvey, then in his seventies, who was the first captain of the Cornell towboat, *Geo. W. Washburn.* (In later years, I served as captain of this same towboat for eight months.) He lived in the Hamilton family homestead in South Rondout, New York, the same house where my grandfather was born. The home was located at the top of a steep hill that overlooked the village, Rondout Creek, and Kingston.

Site of Hamilton family homestead in South Rondout, New York, 1997. (Author's collection)

My grandfather, John Hamilton, married Mary Elizabeth Post in 1865. He was 19 and Grandmother was 18. They built a brick house with a beautiful gingerbread type porch across the front on New Salem Post Road just outside the village of Port Ewen, New York. John Hamilton was captain of the Hudson River sloop, *Ambassador*, owned by Jeremiah Post, my grandmother's brother. As a sloop master, he was responsible for sailing the vessel and conducting all business dealings ashore.

My grandparents' first son, James, was born in 1866 but died in 1874. My dad, Melvin Eckerd Hamilton, their second son, was born September 5, 1870. A daughter, Margaret, was born in 1874, followed by three more sons: Harvey, in 1875; John in 1876; and Jeremiah in 1878.

My grandfather became master of the ice-breaker *Hercules* in the 1880s. This vessel, owned by the Cornell Steamboat Company, was used for ice-breaking duties on the Hudson River in the late 1800s and early 1900s. My dad, Mel Hamilton, was her pilot. Other relatives served as crew. My grandfather died from a heart attack aboard *Hercules* while proceeding through Newburgh Bay in November 1900.

When my grandfather died in 1900, my dad became the *Hercules* captain. He remained in that capacity until WWI. He was then called to be captain of the U. S. Army tug stationed in New York harbor. Its duties were to assist in docking and undocking Army troop transports. During his career he captained many vessels for Cornell Steamboat Company. He last commanded the diesel tug *Jumbo* for Cornell. As her captain, he participated in the pulling of the cables for the George Washington Bridge across the river from Manhattan to Fort Lee, New Jersey. While still active on the *Jumbo* in the Kingston area, my father suffered a heart attack and was rushed to the Kingston City Hospital where he died upon arrival on September 13, 1943, at the age of 72. I vividly recall passing the *Jumbo* that day. I waved to him as I passed while piloting the Day Liner *Peter Stuyvesant*. When I arrived at our New York berth, I learned that less than an hour after I had seen him, he had had a heart attack and passed away.

Author's father, Captain Melvin Eckerd Hamilton (9/5/1870-9/13/1943), longtime Cornell Steamboat Company pilot and captain. (Author's collection)

Of my Hamilton grandparents' five children, only my dad married. In 1910, at age 40, he married Catherine Barton, age 30, at Saint Francis Xavier Catholic Church on 31st Street in New York City. They chose that church, because at that time in the Port Ewen, New York, area mixed marriages were frowned upon. My mother Catherine and the other Catholics lived east of Route 9W, overlooking the Hudson River. That area was called "on the hillside." My dad and the other Protestants lived on top of the hill west of 9W. This separation of people with different religious affiliations was quite common at that time in the Hudson River Valley. The only large hall in town was owned by the Knights of Phythias Lodge, located on the west side of Route 9W. Saturday night dances were held there. My mother told me that if one of the Catholic girls were seen at the dance, the parish priest would announce it from the altar at Sunday morning mass.

My mother was the daughter of John Barton and Bridget McCluskey, who had married in 1863. She had two older brothers, John and Arthur, and a younger brother, Charles. Grandfather Barton owned a fleet of canal boats that operated on the Delaware and Hudson Canal that ran between Honesdale, Pennsylvania and Rondout, New York (Kingston) on the Hudson River. Coal was the major commodity transported on the canal. Grandfather Barton also was very active in Ulster County politics.

As a young woman, my mother was secretary-receptionist for Doctor Joseph Hasbrouck, a brother of New York State Supreme Court Justice John Hasbrouck. When "Doctor Joe" retired, my moth-

called the *Skillypot* or *Tortoise*. With rope ferries, the rope was hung high over the water. The cable for this chain ferry, however, was dropped across the stream and left sitting on the bottom, but securely fastened at each end. This allowed large boats to pass up and down stream without obstruction. A steam-powered engine aboard the ferryboat would grip the chain, which would be raised up temporarily from the bottom during the passage of the ferry in spite of cross current, and provide the fulcrum for traction. The tug *Rob* was needed at times of heavy ice to keep the crossing track clear.

I remember as a very young boy sitting on my grandmother's front porch and watching the string of cars drive by, bound for the Eddyville Bridge

Shamrock on the left and *Jumbo* on the right running cables to build the George Washington Bridge, circa 1920s. (Courtesy of Adam T. Schildge, Jr., of Roebling Engineers)

er oversaw the operation of the Rondout-Sleightsburg chain ferry *Riverside* owned by Doctor Hasbrouck. It was while serving in this capacity that she met my dad, who used the ferry to go home to his parents' house in Port Ewen from the Cornell marine shops when his vessel was in for repairs.

The chain ferry *Riverside* operated at Rondout Creek between the Strand at the foot of Hasbrouck Avenue. It crossed from Rondout to Sleightsburg during the years 1870 to 1922. When the new Route 9W suspension bridge over the creek was opened, the service was suspended. This boat was locally

over Rondout Creek. *Skillypot* only held a few automobiles at a time. There would always be a long line of cars up the Sleightsburg Route 9W hill waiting to board the ferry. The young men of the village would show the waiting motorists the several-mile route around to Eddyville and to Route 9W on the other side of Rondout Creek, and I understand they made a substantial amount of money during the summer vacation months.

Our family's involvement in the region is quite apparent on Rondout Creek. One of the two islands on the creek is called Hamilton Island, and Hamilton Dock, from which the family's sloops

Jumbo abreast of Esopus Light. Photograph taken from the bridge of *Peter Stuyvesant* on September 13, 1943, the day my dad, the *Jumbo's* captain, died of a heart attack. (Author's collection)

sailed, is on the north side of the creek at Wilbur. Dunn Dock is next to Hamilton Dock. Although I am unaware of the exact family connection, I do know that Nathan Dunn was a first cousin of my dad and that Nathan became Steamboat Engineer Inspector of the Albany, New York District. This was before the United States Coast Guard took over the duties from the United States Department of Commerce. Inspectors Dunn and Norton signed my first pilot's license for the Hudson River in 1932. I was nineteen years of age at the time.

I was born at Melvin and Catherine's home in Union Hill, New Jersey on October 1, 1913. Their second son, Melvin was born on October 11, 1917.

When Grandmother Barton became seriously ill, our family moved from Union Hill, New Jersey to the Barton homestead in Port Ewen, New York. However, my brother Mel and I stayed at Grandma Hamilton's home. I attended third grade at the red brick four-room grammar school on the hill. There were two classes to a room. Miss Van Steenburg, whose brother was a Cornell towboat captain, was my teacher. There was a two-room wooden school in the hillside area that had four classes to a room. Again, both teachers, Miss Eigo and Miss Tucker, were daughters of Cornell tugboat captains. Grandmother died in less than a year and we moved to Ridgefield Park, New Jersey.

I married Norma Frances Sowa at Saint Augustine's Catholic Church in Union Hill, New Jersey on January 23, 1938. This year marks our 63rd wedding anniversary. Norma is the daughter of Charles and Alice Sowa of Weehawken, New Jersey. This marriage has been blessed with five children: John Gerard, born November 22, 1938; Patricia Ann, born July 27, 1942; Melanie Frances, born April 28, 1944; Charles Richard, born April 29, 1947; and Terry Maria, born May 1, 1956.

One summer while on summer vacation from high school, I contacted Captain Chapman of the Hudson River night boat *Berkshire* and was hired as a quartermaster (assistant to the pilot). When my dad heard about it, he discouraged my choice. He told me that if I wanted to follow him into the profession, I could come with him and get a more rounded knowledge of the river working on all types of vessels. He proved to be right. At age nineteen, I received a Second Class Pilot license. At age twenty-one, I received my First Class Pilot license, which covered vessels of any type, size, and draft on the waters of New York Harbor, the East River, Newark Bay, Kill Van Kull, and the Hudson River to the Government Dam at Troy, New York. At age twenty-four, I received my Master's license for vessels of any gross tons and draft on the lakes, bays, sounds, and rivers.

A beautiful statue stands proudly on the grounds of the Presentation of the Most Blessed Sacrament Catholic Church, in Port Ewen, New York, overlooking the Hudson River. This Ulster County bluestone sculpture represents Mary, the Mother of God, holding a towboat in her outstretched hands. The statute is dedicated to all who served on the river and was presented to the parish by the New York Towboat Union, Local 333. The site was chosen because Port Ewen gave a majority of its sons to the river to crew its vessels. My Barton grandparents on my mother's side, my mother, uncles, aunts, and cousins all worshiped at this parish church, which was staffed by Redemptorist Order priests.

Author standing by Our Lady of the Hudson dedicated to all who served on Hudson River vessels, June 2000. (Author's collection) The statue stands on the grounds of Presentation of the Most Blessed Sacrament Roman Catholic Church in Port Ewen, New York. Captain John Hamilton and a friend, George Harris, transported the altar statues from this church to Teaneck, New Jersey, where an artist friend of Hamilton, Edward Zucchi, completely refurbished them as a memorial to Captain Hamilton's mother. Hamilton and Harris then returned them to the church altar in Port Ewen.

Crossing the Hudson River on ice from Rensselaer to Albany in the mid-1800s. The sled is leaving from the ferry rack. (Author's collection)

CHAPTER TWO

Hudson River Steamboats
Origins, Early Days and an Overview

The earliest record of an attempt at steam propulsion of a water craft is credited to Blasco de Garay in 1543 in Spain, but it wasn't until 1769 in England that James Watt had success in the development of the steam engine, which in time led to successful steamboat operation.

The prime moving force in a steam engine is the terrifically powerful expansive force of steam, which expands to roughly 1600 times the space of the water required to generate it. The force is measured in terms of the pressure the steam exerts in a closed vessel and is expressed in pounds per square inch of the surface of the vessel. Steam was generated in boilers fired at first by wood and later by coal and oil. If the fire was hot, the steam formed quickly and the piston moved rapidly. If the fire was low, steam formed slowly and the piston moved less rapidly.

There were two types of boilers. In five-tube boilers, hot gases from the firebox exhaust passed through water-filled convoluted tubes inside a large vessel before passing up the stack. The steam was generated inside the boiler shell before being drawn off to the manifold and cylinders. This type of boiler was subject to terrific internal pressures and often led to terrible boiler explosions in the early days of steam power.

In the water tube boiler, which was more commonly used in later years, the hot exhaust gases passed through the boiler shell on the way to the stack. Water circulated through the convoluted tubes inside the shell and was heated by the passing hot gases. As the water inside the tubes turned to steam, it was drawn off to the manifold and cylinders.

Wood was abandoned as a fuel and replaced by coal because coal had a high caloric value per pound and did not pass sparks through the flues. With coal, less weight in fuel had to be carried. Early coal burners were fired by hand shovels and were known as "hand bombers." Eventually, automatic coal stokers were developed. By the 1920s, oil generally superseded coal as the favored fuel on the Hudson River. The last two steamboats to use "hand bombers" were the D. L. & W. ferries, *Binghamton* and *Elmira*, which burned clean anthracite coal.

In a reciprocating steam engine, a piston moved back and forth inside a cylinder. This was accomplished by admitting live steam through a valve into the cylinder to push the piston. This inlet of steam was stopped about halfway through the piston's stroke to take full advantage of the expansive force of the steam. At the end of the stroke, another inlet valve was opened on the other side of the piston again admitting live steam, which pushed the piston back in the opposite direction. Spent steam was exhausted through outlet valves that were mechanically activated in synchronization with the steam inlet valves. More modern engines were very complex and differed in design on vertical and inclined beam engines.

The first individual to make serious sustained efforts toward steamboat development was an

Fulton's North River steamboat *Clermont* abreast of the Palisades circa 1807. (Author's collection)

American, John Fitch. He obtained exclusive steam navigation rights from the states of New Jersey and Pennsylvania in 1786-1787. In 1787, he successfully operated a steamboat on the Delaware River that traveled four miles per hour. Other boats followed this in 1788 and 1790 that operated at seven miles an hour between Trenton and Burlington. Oars propelled these steamboats. In spite of his rapid advances, Fitch's backers were timid and gave him no further support after his fourth vessel was wrecked in a storm. Fitch always seemed on the verge of commercial success that never materialized.

The British, with good reason, claim that the first successful steamboat was William Symmington's *Charlotte Dundas*, which was tried on the Forth and Clyde Canal in 1801. She had paddle wheels and a Watt-built engine, and could pull two 70-ton barges for a limited distance.

Robert Fulton, credited with the development of the first successful commercial use of a steamboat, was born in 1765 at Little Britain,

Connecticut. He was an artist who, as life went on, became an inventor and engineer. In 1796, the American poet Joel Barlow, who was deeply interested in steamboat development, invited Fulton to Paris, France. Fulton lived with Barlow for seven years. During this time, he occupied himself with developing submarines and other experimental weaponry for the French and British governments. While still in France, Robert Fulton met Chancellor Robert R. Livingston, who was then the United States Minister to France.

Livingston was from the great Hudson Valley patent-holding family. He lived on his estate, Clermont, at Tivoli, New York, across the river from Saugerties. He had attended Kings College (now Columbia University), was admitted to the bar and became a law partner of John Jay. Livingston was a member of the Continental Congress and served on the committee to draft the Declaration of Independence. In 1781, he was appointed the first United States Secretary of State. He had administered the oath of office to President

George Washington. From 1777 until 1801, he was the first Chancellor of the State of New York. In 1801, then-President Thomas Jefferson appointed him as Minister to France, where he conducted the negotiations that led to the Louisiana Purchase.

In 1803, Fulton, the poet Barlow, and Livingston pooled their talents and built a steamboat 86 ft. long and 8 ft. wide to operate on the River Seine in France. Livingston held a monopoly from the New York State Legislature for steamboat operation within the State of New York. He now felt he had the right man to bring his steamboat ambitions to fruition on the Hudson River. Fulton and Livingston became partners. Before returning to America, they ordered a steam engine from the English firm of Boulton and Watts to be sent to New York in 1806. When they reached New York, they ordered a hull from the East River Corlear's Hook shipyard of Charles Brown. This vessel was 130 ft. long, 16 ft. wide, and 7 ft. deep. The engine had a cylinder 24 in. in diameter with a 4-ft. stroke.

She was equipped with a low-pressure boiler 20 ft. long, 7 ft. deep and 8 ft. broad. She had two paddle wheels, one on each side, that were 15 ft. in diameter. The vessel was also equipped with masts and sails.

On Monday, August 17, 1807, Fulton's vessel, *North River Steamboat*, with several invited guests aboard, sailed from the foot of Cortland Street for Albany without using her sails against a slight head wind. She arrived at Albany on Wednesday, August 19, with a sailing time of 32 hours. (There was a 20-hour layover at Livingston's estate Clermont that was not included in the 32 hours.) Her return trip to New York City took 30 hours with no stops, again without sails. This experimental trip was so successful that Fulton and Livingston decided to advertise that starting on Friday, September 4th, there would be regular service between New York and Albany.

The partners had a well-organized line operating in very short order. During that first winter, the

Robert Fulton coming upriver off Hook Mountain with the *Hendrick Hudson* in the background circa 1942. Note the shad fishermen in the foreground. (Oil painting by William G. Muller)

steamboat was lengthened to 150 ft. and her paddles were enclosed in a housing to prevent them from being rammed by sailboat men who despised this new competition. Her name was changed to *North River* in 1808. She later became known as *Clermont*, after her homeport.

With this first successful commercial steamboat, the Fulton-Livingston monopoly was put into effect and they enjoyed the right to be the

Redfield, Thomas B. Cornell, Jacob Tremper, Absalom Anderson, Benjamin B. O'Dell and Alfred Van Santvoord also became powerful steamboat operators with Van Santvoord, perhaps, the greatest of all.

The steamboat service on the Hudson River between New York and Albany that started with Fulton's vessel in 1807 continued non-stop until the demise of the Hudson River Day Line in 1948. It

Peter Stuyvesant on the mid-Hudson River circa 1940. (Postcard, author's collection)

only ones to operate steam vessels in New York State. This situation continued until efforts were made to break the monopoly by Thomas Gibbons who operated a ferry from the Battery across the Upper Bay to Staten Island. The Gibbons case finally ended up in the United States Supreme Court. Chief Justice Marshall handed down a decision that opened up the New York State waters to all.

With the death of this monopoly, other operators quickly jumped into the ring. Most prominent among them were Commodore Cornelius Vanderbilt, Daniel Drew, Issac Newton and "Live Oak" John Law. At a later date, William C.

was appropriate that their vessel, *Robert Fulton*, ended the over 140 years of service to the route that began with Fulton's steamboat in 1807.

The *Clermont* had attained a speed of 6 knots. Speed was increased when the new F&L vessel, *James Kent*, made the trip to Albany on May 31, 1824, in 15 hours, less than half the time it took the *Clermont*. In June of 1826, the steamboat *Sun* made the voyage in 12 hours 13 minutes. The steamboats *Rochester* and *Swallow* on November 9, 1836, recorded runs of 9 hours. Speeds of river steamers gradually increased to 20 to 25 miles an hour but never increased beyond that. The fastest time on record for the New York to Albany route was by the steamboat *Chauncey Vibbard,* one of the early Hudson River Day Line vessels. This 267-foot vessel achieved a running time for the route of 6 hours and 20 minutes in April 1876.

The *Mary Powell,* running between New York and Rondout (Kingston) and nicknamed "Queen of the Hudson" was considered the fastest of all vessels in this section of the river. She proved slower than the *Chauncey Vibbard,* however, when she ventured into the shallow waters between Hudson and Albany. The *Mary Powell* was 288 ft. long and was commanded throughout most of her active service by the genial Captain A. Eltinge Anderson of Kingston, New York. This fine vessel regularly steamed along at 23 miles per hour. Her active career as a Hudson River steamboat covered almost 60 years, from 1861 to 1917.

Many fine steamboats plied the river in the early 19th century including the *Paragon, Fire Fly, North America, Chancellor Livingston, Rochester, Swallow,* and *Constitution.* None of these vessels were very large. All were less than 300 ft. long.

Beginning in the mid-1800s, larger, faster, more luxurious vessels appeared. Leading this parade were the *Alida* and *Armenia,* the 321-foot-long *Isaac Newton,* and the original 330-foot-long *Hendrik Hudson,* built in 1847-1848. They were considered the finest night boats on the river. They were also the largest, with elaborate grand saloons. In the next year, the still larger *New World* eclipsed them all. At 353 ft. in length, she was the largest vessel in the world. In 1885, the *Isaac Newton* was cut in two and then lengthened to exceed the length of the *New World.* They made an impressive pair of running mates.

Other fine steamboats that appeared in the latter half of the 19th century include the *Daniel Drew, Sunnyside, Saratoga, City of Kingston, Dean Richmond, Thomas Cornell, City of Troy, St. John, New York,* and *Albany.* When *St. John* was built in 1864 at a length of 393 ft., she was the largest vessel in United States waters, 14 feet longer than one of the giants of North Atlantic service, the Cunard Liner, *Scotia.* The Hudson River Day Liner, *Albany,* built in 1880, was the first iron hull vessel on the river. She served on the Hudson until 1933, when she left these waters to sail out of Washington, D.C., as the excursion vessel,

Potomac. In 1949, she completed 69 years of faithful service. The Cornell Steamboat Company's *City of Kingston,* built in 1884, was the first large propeller steamboat ever built.

The leviathans that plied the Hudson from the late 19th century into the 20th century include the *Berkshire, Fort Orange, Adirondack, Trojan,* and *Rensselaer* of the Hudson River Night Line. They sailed until the demise of the service in 1939. The *Berkshire,* the world's largest river steamer measured 440 ft. in length with a 95-ft. beam. The *Fort Orange,* its running mate, measured 420 ft. long, and 88 ft. wide.

The Night Line boats carried freight (General Electric in Schenectady and Bayer Aspirin in Rensselaer were among the larger shippers). They had four decks of cabins for passengers and served fine food in their dining rooms. They were known for their powerful searchlights that they shone on the shore as they proceeded along.

The Hudson River Day Line fleet of the 20th century, which operated through 1948, consisted of the *Washington Irving, Hendrick Hudson, De Witt Clinton, Robert Fulton, Alexander Hamilton, Peter Stuyvesant, Albany,* and *Chauncey Depew.* All these vessels were very fast, maintaining speeds far in excess of other river steamers throughout the world. This fleet of beautiful, fast greyhounds connected New York City with Albany with way landings at Yonkers, Indian Point, Bear Mountain, West Point, Newburgh, Poughkeepsie, Kingston, Catskill, and Hudson. The high speeds were necessary to meet a schedule that included disembarking and embarking thousands of people en route. A vessel northbound for Albany would unload 2,000 people at Kingston Landing where they took the Ulster and Delaware train to the Catskill Mountains. At Catskill, 2,500 or more would be onloaded, bound for another section of the Catskills. Often, on Saturdays or holiday weekends, a second steamer would be required to assist the first steamer on the Albany route.

These vessels were strictly for passengers and had wide decks for viewing the river and the beautiful scenery of the Hudson Valley. They served excellent meals in their dining room, snacks in the cafeteria; and featured a fine orchestra on the New York to Albany route. As automobile travel became more popular, business dwindled until the line ceased operation in 1948. One family owned the line throughout its existence. It was started by Commodore Van Santvoord, whose daughter married an Olcott who took over at the Commodore's death.

The *Washington Irving*, the largest Day Liner ever built, measured 414 ft. long, 86 ft. wide, and was licensed to carry 6,000 passengers. On the morning of June 1, 1926, while leaving its New York pier in the fog, it was rammed by a tug pushing a steel oil barge. The *Washington Irving* began to sink, but Captain Dave Deming guided the vessel to settle on top of the Holland Tunnel tube close to the New Jersey shore. The two lower decks were under water, while the remaining two decks were above water. Two passengers and a recently dismissed messboy were missing. This affected Captain Deming in such a way that he retired shortly after and died in a few months.

The *Hendrick Hudson* measured 391 ft. by 82 ft. and carried 5,500 passengers. My brother, Melvin F. Hamilton, spent time in her pilothouse after returning from World War Two, where he had captained a United States Army Air Corps crash boat. The crash boats are similar to Navy PT boats and are used to save pilots downed at sea.

The *Peter Stuyvesant* was one of three modern propeller vessels used during the line's existence. She had a passenger capacity of 3,750. I served as pilot of the vessel with Frank Briggs, a very fine gentleman, as her master for several years.

In addition to the Hudson River Day Line and Hudson River Night Line, there were several smaller lines that served specific cities and villages. The largest of these was the Central Hudson Line, formed in 1899 by a merger of three mid-Hudson night lines: Romer & Tremper, formed in 1884, served the city of Kingston; the Poughkeepsie Transportation Company, formed in 1862, served that city; and Newburgh was served by the Homer Ramsdell Company. Major Wilber Harrison Weston, born February 11, 1851, in Manchester, New Hampshire, became president of Central Hudson. His title of major came from his duty with the State Guard. Central Hudson Steamboats served towns and cities between Kingston and New York City: Esopus, Hyde Park, Highland, Poughkeepsie, Milton, Marlboro, New Hamburgh, Newburgh, Cornwall, Cold Spring, West Point, and Cranstons (now Highland Falls).

The line's fleet of side-wheel steamers included *James T. Brett*, *Mason L. Weems* (later renamed *William F. Romer*), *Central Hudson*, *Jacob H. Tremper*, and *M. Martin*. The latter two ran between Newburgh and Albany with all way stops. The line's propeller vessels included *Newburgh*, *Homer Ramsdell*, *Poughkeepsie 1st*, *Marlborough*, *Poughkeepsie 2nd*, *Benjamin B. Odell* (their largest, at 269 feet), and *Hudson Taylor*.

The vessels carried a heavy burden of fruit from the valley to the city. The *Homer Ramsdell* carried fresh milk to New York City out of Newburgh every evening for early morning delivery. She became known as the "Dairy Express."

Major Weston died of blood poisoning on September 27, 1902. He was succeeded as president of the line by Benjamin B. O'Dell, Sr., whose son was Governor of the State of New York. The Central Hudson Line lasted until April 24, 1929, when it filed for bankruptcy.

The Catskill Evening Line was owned by the Beach family, which also owned the Catskill Mountain House and a network of narrow gauge railroads in the Catskill Mountains. This line ran night steamers between Coxsackie and New York City, with way stops at Hudson and Catskill. The vessels engaged in this service were the passenger steamers *Kaaterskill* and *Clermont*, the side-wheel paddle steamer *Onteora*, and the propeller freighters, *Catskill* and *Storm King*. After the line's demise in 1918, the *Clermont* and *Onteora* had their staterooms removed and were operated as excursion boats to Bear Mountain by the Palisades Park Commission.

The Saugerties and New York Transportation Company was established on March 23, 1885. The side-wheel steamboat *Ansonia* was the first vessel on the route. Other vessels to follow were *Saugerties, Ida,* and *Robert A. Snyder*. This line operated between Saugerties and the Christopher Street pier in New York City, with way stops at Tivoli, Barrytown, Ulster Landing, Rhinecliff, and Hyde Park. Henry L. Finger and Robert A. Snyder were the two main stockholders. They were both ex-steamboat captains. This line stopped operating on December 15, 1938.

The first and oldest mid-Hudson passenger and freight line was operated by the Cornell Steamboat Company out of Kingston (Rondout). Boats operated by Cornell were: *Manhattan; Thomas Cornell; City of Kingston*, the first large propeller steamer; and the famous speed queen, *Mary Powell*. With time, Cornell became more interested in towing and became the largest fleet of towboats in the world. The passenger fleet was first absorbed by Romer and Tremper, and then by the Central Hudson line. The *City of Kingston* was sold to Washington State interests and ran on Puget Sound until she was sunk in a collision in fog. *Mary Powell* finally became part of

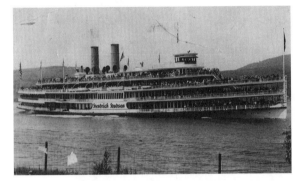

Hendrick Hudson, second largest Hudson River Day Line steamer, approaching Indian Point Park dock circa 1946. (Author's collection)

the Hudson River Day Line fleet. She left Kingston at 6:00 AM making a round trip to New York City, returning at 9:00 PM.

The village of Sing Sing, later renamed Ossining, had its own vessels *Ora*, *Eureka*, and *Sarah A. Jenks* (later *Ossining*).

Between 1841 and 1868, the Erie Railroad operated a line of steamboats between its Duane Street, Manhattan, terminal and its railhead at Piermont, New York. The railroad only had a charter for New York State from Dunkirk on Lake Erie to Piermont. The Erie Railroad terminal was at Piermont Long Dock that extended a mile out into the Hudson where steamers transported train passengers to New York City. Boats that served this route were *Arrow*, *Robert L. Stevens*, *Eureka*, *Thomas Powell*, *New Haven*, *Francis Skiddy*, and *Erie*. When the Erie Railroad received a New Jersey State Charter in 1861 and moved its terminal to Jersey City, the Piermont

operation was terminated. A ferry service was established from the Jersey City terminal to Chambers Street in New York City and, sometime later, also to 23rd Street. During World War One, troops from Camp Merritt were transported by boat from the Piermont terminal to troop ships in New York for overseas duty.

The Fort Lee and New York Steamboat Company began in 1832 and connected Canal Street, 22nd Street, and Spring Street with Weehawken, Guttenburg, Edgewater, Fort Lee, Shadyside, and Bulls Ferry. The vessels on this line included *Erwin*, *Thomas E. Hulse*, *Fort Lee*, *Pleasant Valley*, and *Shadyside*.

The Benjamin Franklin Transportation Company served Yonkers with a steam lighter, the tug *Payne*, and a barge. Many other small commuter vessels serviced Fort Lee and points along the Palisades.

The Lower Hudson Steamboat Company was formed in 1865. The line served Peekskill, Grassey Point, Haverstraw, Ossining, Nyack, and Tarrytown with service to New York City. Their vessels were *Sunnyside*, *Sleepy Hollow*, *General Sedgwick*, *Thomas Collyer*, *Orange*, *Rockland*, *Arrow*, *Broadway*, *Peter G. Coffin*, *John Farron*, *Adelphi*, *Chrystenah*, *Raleigh*, and *Riverdale*. These were all small, paddle wheel steamers that served thousands of commuters daily.

Early Hudson River steamboat captains were primarily business managers. Many owned or shared ownership in the vessel. They were in complete charge of the vessel's business operation, but they did not need or have any knowledge of navigation or piloting. The river's depths, currents, etc., were solely the responsibilities of the pilot in charge. The captain's expertise was in acting as the shipper's agent and disposing of his produce at a satisfactory profit. He also served as host to the passengers. This practice continued late into the 19th century when the Federal Government, for safety reasons, organized the Marine Inspection Service that required all officers on the navigational bridge to be fully trained and licensed navigational officers. From that time on, large Hudson River vessels carried a captain, 1st pilot, 2nd pilot, and a quartermaster for each watch. The purser became the ship's business manager.

Saratoga passing and illuminating with its searchlight the Catskill Evening Line steamer *Kaaterskill* in the Hudson Highlands in 1895. (Oil painting by William G. Muller)

Hudson River Nightboats

Daniel Drew, A. P. St. John, and associates formed the Peoples Line in 1835. Although originally a day service, they soon began night service and were the lineal precursors of the Hudson River Night Line that lasted until 1939.

The Peoples Line had three boats, two for regular service and another as a spare. At the time of incorporation, service was provided by *Hendrik Hudson* (330 ft. long), *Isaac Newton* (320 ft. long) and *New World* (353 ft. long). In order to attract passengers from the new Hudson River Railroad, the line enlarged *New World*, lengthened *Isaac Newton*, and rebuilt both vessels with two tiers of staterooms, which made possible the soaring grand saloons that were to distinguish the steamboats of the late 19th century.

Between 1864 and 1866, this prosperous company enlarged its fleet with the huge *St. John* (393 ft.), the *Dean Richmond* (348 ft.), and the *Drew* (366 ft. 5 in.). *St. John* burned in winter quarters in 1885 but *Drew* ran until replaced by *Adirondack* in 1896. *Adirondack* was a side-wheel paddle steamer with a wooden hull and noticeable hog-bracing, a frame constructed from near the bow of the hull up through the superstructure and back down to the hull near the stern to keep the hull from buckling or getting out of line. However, she did show a clean, modern appearance.

Meanwhile, the Citizens Line to Troy was formed by Joseph Cornell and local interests in 1872. They operated *Thomas Powell* (built in 1846, 231 ft. 2 in. long) and *Sunnyside*. The latter vessel had been built as a day boat to run between Ossining and New York City. That venture did not succeed and she was then placed on a run to Newburgh. She was laid up in 1870, then purchased by Joseph Cornell in the same year and rebuilt to run as a night boat.

Sunnyside sank off West Park on December 1, 1875. It was the high tide era of steamboating on the Hudson River and many fatal accidents occurred. Racing, fire, and collisions caused most, but a few were caused by ice. The sinking of *Sunnyside* was one of these. On November 29, 1875, *Sunnyside* left New York for Troy with a heavy load of freight. The temperature was in the 40s at first, but as she proceeded upstream a severe cold snap set in and the thermometer plummeted to 0 degrees, with ice forming on the river. When she arrived at Troy at 8:00 AM on November 30, it was decided to get the vessel back to New York as soon as possible.

Freight unloaded, the *Sunnyside* sailed at 2:00 PM and began pounding her way through the fast-forming ice. Off Stuyvesant, she encountered the side-wheel towboat *Niagara* with a tow of canal boats and sloops. After freeing the ice-bound fleet, *Sunnyside* continued downstream. Off Barrytown, she was discovered to be leaking water and the pumps were started. The new ice was sharp as a knife and had worked into the seams of the wooden hull, taking out the caulking. As long as *Sunnyside* was moving through the ice, ice stayed in the seams and a small hole in her port bow. Off

Isaac Newton, a famed Hudson River night boat. The third deck tier of staterooms was added in 1885. (Roger Mabie collection)

Esopus Island, she ran out of solid ice into open water. As soon as she sailed into clear water, the ice was washed away and *Sunnyside* began to take on more water than the pumps could handle.

An attempt was made to reach the steamboat dock, but failing that she slid back into deep water. The flood tide swept the bow up river until the pilothouse was filled with water. All that remained out of water was about 40 feet of the hurricane deck aft. Captain Frank Teson ordered the lifeboats put over. The first boat turned over in the drifting ice, throwing its 18 occupants into the icy water. Mate Burhonce somehow reached shore and a rope ferry was established. Survivors were brought ashore in a lifeboat pulled back and forth with the aid of the rope, but eleven people from the capsized lifeboat died of exposure. The survivors made their way to nearby farmhouses where they were given every attention possible. It was now 5:00 AM.

Communications along the riverbank were virtually nonexistent. At the request of Chief Engineer Parsell who lived in Port Ewen, ten miles north, George W. Murdock, a fireman on board, took off at 6:00 AM with the temperature at 6 degrees below zero to summon assistance from Port Ewen. He later stated, "Hiking that distance was rather a task." Murdock became one of the early collectors of historic steamboat material. The following spring, *Sunnyside* was raised and towed to Port

Ewen. The badly damaged hull was broken up. Her replacement was the *Saratoga*.

The fogs of spring and autumn have been the culprits in other steamboat accidents. Fog navigation on Hudson River vessels, before radar, was carried out in a unique manner. During spring or fall, in the early morning hours (usually between 3:00 and 4:00 AM) the difference in temperature between the air and the water was 20 degrees or better, creating fog that covered the river. The Day Line boats, traveling almost entirely in daylight, rarely encountered fog. Ferryboats traveling across the river had a fog bell in operation on the end of the ferry rack at each terminal. For the night boats, which encountered the heaviest fog, courses were timed from point to point, depending on ebb or flood tide. Whistle echoes were used between the vessel and the shore, noting low land, hills or certain structured buildings like ice houses, etc. The time between the blowing of the whistle and the echo return gave us the distance from shore. These measurements were taken in clear weather to be available when fog came. It was not an exact science, but it worked very successfully for years as a night boat navigational aid, when the vessel's speed was controlled. It was more difficult to get an accurate reading with a towboat maneuvering a flotilla tow because the number of units in tow affected the flotilla's speed.

Fog during the early morning of October 13, 1906, led to the collision just south of Saugerties of two of the larger night boats. *Saratoga* of the Citizens Line had left Troy on its regular run to New York, while the even larger *Adirondack* of the Peoples Line had departed earlier from her Manhattan terminal for her overnight run to Albany. The cool autumn air, coupled with the warm waters of the river, had caused fog to form. Both steamers were blowing fog signals on their whistles. Each converging vessel heard the other's signals, and both steamers' officers thought they would clear each other in a routine passing. But the true direction of whistle signals in fog can be misleading. In reality, the two vessels were approaching each other almost head on.

The two steamers loomed up out of the fog, too late to stop their headway completely to prevent swiping each other. *Adirondack* struck *Saratoga's* port mid-section. The grinding crash tore away the outboard housing of *Saratoga's* port paddle wheel and caused the port boiler to roll overboard. The splintering woodwork, crashing smokestack and escaping steam from the ruptured pipes must have made an awesome, deafening roar. Before *Adirondack* came to a complete stop, her main deck and deck housing at the point of impact were completely demolished.

Saratoga suffered the worst. Shortly after the crash, her northbound sister ship, *City of Troy* came alongside and took the passengers off. The wounded steamer's hull was leaking so badly that she was beached on the Hogs Back shoal just north of Barrytown, where she settled to the bottom. *Adirondack*, although badly damaged, continued under her own power to Albany.

In spite of the severity of the crash, only two lives were lost. An oiler on *Saratoga* was crushed and a clerk on *Adirondack* fell overboard and drowned. Other casualties included 35 sheep aboard *Saratoga* that were being shipped to New York in large crates. As *Saratoga* began to settle to the bottom, the sheep were let loose. Only three made it to shore. *Saratoga* was subsequently raised and repaired. She ran through the 1910 season, after which she was taken to Port Ewen and broken up.

For years, old boatmen had the superstition that any steamboat with a name starting in the letter "S" was dogged by bad luck. This sinking was not *Saratoga's* only mishap. She had grounded for weeks on Red Hook Island, collided with the Congress Street Bridge in Troy, and collided with a steam yacht off Stony Point. The steamboat *Swallow* had been involved one of the river's worst maritime disasters in 1845 at Athens, New York, when 5 lives were lost.

Troy Night Boat *City of Troy* during the New York Harbor welcome to Admiral George Dewey in 1898. (Roger Mabie collection)

During General Ulysses S. Grant's last term as president, the Citizens Line built a new elegant steamboat, *City of Troy* to replace *Sunnyside*. It was this vessel that later rescued the survivors off *Saratoga* after the collision with *Adirondack*. *City of Troy* made her first trip on June 15, 1876 and ran for 30 years, providing overnight passenger and freight service to the shirt and collar city after which she was named. Her career came to an abrupt end on the evening of April 5, 1907. *City of Troy* caught fire and was destroyed alongside a dock at Dobbs Ferry. At the time of her last trip, Charles Bruder of Schodack Landing was Captain, William Van Woert of Athens was First Pilot and William Fairbrother of Port Ewen was Chief Engineer.

The steamer had left her New York pier at 6:15 PM with 90 passengers and a heavy load of freight. As was the custom, pilot Van Woert went to his quarters to rest when the steamer left the limits of the harbor, leaving the second pilot, Mr. Bundy, to navigate until the vessel reached Poughkeepsie, the halfway point. Van Woert would take over at Poughkeepsie and pilot the vessel through to Troy.

The fire was first discovered on the freight deck forward at about 7:30 PM as the vessel neared the northern end of the Palisades. After he was informed of the fire, Captain Bruder went to investigate and found two streams of water already playing on the fire and men cutting a hole in the deck above. As many as seven streams of water in all were used in a valiant effort to save the ship.

Captain Bruder woke Pilot Van Woert and told him to make a good dock at Dobbs Ferry. The purser was already calling all passengers. Van Woert took command in the pilothouse and headed the steamer toward Gould's Dock, because there were no buildings there to which the fire could spread. After docking, the gangplank was put ashore; lights were placed all along the dock and the purser, Charles G. Ambler, and the freight clerk helped the passengers safely ashore. As soon as this was accomplished, all cabins were rechecked to make sure that no one had been missed. The officers and crew remained onboard fighting the fire until they were ordered ashore by the local fire department when it became evident that the vessel could not be saved. It was a total loss, but there were no casualties.

Captain Bruder, his officers, and crew were highly praised and honored by the United States Marine Inspection Service for their dedication to duty. The supervising inspector of the U. S. 2nd District considered their actions to be so splendid

Day Liner *New York*, after being lengthened by 34 feet in 1897. (Roger Mabie collection)

Albany of the Hudson River Day Line off lower Yonkers, circa 1925. (Roger Mabie collection)

that he hoped that their example would stimulate others to do as well.

In 1902, Charles Wyman Morse purchased the Peoples Line and the Citizens Line, and formed the Hudson Navigation Company to operate them. With these acquisitions, he then had control over a comprehensive empire of steamboats on the Hudson River, Long Island Sound, New England coast, and elsewhere. It was rumored that he had acquired a twelve-million-dollar fortune, and he was known as a sharp promoter and speculator.

Morse was a "downeaster," born October 21, 1856, in Bath, Maine. His father, Benjamin W. Morse, was a large investor in the towing business on the Kennebec River. Charles attended college at Bowdoin, but scholastic endeavors did not satisfy him. While still in college, he went into business with his cousin, Harry F. Morse. They bought ice from the Kennebec River and shipped it to New York by their own vessel, which they had built. Later, Morse gained virtually monopolistic control of the Hudson River ice harvest by merging his Consolidated Ice Company with the Knickerbocker Ice Company, calling it the American Ice Company and driving out independent dealers. Morse's ice trust more than doubled the price of ice to the consumer.

As soon as Morse controlled the two night boat lines, he made plans for a running mate for *Adirondack* on the Albany route to be called *C. W.*

Morse. She entered service in 1904 as the largest river steamer, an honor she held until the arrival of *Berkshire* in 1913. *Adirondack* ended her career in the mid-1920s. She was laid up at Athens, New York, and broken up in 1927.

In 1907, the Night Line built two new vessels for its New York to Troy run to replace the elderly *Dean Richmond* and *Greenport*, built in 1866 for Boston-Kennebec River service. The new twin steamboats were named *Rensselaer* and *Trojan*.

In 1906, the Hudson Navigation Company began planning a larger version of the *C. W. Morse*. The hull was launched at the New York Shipbuilding Company yard in Camden, New Jersey, on September 21, 1907, and named *Princeton*, in keeping with the collegiate names Morse had given to his Long Island Sound steamers, *Harvard* and *Yale*. Financial difficulties, however, caused *Princeton's* completion to be suspended. In the meantime, Morse had gradually built up control of Atlantic coast shipping with a collection of important lines. He had also been making himself felt in New York City banking circles. Then came the panic of 1907.

Morse was convicted of falsifying books and misappropriating funds of the Bank of North America. In 1908, he was sentenced to 15 years in the Atlantic Federal Penitentiary. After a group of army doctors reported him to be dying of Bright's disease, however, President Taft pardoned him and

Morse went off to Wiesbaden, Germany to restore his health. He had gained his freedom, well ahead of time. He returned to the United States with his health restored, and set about to resurrect *Princeton*.

Finally in 1913, the vessel was completed, but enrolled as *Berkshire*. She made her first regular trip on May 20, 1913. Beam engines powered all four of the company's last boats, although the walking beam was hidden from view by a covered housing.

Morse's interests kept control of the company until 1921, when it went bankrupt. To no one's sur-

Corning) built in 1857 to handle freight and leave space on the passenger steamers for automobiles. This venture failed.

The season of 1927 was the last for *Fort Orange*. She needed new boilers and was laid up at Athens, never to run again. The big *Berkshire*, alternating with *Rensselaer* and *Trojan*, however, provided sufficient capacity to handle the passenger business. Later, the line put into service the side-wheeler *Pioneer* to carry automobiles. She was formerly the Maine Central Railroad car ferry, *Ferdinando Gorges*. She proved too slow for the

Troy Night Boat *Rensselaer* at her Albany dock, July 1936. (Roger Mabie collection)

prise, the receivers quickly changed the *C. W. Morse's* name to *Fort Orange*, the original name for the city of Albany. The night boats had stiff competition from hard-surfaced highways and railroads on both banks of the Hudson, so the company remained in financial difficulties until its ultimate demise.

The company was reorganized again in 1926, as the Hudson River Night Line. Operations continued as before with *Rensselaer* and *Trojan* on the Troy run and *Fort Orange* and *Berkshire* on the Albany route. The company secured two freighters named, respectively, *Green Island* (formerly *York*) built in 1912, and *Cohoes* (formerly *Erastus*

run. Passengers arrived earlier on one of the passenger transportation vessels and had to wait for their cars to arrive.

In January of 1932, the Night Line went bankrupt again. D. F. McAllister, a well-known excursion boat operator in New York harbor, and Alfred Van Santvoord Olcott, president of the Hudson River Day Line, continued its operation on a short-term basis. McAllister withdrew in 1933-1934. In 1935, the line was sold to Samuel R. Rosoff, a New York subway manufacturer. The line's traditional operation ended in 1937. During its later years, Richard Chapman was master of the mighty *Berkshire*, George Warner captain of the

Trojan, and the Rensselaer's master was William Van Woert, who for a long period had commanded the day liner, *Albany.*

As a young boy working with my dad on the Cornell tug *Jumbo,* I was fascinated with the big *Berkshire* as she passed by. The next time we were at the Cornell stakeboat, (a vessel made fast to the shore in Rensselaer, New York, which served as both a dock and office for the Cornell Steamboat Company), I saw the *Berkshire* docked at her Albany pier. I walked across the bridge to Albany and boarded the *Berkshire.* With the permission of

to be the right choice to make. My career on the river had begun.

Some time later, *Berkshire* was laid up at Athens because of a reduction in business. Before she returned to service, she needed to be towed to Teetjen and Lang dry dock in Hoboken, New Jersey, for repairs. The tug *Jumbo,* with my dad as captain and me as a young deckhand, was the towing vessel. After *Jumbo* turned the vessel around to head downriver, a long steel cable was attached from *Jumbo* to the *Berkshire's* bow. She was a fast tow downstream because her paddle wheels were

Adirondack berthed at the Albany terminal circa 1910. Note hog frame required for a wooden hulled vessel of this size. (Postcard, author's collection)

the deck mate, I went to the pilothouse. As I entered, Captain Chapman, First Pilot Benjamin Stanton and the second pilot were all sitting around having a chat. I introduced myself as Captain Mel Hamilton's son and proceeded to inquire about a quartermaster job. Captain Chapman said that Benjamin Stanton's quartermaster was leaving at the end of the month and he would be happy to have me come aboard. He told me they would be in touch. I thanked him and left.

When I told my dad about the visit later, he convinced me to stay on with him and learn how to pilot vessels of every draft and size, which proved

unlocked and their turning helped propel the boat. At times, when we were making sharp turns in the Highlands, she would wander far left or right on the cable, almost reaching abreast of the *Jumbo's* stern.

"Mighty *Berkshire,*" as boatmen and Hudson Valley residents referred to her, had a relatively uneventful career in her 25 years of service as a night boat. After her final trip on September 8, 1937, she was laid up at Athens until 1941, when the federal government acquired her along with *Rensselaer.* During World War Two, she was towed downriver in the ice by the Coast Guard cutter

Berkshire, largest passenger boat on the Hudson. Astern is the largest day liner, the *Washington Irving*. (Roger Mabie collection)

Comanche and laid up at Hoboken, New Jersey. On June 25th, she was towed out of New York harbor away to Bermuda for use as government quarters. Later, she returned to Philadelphia to be dismantled across from her birthplace at Camden, New Jersey. *Rensselaer* was rejected as unsuitable and was dismantled at Providence, Rhode Island.

In the spring of 1939, *Trojan* was refurbished by Rosoff and renamed *New Yorker*. She ran from Battery Park in Manhattan to the World's Fair in Queens. This venture proved to be less than successful. On June 16th, she returned to the New York-Albany night run to supply every-other-night service until September 9, 1939, when the Hudson River Night Line died. *New Yorker* was laid up at Rosoff's sand dock at Marlboro. Early on March 1, 1940, she caught fire and was a complete loss.

The Hudson River Night Line had a reputation as a floating brothel that may have been at least partly deserved, but to a great extent it was the result of a vaudeville joke that got out of hand. However, the fact that the night boats operated completely within one state did remove the vessels from the reach of the Mann Act.

The dining rooms aboard the steamers accounted for a large part of the company's revenues. The assurance of an excellent dinner served on a sail down the beautiful Hudson River led many passengers from the west to leave their train at Albany and continue their trip to New York by steamboat. Another feature attraction was the vessels' powerful searchlights whose beams would be shined on interesting scenes along the river.

Another important line of night boats, the Central Hudson Steamboat Company, was formed in 1899 as the result of a merger of night lines that served New York, Newburgh, Poughkeepsie, and Kingston, and a day light operation from Newburgh to Albany and Troy. The new combined fleet consisted of 9 steamboats constructed in the period from 1853-1887. Others were built and added later. One barge vessel, the *Helen A. Place*, was also in the fleet.

The longest operating of the three night lines that merged into the Central Hudson Steamboat Company was Romer and Tremper Steamboat Company, a direct descendant of the firm Anderson, Romer, and Company of 1884. Its base of operations was Rondout on Rondout Creek. Romer and Tremper had shared the Kingston to

New York route with Thomas Cornell through 1889. Cornell sold his interests in 1890 to become the owner of the world's largest fleet of towboats and tugs. Romer and Tremper had as its night boat *James A Baldwin*. They needed another vessel in a hurry, so they purchased the Chesapeake Bay side-wheel night boat, *Mason L. Weems*. She was renamed *William F. Romer*.

The Poughkeepsie Transportation Company had, for years, run the propeller steamers *Daniel S. Miller* and *John L. Hasbrouck* between Poughkeepsie and New York. These two vessels were uncommon specimens. Each vessel had a propeller fitted with a vertical beam engine, the walking beam of which was positioned athwartship (sideways) and within the superstructure.

The Homer Ramsdell Transportation Company based in Newburgh contributed the iron-hulled propeller steamers *Newburgh* and *Homer Ramsdell* to the newly merged company, with the paddlewheel steamboat *James T. Brett*, as a spare boat. *Newburgh* originally had 2 boilers but later in life was equipped with 4 Scotch boilers. *Homer Ramsdell* originally had 2 lobster back boilers, but also had 4 Scotch boilers installed later. The *James T. Brett* had a vertical beam engine from *Chingarora* with a 40 in. by 12 ft. cylinder.

The steamers *M. Martin* and *Jacob H. Tremper* were active on the Newburgh-Albany day route.

Major Wilber Harrington Weston appeared to be the man who brought these lines together, but it is not clear whether he was acting on his own or serving as a front for others. He was born in Manchester, New Hampshire, on February 11, 1851. After attending the New Hampshire Conference Seminary, he moved to Newburgh at the age of 20 and secured employment with the Erie Railroad, whose branch line connected Newburgh with Jersey City via Maybrook. Later, he became

Hudson River Night Line's *Trojan* passing Beacon, New York, in August, 1933. (Author's collection)

an agent for the New York Central and Hudson River railroads. When he was awarded a contract for carrying mail between Newburgh and the Fishkill Landing railroad station across the river, he got into the transport business and, subsequently, the express, stage, and cab businesses. He also became involved with trolley lines early in their existence. The major (a title that came to him from duty with the New York State Guard) claimed that it was an original idea of his to merge the three steamboat companies.

He began the task early in January 1899. After six weeks of negotiations, he got options to buy. Next, he contacted and interviewed Benjamin B. O'Dell Jr., of Newburgh. O'Dell was born on January 14, 1854. He had studied at Columbia College served two terms in the United States House of Representatives and at that point was chairman of the New York State Republican Committee working for the election of Theodore Roosevelt as governor the following November. O'Dell immediately contacted several capitalists who joined in a syndicate to provide the necessary funding. Subscribers included his father, Benjamin B. O'Dell, E. H. Harrington, and Chauncey M. Depew. The older O'Dell, born in 1825, was a very active Republican politician who had served several terms as mayor of Newburgh.

As a result of O'Dell's efforts, on April 14, 1899, the Central Hudson Steamboat Company came into being. At a meeting of the new board, Wilber H. Weston was elected president, Jacob H. Tremper (son of Captain J. H. Tremper) vice president, Benjamin B. O'Dell, Jr., (the financial power behind the throne) treasurer, and F. G. Kimball secretary.

The initial operational arrangements had Homer Stockbridge Ramsdell (son of Homer Ramsdell) in charge of Newburgh to New York, with his office at Newburgh. Jacob H. Tremper supervised night boat operations north of Newburgh, with his office at Pier 24, North River, New York City. Overseeing Poughkeepsie business was Samuel A. Crum, formerly Poughkeepsie Transportation Company's secretary. Myron Teller, formerly with Romer and Tremper was in charge at Kingston. Teller was also superintendent of the Newburgh-Albany Day Line. Those top management links with the old Romer and Tremper operation were short-lived. In January 1890, an announcement was made that Major Weston had bought the interests of Tremper and Teller in Central Hudson. Conspicuously missing from the new organization was Captain John H. Brinckerhoff, who had controlled the Poughkeepsie Transportation Company when it was sold. Apparently, he chose to step aside.

The aims of Central Hudson were far-reaching. They sought to control the Catskill Evening Line, the Saugerties, New York Steamboat Company, and the side-wheeler *Emeline* of the Haverstraw-Newburgh day route. At one time they had *Emeline* under charter. There also was a rumor that unless Samuel D. Coykendall, president of the Cornell Steamboat Company and the Ulster and Delaware Railroad, agreed to make Kingston Point Park available as a landing, Central Hudson would develop its own recreational resort at Dennings Point in Newburgh Bay. This did not prove true. The local newspaper reported that the rampant rumors could form the nucleus of a free library.

The Central Hudson Line's routes included landings by their steamers as follows:

Newburgh Route: Newburgh, Fishkill Landing, Cornwall, Cold Spring, and West Point to Pier 24, North River, New York City. On Sundays, *Homer Ramsdell* provided a round trip day excursion from New York to Newburgh, as well as operating as the regular Newburgh night boat.

Poughkeepsie Route: Poughkeepsie, Highland, Marlboro, to Pier 24, North River, New York City.

Kingston Route: Kingston, Esopus, Hyde Park, Poughkeepsie, Milton, Marlboro, New Hamburgh, Newburgh, Cornwall, and Cranston's to Pier 46, North River at the foot of West 10th Street, New York City. (The name Cranston's as a steamboat landing, may be unfamiliar to many people. The name came from the large resort hotel built on the top of the cliff 180 feet

Central Hudson Line's *Central Hudson* at her dock on the Rondout Creek, circa 1910. She was formerly named *James W. Baldwin.* (Roger Mabie collection)

above the river and overlooking Buttermilk Falls. Ownership of Cranston's hotel passed in January 1900 to the Sisters of Saint Francis, who converted it into a boarding school for girls called Ladycliff College. Subsequently, this landing was called Highland Falls after the village on the top of the hill.) Later, the Central Hudson moved its line's terminal from Pier 46 North River down to Franklin Street at Pier 10 North River, making that location its sole New York terminal for all steamers.

The Newburgh to Albany day route made stops at almost all communities en route.

Steamboat schedules on the various routes changed little from year to year, but the boats used varied a bit depending on the season or ice conditions.

In 1900, Central Hudson changed the names of their beam engine propeller vessels. *John L. Hasbrouck* became *Marlborough*, and the *Daniel S. Miller* became *Poughkeepsie*. Later, in 1903, they decided to name the *James W. Baldwin* the *Central Hudson*. There was a special reason for that name change. Governor O'Dell's first wife was Estelle Crist, with whom he had three sons. In 1888, Mrs. O'Dell was aboard a sailboat that collided with the *James W. Baldwin* and she drowned. O'Dell later married Linda Traphagen Crist, a widowed younger sister of his first wife, and a daughter was born of that union. It seemed appropriate to eliminate the *James W. Baldwin*, with its tragic associations, by doing a major overhaul and renaming the vessel *Central Hudson*.

In 1902, the *Central Hudson* Line's President Wilber H. Weston ran into the corner of a table and injured his groin. Sometime later, he went home with a chill. He thought he was coming down with malaria, but by the middle of the following week he complained of pain in his thigh. Doctors discovered a large abscess, and an operation was performed on September 25th without anesthesia. Blood poisoning set in and Weston died two days later.

He was succeeded by the senior Benjamin B. Odell, whose son was then governor of New York,

having turned down the Republican nomination for Vice-President of the United States. If he had accepted, he would have been elected along with William McKinley in 1900. When President McKinley was assassinated in 1901, the vice-president, Theodore Roosevelt, became president. It could have been O'Dell.

The *Poughkeepsie*, southbound in adverse weather on her first trip on March 21, 1901, plowed onto the rocks at Stony Point at about 1:30 AM. Her bow was smashed and leaking badly. Lines were run ashore and attached to trees to hold her onto the point. Later on, the ebb tide swung her stern out into the stream as she continued to settle.

Central Hudson Line's *Homer Ramsdell* bound upriver off Manhattan, circa 1925. (Roger Mabie collection)

Her hurricane deck aft was under water. She was successfully raised, however, repaired and put back into service on April 6th.

In 1904, eight steamers were in service: *Central Hudson* and *William H. Romer* on the Kingston route; *Marlborough* and *Poughkeepsie* on the Poughkeepsie run; *Homer Ramsdell* and *Newburgh* on the Newburgh route; and *M. Martin* and *Jacob H. Tremper* on the Albany day route. *James T. Brett* was in reserve.

That year, Herbert R. O'Dell, a graduate of Columbia University, became general manager of the Central Hudson Line. In October, he married Pauline Clarkson Ramsdell, daughter of Homer Stockbridge Ramsdell, in a ceremony that united two illustrious Hudson Valley families. The new manager, assuming the roll of an efficiency expert, cut wages sharply. The wages of chambermaids dropped from $20 to $12 a month (with bed and

C. W. Morse at Albany with *Jacob Tremper* and *Albany* astern circa 1919. (Captain Dick Sherman's collection)

board provided), porters from $25 to $18, and pantry men from $27.50 to $21. The position of headwaiter was eliminated. Captains, who had previously been paid on a year-round basis, were paid for 10 months, unless, of course, weather permitted the steamers to run longer.

The *M. Martin's* hull had deteriorated badly, and in the winter of 1905-1906 a partial rebuilding of the hull and other necessary repairs were done at Marvel's yard. A new boiler from the Hudson River Day Line's *New York* was installed. The old-fashioned, round, "sentry box" pilothouse was replaced with one of more modern design. They even considered renaming her the *Orange* but she came back into service well into 1906 with her original name intact.

On February 23, 1906, while at winter quarters in Newburgh, *Homer Ramsdell* caught fire. The blaze was discovered about 9:00 PM in the kitchen on the main deck aft. The fire damage was confined to this room; however, a dumbwaiter leading to the dining room above served as a flue, and there was considerable smoke damage to the after saloon and to staterooms on the saloon and gallery deck. The ferryboat *Fishkill*, which had been using her searchlights to spot ice fields crossing the river, used this light to aid the firefighters.

On Sunday afternoon about 4:30 PM, on June 26, 1910, the *Poughkeepsie* caught fire in her engine room while loading fruit at Highland. Efforts to fight the blaze failed. The passengers were taken off

safely and *Poughkeepsie* was towed out into the river by the railroad bridge tug tender *Anne*. Then, she drifted to the east shore and sank. The fire from the vessel had jumped to the Highland wharf and destroyed Central Hudson buildings, along with a signal tower of the West Shore Railroad, a house, and a trolley car.

Trouble continued to plague Central Hudson in 1910. *Marlborough*, southbound in the vicinity of 18th Street North River, New York City, had a collision with a car float. Much joiner work was ripped off and about 150 boxes of grapes went overboard.

Central Hudson was withdrawn from service after 50 years on the Kingston route. Her replacement was launched at the Harlan and Hollingsworth yard at Wilmington, Delaware, on December 3, 1910. The entire vessel (hull, superstructure, and engine) was a product of this yard. She was christened *Benjamin B. Odell* after the company's president. There was considerable local criticism that the vessel had not been built in Newburgh at the T. S. Marvel yard, which had produced such notable river steamers as *Hendrick Hudson*, *Robert Fulton*, *Trojan*, and *Rensselaer*. Central Hudson's claim that the Marvel yard was not equipped to build a vessel during the winter was unconvincing.

Benjamin B. Odell was made especially heavy to cut through Hudson River freshwater ice. She reached a speed of 21 3/4 miles an hour on her trial run. She had 60 outside staterooms. Instead of a ladies' cabin in the hold or aft on the main deck, she had two large rooms on the saloon deck with nine berths in each. Forward on the saloon deck was an observation room. Another was located on the hurricane deck. The 100-seat dining room was located aft on the third deck. The vessel's interior was plain but serviceable, a far cry from the New York-Albany day and night lines. The *Benjamin B. Odell* was licensed to carry more than 3,000 passengers for excursion trips. She had great space in which to carry freight, plus two steam elevators to provide entrance and egress.

On Thursday, April 6th, she was inspected by large crowds at Newburgh who were anxious to explore the first vessel built for the Central Hudson Steamboat Company. On the next day, at Poughkeepsie, she provided the citizens of that city the same opportunity. On Saturday, she sailed into Rondout Creek at about 1:00 PM to be greeted by a long succession of salutes until she tied up at the Central Hudson pier. Afterwards, she was open for inspection by the Kingstonians. Then, on Sunday, April 9, 1911, *Benjamin B. Odell* entered regular service as she sailed from Kingston at 5:00 PM. She was advertised as the "handsome and commodious steamer." A one-way trip to New York cost $.90; a round trip $1.40. Staterooms ranged from $1.50 to $3.00.

Adverse weather conditions-fog, freshets, and heavy ice-plagued Central Hudson in 1912. There were no serious accidents however, only schedule delays. Then on July 21, 1913, the northbound *Jacob H. Tremper* struck a rock near Esopus Island, which ripped a hole in her hull and caused her to be beached on the east shore. The small steamer *Elihu Bunker* took off passengers who were bound for Kingston. The rest went ashore to continue by train. Cargo was transferred to a barge and towed to Kingston by the Cornell tug *John D. Schoonmaker*. The *Tremper* got off the rock successfully on July 23 and was towed to Hildebrandt's Shipyard on Rondout Creek.

Service between Newburgh and New York had been maintained for nearly two years straight when ice conditions finally became so bad that the service had to be suspended on February 24, 1914. In that same year, Central Hudson added their smallest vessel to the fleet, the *Hudson Taylor*. This vessel was built at Philadelphia, Pennsylvania, in 1879 for William P. Drake of New Hamburg to run passengers and freight between Newburgh and Poughkeepsie. *Hudson Taylor* was a propeller vessel. On July 7, 1914, she became the sole property of Central Hudson, employed between Albany and Troy through the 1918-1919 season. It is said that her eventual withdrawal from service was the result of running into a bridge.

Central Hudson continued its efforts to attract Sunday passengers out of New York with *Benjamin B. Odell* sailing a round trip to Poughkeepsie, with Newburgh as the main way landing. The Newburgh area had George Washington's Headquarters, Orange Lake Park (which could be reached by trolley) and Mount Beacon as its main attractions. The mountain could be reached by taking a ferry across the river, then a trolley to the foot of the mountain, then the inclined railroad (said to be the steepest in the United States) to the top to enjoy a splendid view and a visit to the Mount Beacon Hotel. At Poughkeepsie, a short tour of the city could be taken by trolley, and Vassar College could be visited. A former ship's officer said that, prior to the commencement of Sunday operations by the Hudson River Day Line in 1918, *Benjamin B. Odell* had capacity loads of passengers out of Franklin Street, New York City, for thirteen successive Sundays and had to pass up large crowds expecting to board her at West 129th Street.

The year 1916 was an important one in the history of the Central Hudson Steamboat Company. First, it marked the launching of a new steamboat with the revived name *Poughkeepsie*, the second and last vessel built for the company. It also seems to have been the last year *William F. Romer* and *M. Martin* took part in regular service. The new *Poughkeepsie* was launched at the yard of Tampa Shipbuilding and Engineering in Tampa, Florida, in May of 1916. After being christened by the four-year-old daughter of the shipyard's president, Marguerite Kreher, *Poughkeepsie* stuck on the ways. A tug tried to pull her off, but the hawser parted, and it was not until Monday the 25th that the launching could be completed. The vessel went into service almost immediately. Her facilities as a freight carrier were excellent, but accommodations for passengers were limited. Additional staterooms were added later.

Central Hudson announced in June 1916 that *Marlborough* was being dismantled at Marvel's Shipyard for scrap, and the dismantling of *James T. Brett* would be completed soon. Then, in 1918, as was the case with many steamboats during World War One, *Newburgh* was employed in U. S. Government service in New York Harbor.

A minor problem arose with *Jacob A. Tremper* on April 18, 1918. She departed Newburgh in a fog and was slowly making her way upriver. Near Roseton, she ran aground on a sand bar with a heavy load of freight on board. The Newburgh office was notified and General Manager Herbert R. O'Dell reached the grounding on the Cornell tug *George Field*, but with the falling tide nothing could be done. Finally, on Sunday, April 21, *Tremper* floated free undamaged and continued up river.

In that same year, the new *Poughkeepsie*, running on the Kingston route with *Benjamin B. Odell*, was sailing into Rondout Creek one morning at about 6:00 AM with an exceptionally heavy

load of freight on board Suddenly, her steering gear failed and she veered into the dock of a shipyard where two barges were under construction. *Poughkeepsie* plowed six feet into the dock, which disintegrated before the onslaught, but she continued unharmed to her own terminal, steering with the hand gears.

In mid-September 1920, it was announced that the *Benjamin B. Odell* was chartered to go to Chesapeake Bay for winter service between Baltimore and Norfolk for the Old Bay Line, while their *Alabama* was being re-boilered. She remained there until the spring of 1921. Later that same year, she returned again to Chesapeake, but this time to the Chesapeake Steamboat Company so that night boats from that line could be withdrawn for service and repairs.

Like all freight-carrying steamboat lines in the 1920s, Central Hudson Steamboat Company was feeling the competition from motor trucks. When the company suspended service one winter during a severe ice problem, some of their business went to trucks and stayed there.

To improve their financial situation, Central Hudson turned more and more to the passenger

The original *Poughkeepsie* aground at Stony Point after running ashore in a dense fog on March 21, 1901. (Roger Mabie collection)

Benjamin B. O'Dell in the East River off E. 71st Street in 1932. (Captain Dick Sherman's collection)

excursion business. They built a small private park, Sunset Park, at Verplanck's Point not far from the Hudson River Day Line's park at Indian Point, but on a much smaller scale. An advertisement for Sunset Park in 1925 read: "Sunset Park, the Hudson's Beauty Spot, and Newburgh. Steamer leaves Franklin Street at 9:30 AM, Battery 10:15 and 129th Street at 11:00 AM. Unsurpassed scenery-Dancing-Restaurant-Parties Accommodated. Round trip $.85, children $.60, Sun. & Holidays $1.00, Newburgh round trip $1.35."

Unfortunately, Sunset Park was not a great success, and the trucks continued to undermine Central Hudson's freight service. On March 16, 1927, Herbert R. O'Dell and George Hutchison, the president of Newburgh Shipyards, Inc., were appointed equity receivers for Central Hudson. Normal operations of the company continued.

In an attempt to hold its own against truck competition in the winter of 1928-1929, Central Hudson tried to continue winter service between Kingston and New York for as long as possible. Windrows (piles of ice built up by the action of the wind) formed the greatest hazard to winter navigation. All went well until late January 1929. On Monday the 28th, *Newburgh* sailed from Kingston at 3:00 PM and *Poughkeepsie* sailed from New York. Both vessels became caught in piled-up ice near Cold Spring. *Benjamin B. Odell*, laid up at Newburgh, sailed to the rescue, but she also got caught in the heavy ice. Finally, on Friday, February 1, all three steamers were free. Later in the same month, however, all three vessels became icebound in Newburgh Bay. This got lots of newspaper publicity and it was enormously expensive. It was yet another severe blow to an organization that was already suffering financially.

On April 24, 1929, the company was the subject of a bankruptcy sale. The highest bid was $200,000, far below the minimum of $425,000. A new sale was ordered for May 8 and the minimum was lowered to $250,000. This time, the high bid was $326,000 plus tax obligations, interest, and an obligation to honor the contracts with captains and pilots and make repairs to the steamers. The total price was considered to be closer to $376,000. The high bid had been tendered jointly by the Hudson River Day Line and the Hudson River Night Line. The sale was confirmed on May 10. The Hudson River Steamboat Company was incorporated to take over the Central Hudson assets, including four steamers. *The Jacob H. Tremper* had been sold for scrap.

The new company continued operating all four steamers until March 1930, when it announced it was selling *Homer Ramsdell* and *Newburgh* for use in the Boston area. Both vessels had their staterooms removed and were converted into daytime excursion boats. *Homer Ramsdell* was renamed *Allerton*. She ran to Nantasket Beach until the early 1950s. *Newburgh* became *Nantasket* and was used on the same run. Both vessels were sold for scrap in 1952.

The two remaining vessels, *Benjamin B. Odell* and *Poughkeepsie*, served the New York-Albany run for a few more years. They were part of the twilight of the night boats on the Hudson.

One hundred miles upriver from the mouth of the Hudson is the village of Saugerties, incorporated in 1885. It was originally called Ulster incorporated in 1831. It had wharves for shipping and receiving on Esopus Creek, a tributary of the Hudson. With a population of two to three thousand, the village was sufficiently important to have a steamboat line, so a boat to carry passengers and freight to New York City was established in the latter half of the 1830s.

On March 23, 1865, a new organization called the New York and Saugerties Transportation Company was incorporated and began to service the route with the side-wheel steamboat *Ansonia*. She made three round trips a week, and served faithfully and well. *Ansonia* was built of wood in 1848 at Burtis and Morgan, Brooklyn, New York. The vessel had been built originally for the Naugatuck River Transportation Company for service between Derby, Connecticut, on the Housatonic River and New York City, and was named after a Naugatuck River town. During the Civil War, the federal government employed her.

Captain Henry L. Finger bought an interest in *Ansonia* in 1848, then acquired full control in 1886. He had previously been a sloop captain; now, he commanded *Ansonia*. In early 1888, he sold his interest in the vessel and became associated with Robert A. Snyder. Together they bought *Ansonia's* docking berth and forced her new owners to seek other docking facilities within the one mile of the navigable waters on the Esopus.

Robert A. Snyder, born in 1836, had become a cabin boy at age 11 on a market barge that ran between Saugerties, Tivoli, and New York. He then moved on to be a fireman on Fall River Line steamers, and then to being the owner of an Erie Canal boat. Later, he purchased the franchise of the Saugerties-Tivoli ferry and captained the ferryboat *Airline*. He became very active in politics, holding elective offices as town collector, town supervisor, sheriff of Ulster County, and member of the New York State Assembly. In addition, he was president of the First National Bank of Saugerties.

The purchase of the dock and the steamboat *Shenandoah* by Captain Finger and Snyder was part of a broader plan. On January 29, 1889, the Saugerties and New York Steamboat Company was incorporated with a capital of $68,000 by Finger, Snyder, James T. and William L. Maxwell, and John and George Seamon. Robert A. Snyder was elected president. Shortly after his election, he and Finger sold the *Shenandoah* and the dock to the newly incorporated company.

Shenandoah was renamed *Saugerties*. She entered Esopus Creek for the first time on April 24, 1889, Henry L. Finger commanding. *Ansonia*, mastered by B. M. Freligh, had started her season on March 17th.

Although both vessels had the same small communities as way landings—Tivoli Barrytown, Ulster Landing, and Rhinecliff—departure dates from Saugerties and New York differed. *Ansonia* departed Saugerties on Monday, Wednesday and Friday, and *Saugerties* on Sunday, Tuesday and Thursday. Both vessels left at 6:00 PM. New York departures were on the following day. Both companies charged the same fares: $1.00 one way, and $1.50 round trip.

Saugerties was advertised as "new and elegant." She had 36 large, well-ventilated staterooms. Cabin berths provided additional sleeping quarters. In the saloon and ladies' cabin, velvet carpeting was used. Chairs, settees, and lounges were upholstered in red and blue velvet plush. Certainly, her accommodations were superior to *Ansonia's* and she would inevitably draw business away from her aging adversary.

She did not complete her initial season on the Saugerties run. The Cornell Steamboat Company, which operated the Kingston-New York night line in league with the Romer and Tremper Steamboat Company, sold its propeller steamer *City of Kingston* to west coast interests in the fall of 1889 and needed a capable vessel to fill in for the balance of the season. *Saugerties* was considered the best available, so a charter was arranged for her. The side-wheeler *W. W. Cott*, built in 1864, replaced *Saugerties* on its regular run for the remainder of the 1899 season. *Saugerties* had the historic distinction of being the last steamboat to serve on the Cornell night line, which Thomas Cornell had founded decades before. Prior to the season of 1890, Cornell sold his operation to the Romer and Tremper Steamboat Company.

In 1891, *Ansonia*, on her first trip of the season, left New York for Saugerties, but now she was operating for the Saugerties-New York Steamboat Company, which had purchased the New York and Saugerties Transportation Company on March 23, 1891. In May of 1891, the New York terminal was moved from the foot of Franklin Street to Pier 48, North River, at the foot of Eleventh Street. Later, it was changed to Pier 43 at the foot of Barrow Street, where it remained throughout the organization's existence. The Saugerties dock property, located on the south shore of the creek, was substantial. There were three large brick storehouses for freight, plus an icehouse, with ample room for two steamboats to dock.

Ansonia was lengthened and so completely rebuilt between 1891 and 1892 at the Burtis Shipyard in Brooklyn that she was eligible to be enrolled as a new steamboat. The renamed vessel,

Ulster, was 205 ft. long (5 ft. longer than *Saugerties*). She had 40 staterooms, 28 cabin berths for men and 20 for the ladies.

On November 11, 1897, *Ulster* had a rather strange accident. She left Saugerties, bound for the usual way landings and New York. There was a strong wind with a flood tide. The captain, A. W. Hale, had turned in for the night. Pilot Ezra Wittaker, who had been pilot of the Cornell side-wheel towboat *Oswego*, was on watch. He kept close to the west bank as the vessel approached Storm King Mountain to be out of the tide's strength. Quartermaster Charles R. Tiffany brought a sandwich to Wittaker, who then turned the steering wheel over to Tiffany while he ate the snack. Then, at Tiffany's request, Wittaker again manned the wheel and Tiffany left for what was intended to be a short absence. About two minutes later, Wittaker was seized with cramps so severe that he released his grip on the steering wheel and fell back into his chair. When he let go of the hand-powered steering wheel, it must have had the rudder over because it swung back to its normal midship position. The wheel spokes struck him in the chest, breaking two of his ribs and cracking another. It was too late for any corrective action to be taken. *Ulster* had yawed off to starboard and went up on the rocks at the foot of Storm King Mountain at full speed. It was just about midnight. The vessel had 20 passengers on board, including two of Captain Hale's daughters, and a heavy load of freight. All passengers were helped ashore. They hiked to the nearest railroad station at Cornwall.

The tracks of the West Shore Railroad go around the base of Storm King Mountain. *Ulster* slid up at an angle of 15 degrees and came to rest within a few feet of the tracks, her jackstaff knocking down a telegraph wire. In addition to the passengers and crew of *Ulster*, one more person was about to receive a great shock that night. The engineer on the northbound West Shore Express rounded a curve and was confronted with what seemed to be definitive evidence that he was about to collide with a steamboat. Before he could react, to his great relief the engine just cleared the vessel.

But it wasn't over yet. The following account, written by John S. Overbagh and Donald C.

Ringwald, appeared in an article in the spring 1978 issue of *Steamboat Bill Quarterly*:

When the tide commenced to ebb, it swung *Ulster's* stern so that she was lying at an angle of close to 90 degrees with the bank. As she swung, the bow cut a deep trench in the shore. The next flood tide resulted in the submersion of the vessel to the maximum extent possible, with little visible aft of the paddle boxes.

Such freight as could be gotten off was removed, and during the day—Friday—a Merritt & Chapman Derrick and Wrecking Co. crew arrived on the scene. Although the wind blew hard and the river was choppy, divers made preliminary examination of the hull.

The foreman of the wrecking operation felt that it was inconceivable that *Ulster*, with her bow perched so high, could possibly slide back into the river. Because of the railroad running across in front of the bow, it was not feasible to put out a secure mooring, but the foreman did have a hawser run out from the steamer to a telegraph pole. Then work was suspended for the day.

Naturally, a watchman was set on the wrecking vessel. About midnight, the man on watch aroused the foreman with word that *Ulster* had apparently sunk completely. Immediately, all hands were called on deck and a lantern swung forward, but no trace of the steamboat could be seen. The foreman was not about to accept the explanation that a wooden-hulled vessel with wooden upper works could sink entirely out of sight, and was quoted as saying to the man on watch, "You have let the wreck slip right from under your nose without giving warning, and now only the Lord knows what havoc she will create." We may sagely assume that what he actually said was worded somewhat differently and more forcefully, since his concern was that another vessel might run into the drifting wreck.

. . .

Lying at the north dock at West Point was a three-masted schooner commanded by Captain John Vought, who had brought up a load of sand from Peekskill. Near midnight the sailor on watch sighted something bearing down on the schooner. Thoroughly alarmed, he called the captain to report that a steamer without lights was about to ram them.

This "steamboat without lights" was, of course, *Ulster*, and even as the captain got on deck, the steamboat caught the schooner and pinned her against the wharf. Captain Vought tried to push the wreck away with a hand spike and, oddly enough, was able to do that, because the waves aided him and the wreck drifted away. Next Vought ran up the hill to the military academy and found two sergeants who returned to the north dock with him and aided him in securing *Ulster* with lines.

. . .

Ulster was raised on Monday, November 15th, and then taken to the Marvel shipyard at Newburgh. Although the upper works were badly damaged, the hull was considered sound enough to merit a rebuilding of the steamer.

Another grave misfortune occurred for the Saugerties-New York Steamboat Company when *Saugerties*, shortly after arrival on Sunday morning, November 22, 1906, caught fire and was a total loss. Her hull was later raised, but found not worthy of repair. It was beached between Saugerties and Malden.

The company decided to purchase *Ida* from the Baltimore, Chesapeake & Atlantic Railroad Company as a permanent replacement for *Saugerties*.

In 1901, Robert A. Snyder and James T. Maxwell purchased the interest in the steamboat company that was held by the heirs of Captain Henry L. Finger, thereby gaining complete control. *Ida* and *Ulster* ran together through the 1920 season, after which *Ulster* was extensively altered. The most obvious change was the removal of the rounded paddle boxes, which were replaced with plain woodwork as *Ida* had. During this overhaul, the name of the vessel was changed to *Robert A. Snyder* in honor of the line's first president.

Until motor vehicle transportation made it obsolete, the Saugerties-New York Steamboat Company filled a need for reliable freight and passenger service between Saugerties, the intermediate landings, and New York City. Northbound cargo consisted of pulp for the several paper mills in the area, general merchandise, and supplies for the Village of Saugerties and the various Catskill Mountain summer resorts. Some farm products were shipped out of Saugerties, as were bluestone slabs, but the principal commodities were paper products. Martin Cantine Company, makers of coated paper, Saugerties Manufacturing Company, makers of business ledgers, Diamond Mills Paper Company, makers of various grades of tissue papers, The Tissue Company, paper converters specializing in crepe paper, and Montgomery Washburn, makers of insulated covers for ice cream and milk containers, all shipped from Saugerties.

The 1931 season ended in early December when a sudden hard freeze brought on severe ice conditions that made it inadvisable for the steamboat *Ida* to depart Saugerties. She had just taken on a load of Christmas trees for the New York market. These had to be unloaded and returned to the shipper for forwarding by other means. Later that winter, a decision was reached to discontinue operations. The competition from over-the-road carriers made it no longer financially practical to continue.

Probably no one felt the demise of the line more keenly than Robert A. Snyder, the grandson of the first president and son of the second, John A. Snyder. As a boy, he had worked at various jobs with the company. After graduating from Dartmouth in 1925, he went with the line full time and became general manager.

Catskill Evening Line night boat *City of Catskill* on the upper Hudson River circa 1882. (Author's collection)

Captains in the line included:

Saugerties—Henry L. Finger, (his son) William L. Finger, and William Tiffany
Ansonia—Robert H. Wittaker, who continued in command after she was rebuilt as *Ulster*
Ulster—A. W. Hale, William J. Snyder, and George Post
Robert A. Snyder—Richard W. Heffernan was master from the time of her rebuilding in 1921 until the company's demise in 1931.
Ida—Captain William R. Tiffany was the long-time commander. He went to Baltimore when she was purchased for Hudson River service, and remained with her throughout her service on the Saugerties-New York line.

Ida and *Robert A. Snyder* remained in quiet retirement at the Esopus Creek dock until the third week of February in 1936, when *Snyder* sank to the bottom because of heavy ice buildup. Later that year, both vessels were auctioned off to Louis Epstein. *Ida* was towed away to New Jersey and broken up for scrap. In August 1938, the federal government at the request of the Village of Saugerties raised *Robert A. Snyder*. Merritt, Chapman and Scott raised what remained of the vessel, and she was towed to Staten Island, where the engine, boiler, and anything else salvageable was removed before the hull was towed to sea and dynamited.

Finally, on December 15, 1938, the Saugerties-New York Steamboat Company, one of the smaller, but proud, steamboat lines, was dissolved.

There is little background history available on the Catskill Evening Steamboat Line. The route was from Coxsackie, Hudson, and Catskill to New York. The Beach family, who also operated the Catskill Mountain House and a network of narrow gauge railroads, owned it.

Steamboats that saw duty on this run in the early years of the line's existence were *New Champion, Andrew Harder, Walter Brett, Charlotte Vanderbilt, William C. Redfield,* and *Escort.* In the early 1880s, two new steamboats slid off the ways to accept passengers and freight: *City of Catskill* in 1880 and *Kaaterskill* in 1882.

On the night of November 8, 1891, *Catskill* found herself fogged in just north of New York City along with two rival steamboats, *St. John* and *Saratoga.* When the fog lifted, the three captains decided to make up for lost time and see who could outrun the others. *St. John* which had a reputation for speed, led all three to Newburgh, but *City of Catskill* had overtaken *St. John* by Poughkeepsie and led the rest of the way upriver. Her reputation was established, and the Evening Line gained stature. *City of Catskill's* days of fame were numbered, however; she burned at Rondout two years later. *Kaaterskill* made her last run in 1913 after many years of faithful service.

Onteora, built in 1898, was the next passenger and freight steamboat built for the Evening Line. She was named after a legendary great sleeping giant of the Catskill Mountains and designed by Captain James Stead of Cairo, New York, a stockholder in the company. Upon entering service, this mid-size night boat could cut through the water at 20 miles per hour with ease and, with a little effort, achieve 23 miles per hour.

As the summer of 1898 wore on, *Onteora* passed other steamboats whose reputation for speed she overshadowed. Her crew began to train their sights in the direction of *Adirondack,* "queen of the night flyers." Captain Ira Cooper, master of the *Onteora,* never wore an officer's uniform—just a dress suit with a cowboy hat. He told me the following story: *Onteora* was late leaving New York, and was just a short distance ahead of *Adirondack.* Coming up through Tappan Zee, Haverstraw Bay, and the Highlands, *Adirondack* was bottled up (as boatmen say). Each time she met a tow, she had to slow down to one-quarter speed to reduce the size of her waves. *Onteora* on the other hand, never made much of a swell, so she did not have to slow down. Consequently, every time the big "A" slowed, *Onteora* ran away.

As *Onteora* was approaching Crum Elbow, *Adirondack* was slowly gaining, "opening up" as they say. It is said that the engineers on *Onteora*

Catskill Evening Line's *Onteora* leaving an upper Manhattan pier on a summer Saturday afternoon, circa 1910. (Roger Mabie collection)

were injecting live steam into her engines and putting shingles between the duck bills of the engine in order to get a shorter stroke on the walking beam and turn the paddlewheels over faster. In any event, because *Adirondack* continued to make the necessary slows, she never did catch the speedy little steamer from Catskill, but old Albany night boatmen continued to defend big "A"as the faster of the two vessels. The Catskill Evening Line changed to opposite night sailings for *Onteora*, so there was never opportunity for a re-run. *Adirondack* holds the record time for a steamboat from New York to Albany with no stops en route: 6 hours and 24 minutes.

In 1911, *Clermont* was built to replace the older *Kaaterskill*. The officers aboard *Clermont* thought she was a fast boat like *Onteora*. This claim to fame, however, was never substantiated.

On a Saturday in 1912, *Clermont* was southbound passing Poughkeepsie just as the screw steamer *Benjamin B. Odell* was getting ready to leave. Both were new ships built in 1911. It did not take long for the *Odell* to catch up to and pass *Clermont*. She arrived in Newburgh when *Clermont* was only passing Roseton. About two weeks later, the Cornell Steamboat Company towboat *Geo. W. Washburn* again whipped *Clermont* in

a race. I know the *Washburn* was an exceptionally fast tug, because in the mid-1930s, I was her captain.

By 1916, the line was in financial trouble. Receivers, including Eben E. Olcott, were appointed on January 4, 1918. They decided to continue freight service, but *Clermont* and *Onteora* were offered for sale. The two steamboats operated in 1918 under charter to the Troy Evening Line, a short-lived attempt by a group of Troy businessmen to oppose the Citizens Line.

Meanwhile, the line operated the freighters *Storm King* and *Reserve*. Then the line reorganized in 1921 and built the steel-hulled *Catskill*. By 1929, Hudson River Day Line ownership increased to over 90%. *Catskill* was sold to operate as a car and passenger ferry across Long Island Sound between Port Jefferson and Bridgeport, Connecticut. *Clermont* and *Onteora* were sold to the Palisades Interstate Park Commission in September 1919. Stripped of their staterooms, they became excursion steamers between New York and Bear Mountain Park. On each was a plaque that read, in part:

> For the service of the public in the enjoyment of the Palisades Interstate Park,

the purchase of this steamboat and its companion was made possible by a contribution equaling their cost made in the loving memory of Laura Spelman Rockefeller.

Storm King was the last of the Catskill Evening Line vessels to run. She made her final trip in 1932. The poor condition of the fruit market in 1929 and succeeding years, increased use of trucks, and the depression combined to eliminate the line's fleet from the river.

Some of the captains of Catskill Evening Line vessels were Joel Cooper, Ben Hoff, James Stead, Ira Cooper, and Bill Burlingham.

The Hudson River Steamboat Company came into being as the result of a high bid at a bankruptcy sale on May 8, 1929. It was a joint venture between the Hudson River Day Line and the Hudson River Night Line. In December 1931, an agreement was made that the

Clermont at the Bear Mountain pier in 1947 when owned by the Palisades Interstate Park Commission. (Author's collection)

Benjamin B. Odell and *Poughkeepsie* would replace the large side-wheel night boats during the winter season on the New York-Albany-Troy runs.

In May of 1932, Judge John C. Knox accepted the offer of Captain D. F. McAllister, an excursion boat operator in the New York area, to operate the Hudson River Night Line but to keep all other activities separate. He named the night boat operation, McAllister Night Line, Inc.

In April 1932, the Night Line sold its half-interest in the Hudson River Steamboat Company. Alfred Van Santvoord Olcott, president of the Hudson River Day Line, now, as sole operator, chose to use *Benjamin B. Odell* and *Poughkeepsie* to run in opposition to *Berkshire*, *Trojan* and

Rensselaer. While *Benjamin B. Odell* was an adequate night boat, it lacked the more luxurious interiors of the much larger side-wheelers. The still smaller *Poughkeepsie* had nothing in the way of passenger facilities. To make up for these drawbacks, the Hudson River Steamboat Company scaled fares considerably lower for these two vessels.

Both the Night Line and the Steamboat Company continued to move freight in large quantities. The Steamboat Company won a round in this economic battle and gained control of the Troy wharfage, forcing the Night Line, which now terminated at Albany, to truck freight overland to the collar city.

In the fall of 1932, new offers for continued operation of the Night Line were submitted. This time, the Steamboat Company's proposal was accepted, to become effective November 1, 1932. The company planned to use its own steamers during the winter. McAllister, in anticipation of his continued lease to operate the Night Line, had chartered two propeller vessels *Hartford* and *Middletown*, from the Connecticut River run to New York. Both vessels were 243 ft. 3 in. long. McAllister used them in opposition to Olcott's Hudson River Steamboat Company. Judge Knox, however, at a February 1933 meeting of creditors and attorneys, refused to approve the sale of the Night Line and returned the steamers to McAllister to operate. McAllister replaced *Hartford* and *Middletown* with the big side-wheelers in the spring.

The Steamboat Company maintained its opposition. As a more suitable running mate for *Benjamin B. Odell*, the line chartered *Southland*, a screw vessel somewhat larger than *Odell*, from the Norfolk and Washington Steamboat Company.

The winter of 1933-1934 was extremely severe with very heavy ice in the Hudson River. On December 29, 1933, at 6:00 PM, *Poughkeepsie* left New York with Captain George Carroll in command and Howard Eaton as chief engineer. (*Middletown* left somewhat later, but had no scheduled stop en route.) *Poughkeepsie* lost time making several landings en route, but she was able to cut out of the track near Castleton and pass *Middletown*, which was icebound. *Poughkeepsie* victoriously led the way to Albany with Middletown following in her wake. *Poughkeepsie* finished with engines at 3:58 PM on the 30th. After discharging passengers and freight, she went on to Troy.

Early in January 1934, a new contract was awarded to the Steamboat Company to operate the Night Line. McAllister had asked to be relieved on the grounds that there was not enough business for two lines, a fact that had been obvious for a long time. The receivers had been complaining about the unsettled debts.

By early February, there was three feet of solid freshwater ice on the river, yet *Benjamin B. Odell* and *Poughkeepsie* continued to run, although far off their scheduled times. It was the worst ice in the history of steam navigation on the Hudson River.

On Thursday night, February 8, 1934, the *Benjamin B. Odell*, commanded by Captain John H. Dearstyne Jr., son of the longtime skipper of the *Jacob H. Tremper*, broke her way out of the ice at her Franklin Street pier and started north for Albany. "Jack," as fellow boatmen called him, later served as a state pilot with the Sandy Hook Pilots Association during World War Two. After the war, he and I were both member/partners in the Hudson River State Pilots Association, piloting deep draft

Trailership *New York* approaching Castleton Bridge through ice in January 1949. (Author's collection)

ships on the waters of New York Harbor and the Hudson River.

The weather that night was bitterly cold. The temperature at 7:25 AM the next morning dropped to 14.3 degrees below zero, the lowest to that date in the history of the weather bureau. The Hudson was covered for almost its entire length with solid ice. The steamer track, created by vessels turning ice up on end as they passed, was frozen even thicker. Sceptics along the river claimed that the *Benjamin B. Odell* would never get anywhere near Albany. On the last previous upriver trip, *Poughkeepsie* got no further than its namesake city.

Captain Jack told me one evening in the Pilot Association's apartment on Chestnut Street in Albany while we both rested for next morning sailings of two ships from the port of Albany, that he felt the *Odell* could make it. She had twice the power of *Poughkeepsie*. Based on past performances, he felt she was the best icebreaker of all the river's passenger and/or freight steamers.

He told me the *Benjamin B. Odell* bucked her way through the ice up to Poughkeepsie, loaded the upriver freight left there by *Poughkeepsie* and continued on upstream. At times, her speed was reduced almost to a crawl, but she kept on going. When she reached New Baltimore, many of those who thought she would never make it that far, now walked out on the ice to greet her. Jack said some of the crew jumped down on the ice and walked alongside. That Saturday afternoon, she arrived safely in Albany.

As she was leaving the next day, the *Benjamin B. Odell* broke her propeller. Since it was impossible to tow the vessel to New York in the heavy ice, she laid up until the tow could be accomplished in the spring.

Mr. Olcott continued to operate the Night Line with the Hudson River Steamboat Company as lessee. He put *Rensselaer*, *Trojan*, and *Berkshire* in commission in 1934 as usual. Then on March 28, 1935, the Hudson River Night Line, including the *Fort Orange*, which had been laid up for a long time, was auctioned off to Samuel "Subway Sam" Rufus Rosoff. *Fort Orange* was sold later that year for scrap.

The Hudson River Steamboat Company was now in deep financial difficulties. In late March

In 1913, opposition appeared on the Albany-Troy night service offering $1.00 fares. *Kennebec* (renamed *Iroquois*) and *Penobscot* (renamed *Mohawk*) made up the fleet of the Manhattan Line. *Iroquois* had been built in 1889 by the New England Shipbuilding Company of Bath, Maine, for use on the Boston-to-Bath run. *Mohawk* had been built in 1882 by Smith and Townsend of East Boston.

To counteract the low fares, Hudson Navigation organized a low fare line of its own. It

U. S. Coast Guard cutter *East Wind* and trailership *New York* passing New Baltimore, New York, in late January 1960. (Author's collection)

1936, Rosoff's offer for the line was approved. In January 1937, *Poughkeepsie* was transferred to the Meseck Steamboat Company and rebuilt into a fine-looking excursion boat named *Westchester*. She operated between Jersey City, the Battery, and Rye Beach Park on Long Island Sound. *Benjamin B. Odell* caught fire and sank at winter layup at the Rosoff sand and gravel dock in Marlboro. So ended the life of the short-lived Hudson River Steamboat Company.

was called the Capital City Line. *Frank Jones* from Portland, and *Kaaterskill* were added to the fleet to cover this service. *Frank Jones* was the first steamboat in Maine waters with an inclined beam engine.

In 1917, *Mohawk* rammed *Berkshire* in the stern during fog. The Manhattan Line lost the court case and Hudson River Navigation Company was awarded $150,000. The Manhattan Line could not pay the award to C. W. Morse's line, so the Hudson River Night Line took the boats over as spares. The competing lines of Capital City and Manhattan both ceased operations by World War One.

Men who served as skippers of this short-lived adventure, included Charles Hallenback, Bill Gates, Frank DeNoyles, Frank Pratt, Bill Newman, Jack Deerstyne, Al Craig, and Bert Briggs. Captain Briggs of Greenport, at age 21, was the youngest of Hudson River passenger masters up to that date.

The "trailerships" were two vessels that plied the waters between New York and Albany daily except Saturday. They were engaged in the overnight transportation of truck trailers. They didn't move the truck tractors so drivers were not needed. They were owned by Mr. Pew, president of the Sun Oil Company (Sunoco). Mr. Crosby, former president of the Hudson River Night Line, was the operating superintendent.

I was the *Albany's* captain, and George Carroll mastered the *New York*. Frank Briggs was my 1st pilot, with Dick Howard my 2nd pilot and Charlie Holliday was quartermaster. It was while I was employed there, that I had my first experience with the actual use of radar on the bridge of a ship. It proved to be a great asset in the navigation of vessels on Hudson River waters, and made me realize what a great job the old night boat officers and Cornell's flotilla tow captains and pilots did in bad weather without this modern aid.

Cornell's side-wheel towboat *Norwich* with flags flying and whistles blowing on her way to participate in the Hudson-Fulton parade of 1909. (Roger Mabie collection)

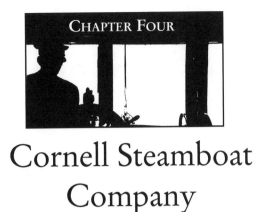

CHAPTER FOUR

Cornell Steamboat Company

The Cornell Steamboat Company was owned by one family. Thomas Cornell started it. After his death, it was taken over by his daughter's husband, Samuel Decker Coykendall, and later by their son, Fred Coykendall, with whom ownership remained until his death. Thereafter, ownership of the fleet spread throughout the industry. The Coykendall family was the premier family in Kingston, deeply involved in politics, property ownership, and charities. They also owned the Kingston Ferry Company and the Ulster and Delaware Railroad.

The Cornell name is first mentioned in Hudson River marine history in 1836. At that time, the 56-year-old Peter, father of Thomas Cornell who later became dominant in Rondout Creek steamboat history, was an agent of the firm of Cornell & Gedney. The firm represented the side-wheeler *Frank*, a 134 ft. 6 in. long vessel built in 1835.

In 1839, Cornell & Bidwell represented Captain David P. Mapes's *General Jackson* and Captain Joseph P. Dean's *Congress*, which was owned by the Delaware & Hudson Canal Company. Captain Dean was a merchant, trader, accountant, walking newspaper, public relations expert and, of course, master, but the one skill lacking was piloting a steamboat. There, he had no talent.

On July 2, 1829, *Congress* carried two of the four locomotives built in England for the Delaware & Hudson Canal Company. One, the *Stourbridge Lion*, cleared Rondout on July 16th and on August 8th ran on the company's tracks between the head of the canal at Honesdale and the coal mines at Carbondale—the first operation of a railway locomotive on commercial tracks in America.

Cornell & Bidwell also provided canal boats for freight consignments along the Delaware and Hudson between Rondout and Honesdale, Pennsylvania. Thomas Cornell, born January 23, 1814, at White Plains, New York, headed the Rondout business. Jacob B. Bidwell took care of the company's New York affairs. In 1840, the firm offered the services of both Captain Mapes's and Captain John Ketcham's lines.

The real forerunner of the giant Cornell Steamboat Company was a partnership between T. W. Cornell, his nephew Thomas Cornell and three other investors in 1846. The steamboat line was named Eddyville, Rondout, and New York Steamboat Company.

In 1847, the side-wheeler *Telegraph* was put into service. Lawrence & Sneden of New York had built her for Asa Eaton, the nephew of Thomas Cornell who was his senior by eleven years. She left Thomas W. Cornell's dock in Eddyville at 4:00 PM on Mondays, Wednesdays, and Fridays, stopping at Andersons' dock in Rondout one hour later. Because no fewer than 5 steamboats were leaving Rondout Creek, *Telegraph* was withdrawn in August 1847 and put into day service between Newburgh, Rondout, Albany, and Troy.

In August of 1848, Captain William B. Dodge, a former Rondout blacksmith, withdrew from the freight and passenger business, selling his route and the steamboat *Norwich* to Thomas W. Cornell and Company. For her new owners, Captain J. Steward Barber, with Nelson Thompson as pilot and John S. Moore as chief engineer commanded *Norwich*. *Norwich* was built in 1836 by Lawrence & Sneden of New York.

The picture was gradually taking shape for years to come. Cornell's vessel ran opposite Romer & Tremper's *Highlander*.

Thomas Cornell and David Abbey Jr. decided to oppose the Peoples Line's *New World* on the Albany-New York run with Abbey's *James Madison*. This venture proved to be a miserable failure. The *James Madison* couldn't hold a candle to the luxurious *New World*. Cornell and Abbey had hoped that their nuisance opposition would cause the Peoples Line to buy them off, but the tactic failed.

In October 1850, Captain William Dodge lost the Delaware & Hudson Canal towing contract to Thomas Cornell. With this lucrative contract in hand, Cornell put *Mohegan* and *James Madison* on the towing route to New York.

In 1851, Thomas W. Cornell withdrew from steamboating and his nephew Thomas assumed control, operating *Norwich* on her route until mid-March. Then, he replaced her with *North America* which he purchased from Captain William B. Dodge. *Norwich* entered Cornell's list of towing steamboats and was enrolled in February.

With 1852 came a considerable change in Rondout steamboat policy resulting from action taken by Thomas Cornell, who was described by a local newspaper editor as "always ready to jump at a conclusion before his neighbors are fairly out of bed." In January, Cornell sold *North America* to Charles Anderson (brother of Captain Absalom L. Anderson) Abraham Sleight, and Jeremiah A. Houghtaling. Cornell became manager of the ferry between Rondout and Rhinecliff that connected with the newly completed Hudson River Railroad running along the east bank from New York City to Greenbush, opposite Albany.

Cornell comes into the picture again on August 23, 1853. Three military companies from Rondout intended to make an excursion by boat to Albany. Cornell provided the side-wheel towboat *Santa*

Claus for their use and even ran the newly built *Walter B. Crane* as a connecting boat to bring passengers down from Eddyville and Wilbur. On September 2nd he made *Santa Claus* available to the fire companies of Rondout and Kingston for an excursion to Hudson.

By that time, Thomas Cornell had attained the rank of major in the state militia. Romer, Tremper & Gillett bought out A. Sleight & Company, kept *North America* for themselves, and sold the rights of the Sleight Line and the surplus *Highlander* to Major Cornell.

During the winter of 1855-1856, Major Cornell purchased a steamboat to replace *Santa Claus*. The side-wheeler *Manhattan* had 45 staterooms, including 8 double rooms for families. It had berthing room for 85 stateroom passengers and 217 other passengers, or 302 in all.

By then, the Major's enterprises were booming. When *Santa Claus* was relegated to his fleet of towing steamers, she joined *Norwich*, *James Madison*, *Mohegan*, *Highlander* and *Emerald*. Cornell also owned an interest in the ferryboat *Rhine*, built in 1852. In partnership with his brother-in-law, Coe F. Young, of Honesdale, Pennsylvania, he owned and operated a fleet of 20 canal boats used in general freighting between Honesdale and New York. Young later became superintendent of the canal, and then general superintendent of the canal company. Cornell eventually became a member of the canal board of managers. Thomas Cornell was rapidly building his fortune and, at the same time, helping to build Rondout.

Spring was late in 1856, so it was not until Saturday, April 5, that *Manhattan* deeply loaded with freight, left New York accompanied by two Poughkeepsie propeller steamboats. With heavy ice ahead, *Norwich* (labeled the "Ice King") led the way. *Norwich* was considered fully competent to break a channel through the ice. As the story goes, the ice was so thick that *Norwich*, after running up on it for a third of her length, was supported by the ice for ten minutes before it gave way. The flotilla reached Poughkeepsie on Sunday evening, and the following day *Norwich* reached Rondout at about 4:00 PM, the first arrival of the season. On Tuesday afternoon, *Manhattan* arrived at Rondout from her Poughkeepsie stop.

On October 14, 1857, fire broke out in a hotel stable in Rondout. It spread to and destroyed the hotel, then jumped to the waterfront sheds of Romer & Tremper. The timely arrival from New York of Cornell's *Manhattan* eased the work of the local fire companies. Her pumps were quickly put into action and extinguished the conflagration.

Major Cornell furnished the *Manhattan* to the Sunday schools of Rondout, Kingston, and vicinity for short daylight excursions, free of charge, during August and September of 1858. The crews, as might be expected, were not overjoyed with this extra duty and daylight frolicking but the captains played affable hosts. Each succeeding one always exceeded his predecessor in bringing goodwill and appreciation to the Major. That fall, *Manhattan* transported 1,207 firkins (quarter barrels) of butter in one haul, guarding her name as the valley's butter carrier. During that winter season, Cornell had considerable overhauling done on *Manhattan*. *Norwich* filled in until her arrival back on the river on March 24, 1859. In spite of her overhaul, *Manhattan* broke a shaft on her southbound trip on June 15th. *South America*, built for service on Albany's Peoples Line, temporarily replaced her. *Manhattan's* cargoes mentioned by the press that year were 36,000 baskets of raspberries out of Marlboro in July, and in September, 1000 Delaware County-reared domestic animals from Rondout.

With the coming of 1860, Thomas Cornell, business genius that he was, looked forward to a most successful season for both his fleet of towing steamers and his sole passenger/freight vessel, *Manhattan*. The Major's career in towing had not hurt his pocketbook in the least, and the steady growth of the freight portion of his business only increased with time. During the 1860 season, Romer & Tremper and Cornell moved their New York headquarters to Jay Street, where Captain A. L. Anderson was already entrenched with *Thomas Powell*. That made the pier headquarters for all who would journey to Rondout.

Boat building became highly contagious. Before Romer & Tremper's announcement of plans to build a new steamboat had time to be thoroughly absorbed, Thomas Cornell announced he was about to build a new vessel 260 ft. in length, with an engine cylinder 60 in. with a 16 ft. stroke. He did not say it would be the fastest on the river, but stated she would be equal to any in beauty and inferior to none in speed.

On April 28, 1861, *Manhattan* steamed out of Rondout Creek with a barge alongside to transport the 20th Regiment, the Ulster Guard commanded by George W. Pratt, bound for New York on their way to the Civil War. Thousands of well-wishers turned out. As the vessel and its barge got underway to prolonged cheers, the ladies waved handkerchiefs and the men waved their hats. Additional thousands at Poughkeepsie and Newburgh stood in the pouring rain to watch *Manhattan* go downriver. At West Point, cadets lined the water's edge to cheer her past. Because this was a three-month enlistment, the 20th Regiment returned to Rondout aboard *Manhattan* on August 1st.

The 20th Regiment was re-formed with enlistees for 3 years or the duration and on October 25th embarked again on a regular trip run of *Manhattan* with Cornell's towboat *John Marshall* carrying the freight and part of the regiment's equipment.

To open the Cornell Line in 1862, *Manhattan*, escorted by *Norwich* left New York on Friday, March 21 and got to Poughkeepsie on Sunday. After *Norwich* made a round trip to New York and back, both steamers left Poughkeepsie at 9:00 AM on Wednesday and arrived in Rondout about 3:00 PM.

This was to be Captain Abbey's last season of command. He had aboard a new clerk, 24-year-old Samuel Decker Coykendall, who had been cashier and superintendent in a Rondout drygoods establishment. In the years ahead, Coykendall was to marry a daughter of Thomas Cornell and eventually succeed to the helm of the Cornell marine empire.

As the summer waned, Thomas Cornell became serious about steamboat building. Romer & Tremper had their new *James W. Baldwin* and Captain Anderson's *Mary Powell* was a girl that had a way of monopolizing publicity. The aging *Manhattan* suffered by comparison. She made her last trip to Rondout on December 31, 1862. Cornell decided to build his new vessel on the grandest scale, a vessel longer than *James W. Baldwin* and with a more plush interior than *Mary Powell*.

City of Kingston shown at her Rondout Harbor berth in the late 1880s. (Roger Mabie collection)

The Civil War made steamboats especially high in demand. Cornell sold *Manhattan* at an excellent price to Anthony Reybold of Delaware City, Delaware, for service in new adventures on the Delaware River, Chesapeake Bay, and the Gulf of Mexico. Thomas Cornell's new wooden-hulled steamboat was built at the Greenpoint, New York, shipyard of Elisha S. Whitlock. The *Thomas Cornell* was launched on January 20, 1863. Modesty was nicely served by design or accident in a newspaper item that said that Mr. Whitlock had named the boat after Cornell; however, name selection is usually far beyond the province of a shipbuilder. Captain David Abbey, Jr., and engineer Oliver G. Fowler, veteran Cornell officers, were to serve aboard in their respective capacities, and they had charge of launching festivities that included dinner, toasts, and speeches.

The *Thomas Cornell* entered regular service in late March 1863. Cornell chartered *Knickerbocker* to fill in until *Thomas Cornell's* debut.

With the *Thomas Cornell* now added to the Rondout-New York service, the three steamboat proprietors—Romer & Tremper and Thomas Cornell of the night lines, and Captain Anderson of

the day line—within four years through their collective efforts had brought to the Rondout Creek area the finest fleet of steamboats to service any Hudson River city except, perhaps, Albany. This fleet of 1863 stayed intact until March 27, 1882, when *Thomas Cornell* ran hard aground on Danskammer Point in a thick fog. The vessel proved to be a complete loss and never ran again. Captain William H. (Billy) Cornell, Thomas' cousin, was master at the time. He was 51 years of age and a life-long bachelor.

Not satisfied with a fleet of towboats and a new night boat, Cornell entered the Rondout-New York day line business by purchasing the *Mary Powell* from Anderson, Ketcham and Hasbrouck on October 10, 1864. On October 17, he sold one-half interest in *Mary Powell* to Daniel Drew; however, in 1867, Cornell bought out Drew and was once again sole owner.

When *Mary Powell* entered service for the 1866 season, Captain Ferdinand Frost from Nyack was in command (Captain Anderson had retired). The traveling public was amused by the story that morning sailings were quite cold "because there was Frost aboard." The purser was William H.

Cornell, Thomas Cornell's cousin, and Guernsey B. Betts was back as first pilot. William Cornell also served for a time as the vessel's master.

While Cornell owned her, he put a few of his own special touches in the *Powell's* management. For the 1867 season, he experimented with not serving hard liquor at the bar of either the *Mary Powell* or the *Thomas Cornell*. It was a short-lived temperance experiment. On Election Day, Tuesday, November 3, 1868, he offered free passage to all who wished to vote at all landings as far as Catskill, regardless of political affiliation. Cornell was running for re-election to the United States House of Representatives that year, and he lost.

In December of 1868, Cornell and Alfred Van Santvoord commenced complicated negotiations revolving around *Mary Powell*. Santvoord, in addition to his interest in what became the Hudson River Day Line, controlled a majority of shares in a towing line started by his father. This towing line had suffered a sizeable loss in 1868, and Santvoord was interested in disposing of some of its fleet. Cornell, on the other hand, was interested in increasing his own towing fleet. Towing was becoming his major enterprise. It was far more profitable for him than his night line or his sortie into the day boat operation with *Mary Powell*.

Van Santvoord's company bought *Mary Powell* and Cornell's Rondout day route for $180,000. Cornell got the *Oswego*, the first large paddle steamer actually built specifically for towing on the Hudson at a time when major towing vessels were merely remodeled passenger vessels. In addition, Cornell got *New York* and *Baltic*. After much horse trading with Schuyler's Towing Line, Cornell gained control of the towing business between Rondout and Albany.

To replace the loss of their steamer *Thomas Cornell* in 1882, Cornell Steamboat Company departed radically from the traditional Hudson River design of the wooden hull, side-wheel, beam engine steamboat. Major Cornell sought out Harlan & Hollingsworth of Wilmington, Delaware, to build him an iron hull propeller steamer named *City of Kingston*. The old colonial town of Kingston, first capital of New York State, was to be the homeport of this new sleek and graceful vessel.

During the two years between signed contracts and completion of the vessel, Cornell chartered several steamboats to run at night opposite Romer & Tremper's *James W. Baldwin*. For the 1882 season, *City of Catskill*, a new steamboat only in her second year, was chartered from the Catskill Evening Line.

Bad luck continued to plague Cornell. On February 11, 1883, the Cornell Steamboat Company's large office building caught fire. The blaze jumped to the *City of Catskill*, tied up in winter quarters behind the building. The vessel, which was locked in solid ice and could not be moved, burned to a total loss.

City of Kingston was launched on the Delaware River on March 11, 1884. She was smaller than the side-wheelers in similar service, but her machinery took considerably less space. The result was that she was about equal to them in capacity. The new vessel left Wilmington on May 24, 1884. She sailed down the Delaware around Cape May, then up the Jersey coast to her New York pier in just 14 hours.

On Saturday, May 31, at 1:27 PM, *City of Kingston* left on her maiden voyage up the Hudson to Rondout with no freight and a few invited guests as passengers. The Cornell Line propeller towboats *Hercules*, *S. L. Crosby*, and *Edwin Terry*, gaily-decorated, escorted the new steamer up river through the harbor. *City of Kingston* appeared off Rondout Light at 6:22 PM and steamed slowly up the creek to Rondout, where a large crowd greeted her.

She began regular service on June 2, 1884. She left Rondout at 6:00 PM on Mondays, Wednesdays, and Fridays, and after making landings at Esopus, Poughkeepsie, Milton, Marlboro, Newburgh, Cornwall, and Cranstons (Highland Falls), she would arrive at her Harrison Street pier in New York in the early hours of the morning. On Tuesdays, Thursdays, and Saturdays, *City of Kingston* left New York at 4:00 PM, arriving in Rondout at 9:00 PM. The downriver schedule was mostly for the purpose of getting produce from the Kingston area and the Catskills to New York markets before dawn. Passengers could remain resting in their cabins until 8:30 AM, not an easy task with freight being trundled off the cargo deck below. On summer Saturdays, she left New York at 1:00 PM, made no way landings, and arrived in Rondout to connect with a special Ulster & Delaware Railroad train that took passengers right from the dock to the Catskill Mountains resorts. On Sunday nights, she met a train from the mountains and sailed directly to New York, leaving Rondout at 11:00 PM or as soon as the train arrived. After her early Monday morning arrival, she deadheaded back for her Monday evening sailing out of Rondout.

U. S. Coast Guard identification card for the author's father, Captain Mel Hamilton, dated November 13, 1941. These cards were carried by all licensed masters and pilots granted entry to security areas throughout New York Harbor and the Hudson River during WWII. (Author's collection)

In her early years, *City of Kingston* had a reputation for being a cranky boat that was hard to handle, vibrated terribly, and backed poorly, thus taking longer to make her landings. This label was largely undeserved. I know from my time on the Day Line's *Peter Stuyvesant* that there is a big difference between maneuvering a side-wheeler and handling a screw propeller vessel. Former Cornell propeller towboat pilots replaced the City of Kingston's paddle steamer pilots, and her handling problems disappeared. The new propeller added in her third season lessened her vibration and subsequently improved her backing power.

She was involved in only two accidents while in Hudson River service. On June 23, 1886, she left Cranstons Landing at 9:40 PM, well ahead of schedule. She was traveling at two-thirds speed on a still, hazy night off Manitou in the Hudson Highlands. It was the kind of a night when the smoke from passing trains lay low over the water. Captain Van Keuren and both pilots were in the pilothouse, scanning the dark water for other craft. Suddenly, without warning, they spotted a schooner dead ahead, drifting with the ebb tide and too close under the steamer's bow to avoid a collision. The *Mary*

Atwater had sailed that morning from Rondout with 50 barrels of cement. *City of Kingston* had not seen her earlier because she carried no lights. Sloop and schooner men often kept their boats dark on these still nights so as not to attract mosquitoes and other insects. They would keep a lantern ready in the hold, and when they heard the steady splashing of an approaching steamboat, they would quickly run the lantern up the mast. *City of Kingston*, known as "the sneak" by schooner men, was a propeller boat that hardly made any stir or noise as she cruised through the water. The *Mary Atwater's* helmsman had not heard the approaching steamer and had failed to raise the lantern. The steamer's knife-like iron bow sliced the schooner in two. With her cargo of cement, *Mary Atwater* went to the bottom in less than a minute. The steamer's crew picked up the helmsman, but his father (who owned the vessel) and the cook, both of whom were sleeping below, were drowned.

The only other accident that *City of Kingston* was involved in took place on June 5, 1888. Just as the steamboat left her New York pier for her run up the Hudson, the steam yacht *Meteor* was getting underway from her anchorage off 24th Street in the North River. When the two vessels came together, the bowsprit of the yacht caught *City of Kingston* just aft of the forward gangway. Before it snapped off, it tore a large gash in the main deck bulkhead. In the investigation that followed, the captain of the *City of Kingston* was found blameless while the yacht's captain's license was temporarily suspended.

On Saturday, July 2, 1887, *City of Kingston* pulled out of her Harrison Street pier at 1:03 PM, crowded with passengers. *Kaaterskill* of the Catskill Evening Line left its pier nine minutes later. A good ebb tide was running. After the vessels cleared the harbor, the *City of Kingston's* crew could hear the rapid thunder of *Kaaterskill* well behind them. As City of *Kingston* entered Newburgh Bay, *Kaaterskill* had just rounded Magazine Point. Although *City of Kingston* lost nine minutes landing at Newburgh and Poughkeepsie while *Kaaterskill* made no landings in this section of the river, *City of Kingston* sailed into Rondout Creek at 6:16 PM, the winner of the race by four minutes.

During the summer of 1889, Captain D. B. Jackson, operator of the Puget Sound and Alaska Steamboat Company, came east looking for a good steamer. *City of Kingston* especially caught his eye and he made a very attractive offer to the Cornell Steamboat Company for the vessel. Cornell, at that time, seemed to have every intention of operating the steamer for many more years. Plans had been made for many alterations, including a glass-enclosed dining room aft on the gallery deck. Cornell was ever the astute businessman, however, and showed no aversion to selling if the price was right. Apparently, it was. Toward the end of September 1889, even before the season was over, Cornell announced *City of Kingston* had been sold for service on the west coast. *Saugerties,* from the Saugerties-New York Line, was chartered to complete the season in *City of Kingston's* stead.

On September 30, 1889, *City of Kingston* made her last official regular trip out of Rondout. She was taken later to Marvel's Shipyard in Newburgh to be properly prepared for her long voyage to the North Pacific. Her guards were reinforced, windows boarded up, and two large masts were stepped and rigged for sails to steady her in heavy seas and to supply emergency power.

City of Kingston sailed out of New York Harbor on September 30, 1889, and began her long trip. This relatively small Hudson River steamboat's voyage took her all the way down the Atlantic coast of South America (there was no Panama Canal then), through the Straits of Magellan, and then up the Pacific coast of South

America, Mexico and California to the entrance of Puget Sound at the northernmost corner of Washington State. She made stops at Barbados and Rio de Janeiro for coal. After passing safely through the Straits in early January 1890, she spent two weeks in Valparaiso taking on coal and having minor repairs made to her engine. Other coal stops had to be made in Mexico and California.

City of Kingston sailed into the Strait of San Juan de Fuca on February 17, 1890, and docked at Port Townsend, Washington. With heavy weather following her most of the way, she had taken 86 days and 12 hours for the voyage, of which 61 days had been spent underway. The next day, she proceeded down Puget Sound to Seattle, where she was given a rousing welcome.

In order to have his newly-owned steamer manned by people familiar with her operation, Captain Jackson asked her captain, Melville Nichols, her engineer, George H. Lent, and her second pilot, John Brandow, all of whom were aboard the steamer on her long voyage to the west coast, to stay with the vessel. They agreed. Jackson had also been very favorably impressed with the skills of first pilot William H. Mabie, who had been able to bring *City of Kingston* to a stop alongside the dock with the ease of a side-wheeler. Captain Mabie, a true Hudson River man, declined Jackson's offer and remained in Hudson River service to become pilot of the Central Hudson Line's *William F. Romer.*

The *City of Kingston's* new route called for her to connect with Northern Pacific Railway trains at Tacoma and sail up Puget Sound to Bellington in northern Washington, with stops at Seattle, Port Townsend, Anacortes, Fairhaven, and Whatcom. Shortly thereafter, she was shifted to the more lucrative run from Tacoma to Seattle, Port Townsend, and Victoria, British Columbia. She ran this route without incident for nine years. *City of Kingston,* built originally for her short, 90-mile Hudson River route, had not only circumnavigated the Americas, but was one of the first steamboats to make the 1,000-mile, perilous inside passage to Skagway, Alaska.

The newer *City of Seattle* took over the Victoria route, and when the *City of Kingston* returned from Alaska, she was assigned back to the

Tacoma-Bellington route. On April 23, 1899, City of Kingston was making her way south from Seattle to Tacoma in a thick fog. First pilot John Brandow, who had been with the vessel since her days on the Hudson, was in the pilothouse. At about 4:30 AM, she was passing Brown's Point just outside Tacoma Harbor when Brandow was able to make out a large freighter dead ahead in the fog. This turned out to be the British vessel *Glenogle*, which had just left Tacoma bound for the Orient. Records show that both vessels were proceeding very slowly. Brandow ordered *City of Kingston* full speed ahead in an effort to avoid a collision by pulling out of the way across *Glenogle's* bow. Failing to clear, *City of Kingston* was struck on her starboard side 85 feet aft of the pilothouse. With a gash in her hull five feet deep, she sank in three minutes. Luckily, all on board, passengers and crew, escaped with their lives by climbing onto parts of the wooden upper deck that floated free when the iron hull sank. And so, this pioneer propeller steamer that served both American coasts was lost after 15 years of service.

The Cornell Steamboat Company operated side-wheel paddle towboats from the mid-1800s through 1918. Most were remodeled passenger vessels with their staterooms removed. There were, however, seven vessels actually built as towing steamers. The first two, which were built for Schuyler Towing Line, were *Oswego* and *Cayuga*. Many of the side-wheel towing steamers in Cornell's Hudson River service, along with many of their captains and engineers, are listed below:

Towboats	Captains	Chief Engineers
Mohegan	Sam Overbagh	
	Ed Pierce	
James Madison	Will Hayes	
Norwich	Harry Barber	Frank Van
	Will Hayes	Housen
A. B. Valentine	Chas. Conklin	H. Metcalf
	Jerry Patterson	
William Cook	Geo. Gage	Ike Van
		Walkenbore
George A. Hoyt	Jerry Patterson	Douglas Fowler
	Sandy Forsyth	
Washington	Geo. Dubois	Abe Van Vliet
Pittston	Billy Roberts	Doug Barber
	Geo. Dubois	
W. B. Crane	Jim Dubois	Dave Eighmey
Maurice Wurtz	Sandy Forsyth	Tom Harmon
Ceres	Dan Cogswell	Luke Smith
Marshall	Billy Ward	Pop Smith
Syracuse	Ben Wells	Doug Barber
Austin	Chas. Conklin	
General	Lon Sickles, Sr.	
McDonald	Will Brooks	
Sylis O. Pierce		
Niagara	Will Brooks	Doug Barber

Towing by hawser was first adopted by the Schuyer Towing Line in 1860. Previously, barges were towed alongside the towing steamboat.

The fleet of the Cornell Steamboat Company's propeller towboats and tugs included the large flotilla towboats. *Cornell's* engine developed 1433 horsepower, exceeding any other Cornell towboat of her time by more than 500 horsepower. Boatmen referred to her as the "Big *Cornell*." This coal burner was very hard to fire, and turnover of firemen was rapid. Because of her size and draft, she was used almost exclusively on the river south of Rondout. The upper river had not yet been dredged for deep-draft vessels.

The winter of 1910 was very severe. A huge ice jam formed south of Albany, causing the river water to back up and flood the downtown areas of Albany and Rensselaer. The federal government's plan was to dynamite the ice jam and charter the most powerful vessel they could find to break up the ice and force it downstream. The "Big *Cornell*" was chosen for the job.

Normally, *Cornell* was too deep in draft for the job, but because of recent warmer weather the river was at flood stage and there was sufficient deep water north of Athens to accommodate her. She left Rondout on March 3, 1910, with the small tug *Rob*. Ulster Davis, Cornell's agent at Rensselaer, was in charge of the operation. *Cornell's* regular crew, captain Tim Donovan, pilot Irving Hayes, and chief engineer Nippy Parsell, were aboard. She encountered heavy ice over two feet thick to Athens, where she went up the wider west channel, passing on March 5, 1910. *Cornell* arrived at Albany-Rensselaer on March 6, 1910, the ice jam broken and the ice moving downstream.

S. L. Crosby on the lower Hudson River circa 1934. (Captain Dick Sherman's collection)

Once the ice jam let go, the water immediately began to drop at Albany, so there was concern about getting *Cornell* back downriver over the rocks, reefs, and shoals of the upper river. The *Cornell* took on coal, fresh water, and food at Rensselaer. Then, with the help of the tug, *Rob*, she turned and headed downstream. At first, they were going to wait for daylight, but because of the rate the river's water was falling, they decided to leave right away. The current was running downstream so fast that they kept the engine at dead slow speed, just enough to keep safe steerage. The men in the pilothouse were reluctant to travel any faster for fear of scraping or hitting bottom, possibly smashing her rudder shoe or breaking her propeller.

Everything went fine until the two tugs reached Dover Platte Island off Coxsackie. Captain Donovan knew that there was a sand bar there, and he figured the freshet may have built the bar up even higher. They stopped the engine and just let *Cornell* drift. Sure enough, when they reached the bar, *Cornell* stopped and rolled slightly to port. They sounded all around the vessel and found only sand. *Rob* then put a hawser on *Cornell* and both vessels called for full speed ahead. In a matter of minutes, *Cornell* jumped over the sand bar. She leaped ahead so fast that she almost ran over the small *Rob* before they could get the engine stopped.

A quick cut with a sharp axe to the hawser by the *Rob's* deckhand saved the day. From that point back to Rondout, they did not encounter any more difficulties. Thus ended the only trip the "Big *Cornell*" made to Albany.

Her continuing trouble with keeping firemen aboard ended her career on the Hudson. In 1917, she was sold to the Standard Oil Company of Louisiana. Her new owners named her *Istrouma*, converted her to an oil burner, and operated her on the Mississippi River out of Baton Rouge, where she remained in service until 1956.

The Cornell Steamboat Company had said that it was not feasible to convert *Cornell* to an oil burner because it would not be possible to install sufficient oil storage aboard her. It has since been learned that before purchasing her, Standard Oil, unknown to Cornell, sent some men to him who hired out on *Cornell* as firemen. These "industrial spies" thoroughly examined *Cornell* and apparently concluded she could successfully be converted to oil firing. As with the *City of Kingston*, if the price were right, Cornell would sell.

The Cornell Steamboat Company had, at one time, two stake boats anchored with mushroom anchors just west of mid-stream off the Weehawken shore. They were anchored one behind the other about a quarter of a mile apart. Later, there was only one. The last was built from the hull of the Rondout-Rhinecliff ferry, *Transport*. Tugboats from the metropolitan New York area would bring scows, barges, etc., bound for upriver points to these stake boats. Each stake boat had living quarters and storerooms aboard and a captain whose duty it was to see that the units arriving were set in their proper place so that the flotilla tow's helper tug could release them for delivery along the river.

One stake boat accepted units for points as far north as the traprock quarry at Clinton Point, just south of Poughkeepsie. The other stake boat accepted units for delivery as far north as the St. Lawrence River at Sorel and to Buffalo through the Erie Canal. This tow was called the Beverwyck tow, and it was Cornell's flotilla tow's responsibility as far as Albany-Rensselaer. From there, other small Cornell tugs or vessels of other lines made deliveries north or west.

On the New York City end of the river, one of the larger towboats like *John H. Cordts*, *Geo. W. Washburn*, *J. C. Hartt*, *Edwin H. Mead*, or *Perseverance* handled the Beverwyck tow. They would meet the downtow from Albany in the vicinity of Poughkeepsie and change tows in midstream. While this procedure took place, the helper tug for each held the tow. *Pocahontas*, *Osceola*, and *Lion*,

among others handled the downtow. The New York tug returned to New York with the downtow, and the Albany tug returned north with the uptow.

John H. Cordts, a large propeller towboat, was built in 1883 for the Washburn Brick Company of Glasco, New York, then purchased by Cornell. She was the first tug on the east coast with two smokestacks crossways. Later, when rebuilt, she had one stack. Her captains included Charles Coughlin, Tim Elvandolph, Lynn Relyea, Jim Monahan, and Ira Cooper.

J. C. Hartt, built for Cornell in 1883 by Nalfie & Levy in Philadelphia, was another of the large, propeller, flotilla tow tugs. Her captains included Charles Terwilliger, Washington Saulpaugh, Ben Hoff, and Ira Cooper. During the freshet of March 1893, the *Hartt* got up steam and rescued the more than 50 tugs and barges swept out of Rondout Creek by the raging waters.

Edwin H. Mead, built in 1892 for Cornell by Thomas Marvel & Sons of Newburgh, had a slightly larger engine than the *J. C. Hartt*. As with all Marvel-built tugs, she had beautiful stature with fine lines. *Edwin H. Mead* served the Cornell Steamboat Company well during her 50-year career. The year before we moved to Port Ewen, New York, to take care of my ailing grandmother, my dad was captain

Edwin Terry in New York Harbor circa 1940. (Captain Dick Sherman's collection)

Syracuse on the Hudson in the 1890s. (Author's collection)

of the *Edwin H. Mead*. He always spoke of what a fine and perfect towboat she was. During her active lifetime, she was commanded by Abe Wells, Tim Donovan, Charles Warner, Herb Dumont, my dad, Alex Hamilton (my second cousin), and Al Walker. She was broken up in the early 1930s.

The "Greyhound of Towboats" was the name given to the very fast *Geo. W. Washburn*, built in 1890 for Washburn Brick Company of Glasco, New York, by the Thomas S. Marvel Yard at Newburgh. She was one of the towboats Cornell purchased from the Washburn Brick Company to ensure that the brick scow-towing business would be handled by the Cornell Steamboat Company. The *Washburn* was known for her ability to pull unloaded tows but she could not compete with the more powerful *Perseverance* on loaded larger tows. She was said to be the fastest running towboat on the east coast, rivaled only by the Berwind & White Coal Company tug, *Admiral Dewey*.

The *Washburn* always burned soft coal. When she passed through the Hudson Highlands on a still night, she would lay heavy clouds of smoke in the valley blocking out visibility, sometimes even for her own pilothouse crew should a stiff stern breeze be blowing. Whenever the *Washburn* was running light, the crew took any opportunity to hook up with one of the night boats in a race, and they won numerous times.

Washburn had an unusual setup of the master's living quarters. Unlike all of the other larger Cornell towboats where the captain's room was just aft of the pilothouse, on *Washburn* it was way aft on the main deck and ran the full width of the deckhouse. The following men captained *Washburn* down through the years: Bill Ward, Harvey Hamilton (my grand uncle), Alex Hamilton (his son), Jim Dee, Al Walker and myself. I served as her last captain. *Washburn* worked long and well until being taken out of service in 1943. She was sold in 1949 and scrapped.

Osceola was built by Ward & Stanton at Newburgh, New York, in 1884 for the Ronan Towing Line. When Cornell took over the Ronan Line, *Pocahontas*, *Ellen B. Ronan*, and *Mabel* came with *Osceola*. The *Arthur* was not taken.

Osceola and *Pocahontas* handled Cornell's Beverwyck tows on the upper river for years. H. Pratt, John Hickey, John Skean, and Howard Palmatier were captains of the *Osceola*. She made her last trip on the Hudson on a Sunday in late October 1929. She had a southbound Beverwyck tow and was assisted by her long-time mate, *George W. Pratt*. The big, lower river towboat, *Edwin H. Mead*, which was running light from New York, relieved *Osceola* of her tow off Rondout Creek Lighthouse. When the towing cables were made fast, the *Mead* blew a three-whistle parting farewell salute to *Osceola* as she turned and headed for the creek. Then, as *Osceola* was

years, it also was towed to Port Ewen in the late 1940s and abandoned.

Pocahontas was similar to *Osceola*. She was built at the same Newburgh shipyard in the same year. Both vessels were used on flotilla tow service on the upper Hudson. One would leave Albany one night, and the other the following night with the daily (except Sunday) downriver tow. *G. C. Adams* was the helper tug for *Pocahontas* on this route for many years. *Pocahontas* last ran in 1937, and she was broken up in 1938. Many of the same captains that served on *Osceola* served on the "Pokey" including, John Sillerman, Aaron Relyea, and Howard Palmatier. In my earlier piloting days,

A Cornell flotilla tow with the side-wheel towboat *General MacDonald* as the towing vessel and *S. L. Crosby* as the helper tug. (Postcard to Henry Edwards dated 1905, author's collection.)

going between the dykes, *George W. Pratt,* her helper tug for many years, blew her a good-bye salute with the knowledge that her long-time partner would never sail again.

Cornell intended to remove *Osceola's* engine and boiler from the old worn-out hull at their Rondout shop and place them in a newer hull that was already available. Charlie King, who was the superintendent of the Cornell Machine Shop, was my cousin by marriage. After the machinery had been removed, the *Osceola's* hull was towed to Port Ewen and stranded on the riverbank. The Great Depression settled in and all work stopped, never to be finished. After the new hull had lain across the creek at Sleightsburg weathering for another 20

I was pilot for short periods to Aaron Relyea. Bill Coughlin was her chief engineer for a long time.

The *Hercules*, built in 1876 at Camden, New Jersey, for the Delaware Bay pilots, was purchased by the Cheney Line in the late 1800s, and was later bought by Cornell. She was nicknamed the "moneymaker" because of her varied service as a tugboat, a towboat able to handle big flotilla tows, and as an icebreaker. She had a reinforced hull and bow covered with heavy copper sheathing for icebreaking duties.

Hercules was making her way upriver on one trip with a flotilla tow of 40 units in a strong wind when, suddenly, one of the rope hawsers parted and flew into her propeller. *Hercules* was disabled and the helper tug, *Victoria*, did not have sufficient power to manage the tow. It started to blow ashore. Luckily, the three schooners on the tow's starboard side fetched up on the soft bottom, holding the tow from going ashore until the towboat *J. C. Hartt* arrived.

Under Cornell's ownership, my grandfather and my dad commanded *Hercules* for many years. Among her other captains were Martin Carney and Bill Dittus. Ned Bishop was her longtime chief engineer. I served as deckhand aboard *Hercules* one summer while on vacation from school. The hardest part of the job for me was hoisting buckets of ashes from the fireroom by a pulley system, and then lifting them over the rail to dump them overboard. Fortunately, other members of the crew saw my predicament and readily helped.

Hercules last ran in 1931, and was broken up in 1940.

The Cornell Steamboat Company's largest and most powerful propeller towboat exhibited a combination of many talents. The wooden hull was built in Fall River, Massachusetts, for the United States Shipping Board late in the First World War. Cornell purchased the hull and towed it to its Rondout shops. A new engine was purchased from the government. Everything was assembled at the Cornell Shops, including all joiner work for the pilothouse and living quarters. When finished in 1919, she emerged as the giant river tug *Perseverance*. An exceptionally large four-blade propeller was installed. According to the chief engineer, Bill Whitmore, she developed 1,800 horsepower. I recall once speaking to Bill, a man many years my senior, when we had an exceptionally large and heavy tow and were about to buck a strong tidal current. His answer was, as it would always be, "Jackie boy, whatever you need, I'll see the 'Persy' has." The "Persy" like many other large towboats, had her three towing bits on the upper deck. Her propeller did not give her the speed to challenge *Geo. W. Washburn*, but when it came to pulling power, she had no equal.

I spent many of my younger years on her as pilot, with my dad as captain. Later, I was her cap-

The steam tug "Big Cornell" running light off Newburgh, circa 1910. The *Cornell* was the largest and most powerful tugboat on the river. (Roger Mabie collection)

tain myself. Anything the *Perseverance* hooked up to, no matter how large, she moved. One spring we left the New York stake boat with 108 units in tow, and we moved upstream with no problem. This was not always the case with a flotilla tow. I recall being southbound aboard *Jumbo*. When the flood

street number to get the pier number, because the streets of lower Manhattan are not numbered, but named streets.) Events usually unfolded like this: while the deckhands were reeling in the towing cables on the winches, we could see several tugs seeking scows and barges from within the tow for

Wm. S. Earl with Kingston, New York, ferry *Transport* circa 1930s. (Drawing by William H. Ewen, Jr., author's collection)

tide hit us, we were abreast of 125th Street, North River, and by the time the next ebb arrived, we had been pushed backward beyond the George Washington Bridge.

I always felt that a good, powerful steam towboat was a better puller than a diesel, although I must admit the weight of the towing steamer must be taken into consideration. I would like to see some diesels rated at 3,000 horsepower pitted against the *Perseverance*. I am sure she would easily outpull them. (I suspect diesel horsepower is from ponies, not full-grown horses.)

Typically, the "Persy" would land her flotilla tow at the 30th Street Pier 70. (You add 40 to the

delivery throughout the metropolitan area. With the towing cables safely coiled on the stern deck, we would proceed to Pier 93 (53rd Street), where Cornell's New York office was located. Upon arrival, the officer on watch would present the tow's log to the office and pick up the log for that night's upbound tow, as well as take care of any other necessary business. In the meantime, the cook would head for the ship chandler's store located at the corner of 11th Avenue and 51st Street, where he would order the food and supplies for the next round trip.

Food served on board the *Jumbo* included breakfast at 6:00 AM, dinner at 12:00 noon, supper at

6:00 PM, and snacks always available in the evening hours. The cook on this tugboat spent long hours in the galley.

Breakfast was plentiful. It consisted of fruit juices, various hot and cold cereals, either steak, chops, ham slices, omelets, or the usual bacon and eggs (any style), with home fried potatoes, cake, donuts, various toasts, homemade biscuits, and coffee or tea. The varied menu was dictated by the fact that some of the crewmembers were just coming off watch, while others were going on.

Dinner, served at the noon hour, consisted of either roast beef, prime rib, leg of lamb, roast lamb, pork roast, roast chicken, roast turkey, spaghetti and meatballs, corned beef and cabbage, or fish, soup or clam chowder, salads, a variety of vegetables, rye or white bread, cake, pie, or pudding for dessert, with tea or coffee. No beer or hard liquor was ever served on board.

Supper consisted of either cold slices of the dinner meat, hot dogs, hamburgers, fish, or crab cakes, plus various vegetables, french fries, tea, coffee, soda, and dessert.

On the *Jumbo*, the deckhand and oiler on watch, when available, helped the cook prepare the meals, clean up, and wash the dishes afterwards. Other members of the crew also helped. On the larger towboats like the *Perseverance*, *Cornell*, *Geo. W. Washburn*, etc., they had a dining room where the officers ate while the crew ate from the galley table. The large towing tugs had two mess boys to assist the cook.

I have found many wonderful cooks serving on Hudson River vessels. First, there was Augustus (Gus) Hargrave. He was the cook on the tug *Jumbo* for many years. Gus never married. He lived with his mother in Kingston. His dining table was always filled with an abundance of good food. He baked his own cakes, pies, puddings, and breads.

John Van Wagon of Ellenville, was another prized cook on the Cornell Line. He served the typical roasts, etc., however, he was especially known for always having twelve different vegetable dishes on the dinner table.

Paul Goguskie of Kingston, who had served as cook on many Cornell Line tugs, was my chef aboard the trailership, *Albany*. Meals were served family-style, as they were on the tugs, but there were many more mouths to feed, so Paul had an assistant cook.

At that time, whole families lived in the cabin of the canal boats loaded with grain that sailed on the Hudson River on their way from Buffalo to New York. Husband, wife, children, and sometimes, dog, cat, and pet bird all shared the cramped cabin area. They carried basic food with them for the whole trip or received supplies from the "bum boats" en route.

"Bum boats," small provision vessels, were used at Newburgh and Kingston to meet the flotilla tows and supply the canal boats, barges, scows, etc., with meat, fowl, fresh vegetables, and anything else anyone might need while being towed. These boats also served as the mail distributor, bringing mail out and taking letters ashore for posting. In later years, this became a task for the helper tug. These "bum boats" ceased operation when refrigeration became popular.

Many times, when our tug was positioned alongside a canal boat, we would invite the family aboard to have dinner with us. They were always most appreciative because our varied and plentiful menus were not what they were used to having. Our cooks bought everything fresh and made desserts from scratch. Canned goods were the exception.

The cooks were always the targets of good-spirited humor. Crewmembers would step out on the deck and drop a helping of bread pudding overboard. If it sank, no one would eat the pudding.

On the Day Line and Night Line steamers, crew meals were served restaurant style in their dining room by a waiter. We ate well and in style among our many guests. There was not the choice one had aboard a tug; it was more like eating in a fine restaurant ashore.

As a river pilot aboard ship, I received my meals on the navigation bridge while underway. If the ship was at berth or anchored, I ate with the captain in the dining room. The quality of the food and the menu depended on which nation was the ship's homeport. I especially enjoyed the food on American, Swedish, Norwegian, Danish, Italian, Spanish, German, and French vessels.

Rob breaking ice in Rondout Creek circa 1920s. (Author's collection)

After the grub has been delivered and all other business matters have been completed, we head for the Delaware Lackawanna Railroad coal dock at Hoboken. We coal up the "Persy" with anthracite coal, which produces substantially less smoke than the fuel used by *Geo. W. Washburn*. We pull the "Persy" along the pier's north side with her port side to the dock. Several steel plates are removed from the deck and the coal dock's shoots are placed in the vessel's hold. We can only half-fill the coal bins before the "Persy" is leaning heavily toward the left and her smokestacks are almost touching the pier's upper structure. We then turn the vessel and fully load the starboard side bunkers, after which we turn around again and finish fully loading the port bunkers. While all this is taking place, we also load a freshwater tank with water for drinking and cooking.

Refueling accomplished, we cross the river to the Barrow Street pier where a water hydrant is located. We hook up a hose and take on water for the boilers. We are now ready for the night's upriver tow that usually is ready to leave the stake boat at about 9:00 PM. It is not unusual for the tug *Alexander Roe* to be late arriving with her light traprock scows bound for the river's stone quarries. Many times, we would have to go down the harbor and the upper bay, and even into the Kill Van Kull,

looking for her. When she was found, we would put a rope hawser on her bow bits and give *Alexander Roe* and her tow a fast ride to the stake boat.

As pilot, I will stand the midnight watch. When I step out on the deck from my cabin into a beautiful moonlit night, I notice *Perseverance* is heading south after exchanging our northbound tow with *Lion's* southbound Beverwyck tow. I approach the galley for a cup of coffee and a snack before reporting to the pilothouse duty and notice Diamond Reef's lighted buoy just ahead. Assistant engineer John Garavan, deckhands Anthony Pendergast and Charlie Barton (my cousin) and oiler Dick James are already enjoying the goodies in the galley.

Later, as I approach the pilothouse, I notice our helper tug, *R. G. Townsend* captained by Joe Barton, leaving Jova's brickyard at Roseton with two brick scows to add to our flotilla tow. The *Townsend* showed two white lights in vertical order on her aft staff pole, indicating she was towing a unit or more alongside. *Perseverance* had three white lights vertical on her staff, indicating she was towing a hawser tow. If the vessels were running light, there would have been just one white light on the aft mast, 15 feet higher than the forward white light.

On all river vessels, atop the forward mast (if no mast, atop the pilothouse or nearby in the center of the fore part of the vessel) is a bright white light so constructed as to show an unbroken light over an arc of the horizon of 20 points of the compass, 10 points on each side of center (from right ahead to two points abaft the beam on either side), visible at least 5 miles.

There is a green light on the starboard side so constructed as to show an unbroken light over an arc of the horizon of 10 points of the compass, so fixed as to throw the light from right ahead to two points abaft the beam, visible for a distance of at least 2 miles. There is a red light on the port side, of the same construction and character.

A sailing vessel, however, carries only the green and red side lights, and rowing boats are to carry a lantern at the ready, to be shown in sufficient time to avoid a collision.

When I enter the pilothouse and say hello to my dad, he advises me that the tow's log is on the chart desk and we have 43 units in tow. He also indicates that the northbound Central Hudson Line steamboat *Benjamin B. Odell* was landed at Poughkeepsie as he passed by. The Troy night boat *Trojan* had paddled by, and the Albany night boat *Berkshire* could be seen coming north off Newburgh. He indicates we have not met the northbound Clinton Point or Beverwyck tows yet. My dad says good night and enters his cabin aft of the pilothouse to rest until 6:00 AM, leaving the safe navigation of the *Perseverance* and her tow in my hands.

I hear the three short blasts of our helper tug's whistle. This is a Cornell Company signal asking me to slow down so the tug can attach two brick scows to our tow. That accomplished, they signal three long blasts and three short blasts, which indicate we can resume full speed. The tug heads to Rose's brickyard to pick up another scow. This continues through my watch as *Townsend* picks up brick scows at the Brockaway and Dennings Point yards, and coal barges at the New York, Ontario, and Western Railroad coal yard at Cornwall.

As *Berkshire* is about to pass, pilot Ben Stanton flashes his powerful searchlight as a greeting, which I return with ours. He uses the light to greet us because the vessel's steam whistle would wake up sleeping passengers.

Our tow on this night has on its starboard side a schooner loaded with sand from the dock below Coxsackie. The loaded schooner has a draft of 18 feet. This presents no problem to *Perseverance* because her draft is also 18 ft. deep, but it would be a problem for the lighter drafted *Geo. W. Washburn*, *J. C. Hartt*, *Jumbo*, etc., when they were bucking a flood tide close to shore along the Palisades to stay out of the current's strength. The schooner's deep draft would force them to move further off shore into deeper water with the strong current against them. *Perseverance*, with her 18-ft. draft, was always forced into this position, but it did not matter much. She always forged ahead.

In the early hours of the morning, we pass the northbound Clinton Point tow pulled by Captain Jim Dee's *Geo. W. Washburn*, and the Beverwyck tow in the charge of *J. C. Hartt*, captained by Ira Cooper. My dad relieves me after his 6:00 AM breakfast.

This midnight watch was typical. Crews worked six hours on watch and six hours off. Usually, they had 24 hours off on Sundays. In later years, crews worked two weeks aboard their vessel, and one week off.

In the early hours of one late-September Sunday morning about 7:00 AM, I was captain of the *Perseverance* proceeding downriver on the ebb tide with a large flotilla tow. There were three, flexible, 200-yard-long steel cables as tow lines between the towboat and the head barges of the tow. We were

Scows hanging on stakeboat in New York Harbor circa 1938. *R. G. Townsend* in attendance. (Author's collection)

John H. Cordts with *J. C. Hartt* in the background changing tows in the mid-Hudson River circa 1920s. (Captain Dick Sherman's collection)

in a thick fog and I was using the known compass courses and the whistle echoes as my navigational guides. There was no radar aboard vessels in those days. As I rounded the Gees Point Light at West Point, I heard the ring of several fog bells ahead, which meant that vessels were anchored there. My knowledge of the river's currents told me that the current at this sharp bend went first to the east shore above Garrison, and then, after hitting the shore, turned sharply toward the dock at the West Point Military Academy. I quickly headed the *Perseverance* at an angle toward the west shore. I knew that if I had any chance of my tow clearing the anchored vessels, this was it. The powerful "Persy" would be able to keep her tow directly behind her, and it would not be swinging around left or right. This was to be a major factor in safely passing the obstacles. I also knew that any vessel at anchor had to allow sufficient room at its anchor point to safely swing around in a tide change in order to clear the shore, leaving me clearance between the anchored vessel and the shore. I steered the *Perseverance* and its tow safely past this hazard with local knowledge, good luck, and, I am sure, with God's help.

The fog cleared as I was passing Bear Mountain. I later learned from the crew of my helper tug, *Edwin Terry*, which was attached to the west side of the tow, that we had come very close to the west shore line. As we learned later, a fleet of

seven Navy destroyers had brought the Annapolis midshipmen on a visit to the cadets at West Point. Had a towboat with less power than the "Persy" been in charge of the tow that morning, there would have been a very different, and disastrous result.

Tom Purvis, John Cullen, John Hickey, my father, and I served as masters of the *Perseverance*. She was sold for scrap in 1950 and towed to Staten Island to be dismantled.

The *E. L. Levy* and the *E. C. Baker* were two other fine steam tugs in Cornell's fleet. The *Levy* was build by Nafie & Levy at Philadelphia in 1888. Jim Welch was her captain. She was sold to Scully Towing and became *Mary Scully*. She was later sold to Moran Towing , where she lived out her life as the *Marion Moran*. *E. C. Baker* was built by Nafie & Levy in 1889. She was sold to Scully and named *Thomas J. Scully*. When she was subsequently sold to Olsen Towing, she was renamed Revere. Both of these vessels were of light draft. I recall seeing *Revere* on occasion pass through the open drawbridge at the mouth of Wappinger Creek on rising water to deliver an oil barge to the village about a mile upstream.

The wooden hulls of *Jumbo* and *Lion*, Cornell's two large diesel tugboats, were built for the government at New York, New York, in 1918. Their engines were installed later at Nelseco, New London, Connecticut. Cornell purchased both vessels in 1924. Both were 95 ft. 9 in. long, 25-ft. beam with 14 ft. draft. They had 217 gross tonnage and produced 750 horsepower. The similarities ended here. *Jumbo* was the better puller, but *Lion* had more rudder power for handling vessels alongside.

The Cornell Steamboat Company was active in building the George Washington Bridge, and the tug *Jumbo*, captained by my dad, along with the tug *Shamrock* ran the original cable for the bridge across from New York City to Fort Lee, New Jersey. *Jumbo's* service was mostly on the lower Hudson, New York harbor, and vicinity, while *Lion* was mostly confined to the Albany Beverwyck tow route.

My experience on the river began in 1929 as a deckhand on the Cornell Steamboat Company's *Jumbo*. I rose at 6:00 AM, climbed out of the fo'c'sle (the forecastle), washed, dressed, and had a hearty breakfast before relieving my fellow deckhand, Bill Barry, who later became the postmaster at the Kingston Main Post Office. My first duties were to wash down the entire tug with fresh water, shine all the brass (there was a <u>lot</u> of brass on boats back then), splice rope as needed, and help the cook. These tasks were carried out when not busy with the usual deckhand duty of handling lines in picking up scows and barges.

Being deckhand also gave me the opportunity to learn the rudiments of how to operate the tug and navigate the various river channels. When you were towing a large barge or unit alongside the tug and the captain or pilot could not see ahead to navigate, the deckhand had to stand on the unit in an area where he had good vision ahead and direct the captain in the proper course procedure. This task had to be done in both clear and bad weather, and was a very unpleasant job at times.

The morning watch ended at noon. After being relieved by my cohort, I had dinner. I was then free to sleep or do as I pleased until 6:00 PM. Then, I had supper and was on watch till midnight.

The fo'c'sle, where the deckhands and oilers slept, was in the forward part of the tug's hull. Officers slept on deck in their individual rooms, and the captain slept in his cabin behind the pilothouse. The forecastle (fo'c'sle) was a well-lighted area containing several bunk beds with drawers underneath, chairs, and individual closets and mirrors. You had to climb the ladder-like stairs to the deck to use toilet facilities. As time moved on, I advanced in grade and moved up to my own room on deck and then to the captain's cabin.

One time, early in my career as a very young pilot with my dad on the tug *Jumbo*, I received word that Mr. Coykendall would like to see me in

Geo. W. Washburn, Stirling Tomkins, and *Perseverance* at the Cornell Shops on Rondout Creek in June 1949. (Author's collection)

his office. Mr. Coykendall had great respect for my father, and they had been friendly for years. Why did he want to talk to me? To my surprise, he offered to pay my tuition to attend Columbia University, and after graduation from Columbia he would sponsor me to study law at Brooklyn Law School with a major in maritime law. His only requirement was that I agree to represent the Cornell Steamboat Company as their marine lawyer after I passed the bar. He would not restrict me from having other clients.

At that time, Mr. Coykendall was president of the board of trustees of Columbia University. It was a very honored and powerful position. I carefully considered the offer. I had not graduated from high school, and so I would have to return for two more years and then spend at least four years at Columbia. Adding on the years needed to graduate from law school, I was looking at ten years of my life. I would be 29 at the completion of my studies.

I had a job and was earning a decent living. Looking forward to ten years with little or no money in my pocket was not a pleasant prospect.

After deep thought and much soul-searching, I met again with Mr. Coykendall and thanked him but refused his generous offer. I will never know if I made the right choice or not. He never held it against me, because many years later he offered me the position of superintendent of the line, in charge of full operation of the boats and oversight of the crews. I again turned down his offer because I had other career goals in mind. I know I made the right decision that time, because Mr. Coykendall died a few years later and the fleet was split up and spread among the industry.

In my deckhand days, the crew was paid on the 5th and 20th of every month. During severe winters when Hudson River ice became too heavy for the barges and scows to run without damage, many of the Cornell tugs were taken out of service, but captains and chief engineers were kept on full salary regardless. The captains went to the Cornell office at Pier 91 North River, (51st Street New York City) to receive the entire crew's salary in cash. Once, my dad and several other captains were met at the office by a group of bandits and relieved of all their crews' pay.

Geo. W. Washburn running light in New York Harbor circa 1930s. The author, his father and his grandfather all served as skippers of the *Washburn* at various times. (Author's collection)

Pocahontas, freshly painted and flying a big American flag. This photo was probably taken on an early summer holiday, circa 1925. The *Pocahontas* was used almost exclusively for towing the Beverwyck tows north of Poughkeepsie. (Roger Mabie collection)

One season, as a young twenty-two-year-old pilot, I was assigned as pilot on the tug *Lion*, captained by Arthur "Chinney" Newman, handling the Beverwyck tow out of Albany. *Jumbo*, which had been running the same route opposite *Lion*, was needed for lower river duties on the Tomkins Cove stone tow. I had been pilot on *Jumbo* with my dad, but after discussing the matter with him, I agreed, and I piloted the *Lion* with Captain Newman for about a month.

Pocahontas was brought out of lay-up to replace *Jumbo*. Captain Howard Palmatier and pilot, Bill Benson, who both previously had been aboard *Lion*, were reassigned to *Pocahontas*, a coal burner. By this time, there was no longer a dock in the Albany area to coal up the vessel. The stake boat, made fast to the Rensselaer shore, just south of the Dunn Memorial Bridge, served dual roles— as an office and a place from which the tows started. A deck scow was filled with coal at Rondout's coal terminal, towed up river and berthed alongside the stake boat. *Pocahontas* was coaled up every other day from the scow. The entire crew carried out this back-breaking work by hand and shovel.

Lion, a diesel tug, fueled up once every week at the Socony terminal across the river. I had no problem with *Pocahontas'* officers, whom I knew well. I had served as pilot aboard the *Pocahontas* with Captain Aaron Relyea. He and I refused to coal up the *Pocahontas* by hand, and he refused to order the crew do it either. George McCabe, Cornell's agent at Rensselaer, had to hire shore people to do the job.

The men of the *Pocahontas* showed an entirely different attitude toward Captain Newman. When both vessels lay alongside each other at the stake boat, they would not socialize with him or even talk directly to him. An attempt was made to use me as a go-between for any necessary orders or messages, but I would have none of it. I truly felt sorry for Captain Newman's situation, because I found him to be an excellent shipmate.

It was common knowledge that many upriver men did not relish strangers in their domain, and it was obvious that Captain Newman and I were aboard a clean diesel tug while they were relegated to coaling up *Pocahontas* by hand. Within a month, Captain Newman was relieved and returned to duty on a New York harbor tug. I returned to the

Osceola with helper tug *G. C. Adams* at the mouth of Esopus Creek circa 1929. Saugerties Lighthouse is on the right. (Captain Dick Sherman's collection)

Jumbo. Captain Palmatier and pilot Bill Benson returned to *Lion* and peace and harmony were restored on the upper Hudson.

Years later, I was working for the Cornell Steamboat Company one winter while the Day Line steamers were out of service. Mr. Oliver, the superintendent, called me to his office one day and he said that they had an opportunity to lease the large diesel tug *Lion*, sister ship to the *Jumbo*, to the Tracy Towing Line at a good profit. Cornell did not need the vessel on the Hudson until the ice thawed in the spring. She would be used in the coal trade between Communipaw Coal Docks in Jersey City and Hunts Point in the East River. The *Lion's* captain was not licensed for those waters, but I was. This would be a one-crew, day-boat job. I was offered an excellent salary and I took the job. I agreed with the Tracy's dispatcher to work eight hours one day and twelve or more hours the next, with Sunday off. We lay up for the night on the south side of the ferry racks on 42nd Street in the North River. It was very handy to cross by ferry and take the train to my home in Teaneck every other night. This assignment turned out to be profitable for the company and me. The job lasted through late March, and they even gave me a good bonus in addition to my salary.

For years, *Jumbo* was assigned the evening loaded stone tow from the stone quarries at Tomkins Cove and Verplanck Point. After delivering the tow to New York, she would run back up light to repeat the same run the following night. The light scows were delivered to the quarries from the northbound Clinton Point tow on the previous night.

Captains aboard *Jumbo* included George McCabe and my father, while *Lion* was mastered by Aaron Relyea, "Chinney" Newman, George Carroll, Howard Palmatier and me. *Jumbo* last ran in 1955 and was broken up at Rossville, Staten Island, in that year. *Lion* also ended her career in 1955.

S. L. Crosby, one of the finest-looking tugboats ever in Cornell's fleet, was built by Nafie & Levy at their yard in the suburbs of Philadelphia at Pennington, New Jersey, in 1883. This beautiful vessel had John Anthony, Charlie Warner, and Aaron Relyea among her masters. My former schoolmate, Bill Benson, served as deckhand for Captain Relyea early in his career.

When coal was a popular fuel, the Cornell Steamboat Company had a coal tow route that started at the Erie, Susquehanna & Western coal docks in Edgewater, New Jersey, with pickups at the New York, Ontario, & Western dock in Guttenburg, and the Delaware, Lackawanna, & Western dock in Hoboken for deliveries in the East River and to 96th Street for Harlem River points. Although many tugs served this route, two of the most frequently seen were the *Bear* and *Burro*. They also served regular harbor duties. The *Bear* and *Burro* had identical dimensions. The U. S. government built them at the end of World War I at Sturgeon Bay, Wisconsin.

My uncle on my mother's side, Jack Barton, served for a long time as the *Bear's* captain, as did Tom Fitzgerald, Bill Warner, and Bob Kivillian. *Burro's* captains were Ben Van Steenburg (a brother of a 3rd grade school teacher that I had in Port Ewen), Al Walker, and John Barton. *Burro* was sold to Barrett Towing Company and became *George N. Barrett,* continuing her duties as a harbor tug, including ship docking. *Bear* was broken up in 1950.

Senator Rice was built at Rondout for Schoonmaker & Rice in 1902. Cornell soon purchased this vessel, which had a license to carry passengers. She was chartered to the New York Central Railroad, where she shifted rail car floats around New York harbor for a year. My dad was assigned as her captain during this period. Abe Wells, C. Tobbey, and Jim Flynn were also master on her. She was broken up at Rondout in 1946.

R. G. Townsend was built for Cornell at Philadelphia in 1882. She was rebuilt in 1936, and sold to McAllister Towing in the 1960s. The *Townsend* served most of her career as a helper tug on flotilla tows. Charlie Warner, J. Suriene, Will Durrundo, Will Warner, and Joe Barton were her captains.

G. C. Adams was originally built for Schuyler Towing, but she served longest for Cornell as a helper tug for *Pocahontas* on the upper river. She was taken out of service in 1938. I am sure several men served as her captain, but in my memory Ed Van Woert and his son, Arthur, always seem to be leaning out of the pilothouse window.

George W. Pratt was built in Rondout in 1863. She accompanied

Osceola as helper tug for years. Will Van Woert and Tom Brennan were two of her masters. She ended service in 1950.

W. N. Bavier was built for Cornell at Port Richmond, New York, in 1901. Jim Relyea, Herb Dumont, Lou Miller, and Ace Gritman were her captains. She mostly served as a helper tug on lower river tows. She last ran in 1934, and sank in 1940.

Victoria was built at Camden, New Jersey, in 1878. She ran until 1934. Jack Hamilton (my uncle), Jim Flynn, Joe Eigo, Al Walker, and others captained this tug.

Edwin Terry was built at Camden, New Jersey, for the Washburn Brick Company of Glasco, New York, in 1883 and rebuilt in 1919 after running onto Con's Hook Reef. She came to Cornell when they took over Washburn's brick towing, and she served in general towing and as a flotilla tow helper until she was sold to Carroll Towing in the 1960s. Her captains included John Vantine, Frank Carroll, Joe Eigo, George Munson, and Morris Flynn.

Ellen M. Ronan was built in 1883 at Athens, New York, for Ronan Towing, which was taken over by Cornell. She last ran for Cornell in 1934. She sank in 1949.

John D. Schoonmaker was built by McCausland in Rondout in 1888. Barnett and Abe Van Aken were among her many captains.

Osceola on the upper Hudson River circa 1929 running light at full speed, showing what is called a "bone in her mouth." (Captain Dick Sherman's collection)

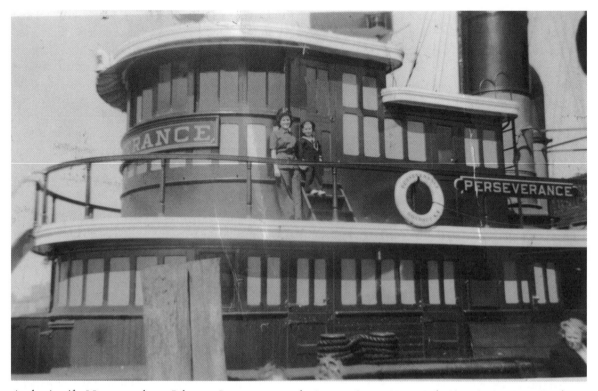

Author's wife, Norma, and son, John, on *Perseverance* at the Barrow Street, New York City pier in 1940. (Author's collection)

Rob and the *Wm. S. Earl* were two small-screw, high-pressure tugs that were stationed by Cornell generally in the Rondout-East Kingston area. *Rob* was built in 1902 at Sleightsburg, New York. She last ran for Cornell in 1940, and was sold to Hilderbrandt. She was then rebuilt into a diesel and sold to Reinauer.

Wm. S. Earl was built by the famous Kensington shipbuilders, Neafie & Levy, in 1859. Until she was "finished with engines" on July 20, 1949, she was the oldest steamboat in the world.

Cornell # 41 was originally the *Eli B. Conine*, built in 1900 at Wilmington, Delaware, for the Rose Brick Company. She was later taken over by Cornell, and in 1925 was rebuilt into the diesel-powered *Cornell #41*. This vessel ran into the 1960s. Pete Henry and Frank Carroll served as her captains. My first job as a licensed pilot at age 19 was aboard this vessel with Captain Frank Carroll. At that time, I had a 2nd class pilot's license, a type no longer issued. At age 21, I received a 1st class pilot's license.

Cornell was originally the steamer *Charlie Lawrence*, built in Philadelphia in 1874 for the Knickerbocker Ice Company. She came to Cornell when the company took over the Knickerbocker fleet. In 1925, she was rebuilt and refitted with a diesel motor. When Cornell became interested in towing on the Erie Canal, she was assigned to that route. She had very little freeboard (the area on a vessel between the upper edge of the hull and the waterline). Some years later, when she returned to the Hudson River, she swamped and sank in a storm off Tarrytown on November 4, 1955.

Cornell #21 was originally the *J. H. Williams*, built in Newburgh in 1904. She was converted from steam to diesel in 1926 and bought by Reichert Towing in 1959.

The *Wm. E. Cleary*, unlike the *J. H. Williams*, remained a steamboat throughout her career. She was scrapped in 1949.

Coe F. Young was built at Sleightsburg in 1872. She was abandoned and sank on March 3, 1936. DeForest Rainey and Aaron Atkins served as her masters.

Cornell #20, originally *Frank*, was built at Rondout for McCausland in 1893. She was a small screw tug that was converted to diesel in 1926. As *Cornell #20*, with Tom Hillis as captain, she was the first Cornell tug to reach Buffalo, in May 1928. She sank off Sandy Hook on February 1, 1953.

Saranac was built in 1886. She was cut down for canal service in the mid-1920s and was abandoned in 1949.

Geo. N. Southwick was built in 1891 in Alexandria, Virginia. She last ran in 1936, was broken up, and her hull was abandoned at Port Ewen in 1943.

Cornell took over several tugs from Newburgh owners: *George Field*, built in 1882; *R. G. Davis*, built in 1891 (then rebuilt and renamed *George B. Hance*), and *M. Conway*. *George Field* was built at Buffalo. She ran for Cornell until 1920, when she was sold to Matton Towing. George Field (the original owner of the vessel), Harvey Hamilton (my granduncle), Bill Norton, and Al Walker were among her captains.

Wilson P. Foss was built in Brooklyn in 1899. She ran until 1935 and was broken up in 1949.

Geo. W. Decker was built at Marvel's Shipyard in Newburgh in 1900. Tom Hillis was her captain for a long time. She was abandoned in 1949.

J. G. Rose was built in 1900. She was used for general towing on the Hudson River and later in her career became a canal tug.

H. D. Mould was built at Athens in 1896. She was primarily stationed in the Haverstraw Bay area feeding the *Jumbo's* traprock tow from Tomkins Cove and Verplanks Point. DeForest Rainey and Art Post were her captains.

Harry was a small screw tug that was built in 1892. She served the brick and cement yards at Catskill, Athens, and Hudson. She was broken up in the 1930s.

Eugenia was built in 1865 in Buffalo as *Saratoga*. She was broken up in the 1930s.

A. C. Cheney was built for the Cheney Towing Line in 1877. She came to Cornell when the Cheney fleet was taken over and ran until she was broken up in 1910. Jerry Relyea and Ben Hoff were among her captains. Ed Smith was her chief engineer.

Adriatic was built for Cheney in 1860 and acquired by Cornell in 1886. She was sold and became the *H. L. Finger* in 1896, then renamed *Gladys* in 1903. She was abandoned in 1913.

Ambition was built for Cheney in 1864, acquired by Cornell in 1864, and broken up in 1897.

Bismark was built for the Knickerbocker Ice Company in 1888, acquired by Cornell, then sold to Cahill Towing.

Britannia was built for Knickerbocker Ice Company in 1879 and also was acquired by Cornell. No further information is available on *Britannia*.

C. D. Mills was built in 1864, and broken up in the early 1900s. Ben Gage was among her captains.

Christianna was built in 1864 as *Amaranthus* for Cheney, and acquired by Cornell in 1892. Jerry Relyea and Ben Hoff were among her captains.

Conqueror was built as *Dictator* in 1862, then renamed *Sweet Brier*. Cornell acquired her in 1892.

Columbia was built in 1863 and acquired by Cornell in that same year. She ended her service in

E. L. Levy with her captain, Irv Hayes, standing on the ladder in front of the pilot house circa 1910. (Captain Dick Sherman's collection)

Senator Rice on the lower Hudson River circa 1914. (Captain Dick Sherman's collection)

1900. Her captain was Frank Hallenbeck, with chief engineer F. Van Hoosen.

C. W. Morse was built at Bath, Maine, for Knickerbocker Ice Company in 1889. This large towboat came to Cornell with the rest of the Knickerbocker fleet. She went to sea from Philadelphia in 1916 and was never heard from again. Will Schultz and John Hickey mastered her when she ran on the Hudson.

Dr. David Kennedy was built at Rondout for Jacob Tremper in 1880. She was sold to Cornell, ran until 1929, and was broken up in 1936.

The small screw tug *Empire* was built in 1889, ran until 1936, and was broken up in 1958.

Engles was built in 1899 and sold to O'Brien Towing in 1921.

General Sheridan was built in 1864 and scuttled in 1887.

George C. Van Tuyl Jr. was built in 1900 and broken up in 1936.

Honeysuckle was built in 1862 for Cheney as *William G. Fargo*. She was acquired by Cornell and broken up in 1886.

H. T. Caswell was built in 1882 for Washburn Brick Company and came to Cornell with the fleet. Later, *Rob* inherited her engine.

Ice King was a large, ocean towboat originally built as *Greyhound* for Knickerbocker Ice Company in 1877. She came to Cornell with the Knickerbocker fleet in 1886. *Ice King* was lost on December 26, 1913, when she stranded on the quicksands of Romer Shoals near Sandy Hook. Charles Toby was her master on the Hudson.

Imperial was built for Knickerbocker at Baltimore, Maryland, in 1904. She came to Cornell with the fleet and was sold to Cahill Towing. *Princess* had a similar career. She was also built for Knickerbocker at Baltimore in 1906, acquired by Cornell and sold to Cahill Towing.

Ira M. Hedges was built in 1883 at Camden, New Jersey, for Washburn Brick. She was acquired by Cornell and broken up in 1926. Alex Hanlon was her captain and Bob Tierney was the chief engineer.

Isaac M. North was built in 1862 as *Poppy*, and acquired by Cornell in 1865.

Tug Victoria circa 1930 at Cornell Repaair Shops, Rondout Creek

Victoria at Cornell's shops on Rondout Creek circa 1930s. The author's uncle, John Hamilton, was a captain on the *Victoria.* (Captain Dick Sherman's collection)

James H. Scott was built in 1897 and continued in service until 1936.

J. Arnold was built in 1893 and ran until 1934, mostly in the Albany and Erie Canal area.

John T. Welch was built in 1899. No other information is available except that Frank Spinnerweber and George Munson served aboard.

Thomas P. Fowler was said to be about the same size as *Edwin H. Mead.* She was built of steel in 1893 for Cornell. She was sold to the U. S. government during the Spanish American War and became *Mohawk.* Charlie Warner was one of her Hudson River captains.

W. E. Street was built in 1881 for Cornell. She was about the same size as the *S. L. Crosby.* I have been told that Acor Wells, her captain, was always in bare feet, wore a straw hat and short sleeves in winter and summer, and had a rope belt. The vessel was out of commission before 1910.

Sammy Cornell was built in 1867. This small tug sported a giant steam whistle with a deep bass tone. She was broken up in 1891.

Julia A. Brainard was built in 1872, and went out of service in 1924.

Primrose, built in 1902, ran until 1936.

Thomas A. Dickson, built in 1872, ran until 1924.

Terror was built in 1854, and acquired by Cornell in 1892.

Watchman was acquired by Cornell from Card Towing in 1919. She was never put in service and was abandoned in 1949.

W. A. Kirk was built in 1905 as *Walter B. Pollock* and acquired by Cornell in 1913. She ran on the New York State canals.

Stirling Tomkins, built as *Artisan* in 1919, was purchased from Card Towing in the 1930s. As a young deckhand I accompanied my dad to board *Artisan* at the Tietjen and Lang shipyard in Hoboken, NJ when she was delivered to Cornell from Card. Our mission was to see whether she was properly fitted out for Hudson River flotilla towing. Bob Fitch later became her master.

Thomas Cornell, built in 1944 as *U. S. L. T. #494,* was bought by Card Towing and renamed *Harry Card.* She was purchased by Cornell and rebuilt as a diesel. She was sold to west coast interests in 1959.

Mary A. Cornell, formerly *U. S. L. T. #374* built in 1944, was bought by Robert Wathen and renamed *Jack,* until she was also purchased by Cornell and rebuilt as a diesel. She joined *Thomas Cornell* on the west coast in 1959.

Rockland County, a diesel push tug purchased in 1960, was sold to Red Star Towing in 1964.

Rocktow, formerly *Magnetic*, was purchased in 1950 and sold to Carroll Towing Corporation in 1959.

The following tugs were also part of the Cornell fleet at some time in its long history:

J. W. Conklin	acquired in 1846
Knickerbocker	built in 1846
Mabel	built in 1893
Triton	built in 1890
Volunteer	built in 1888, abandoned at Rondout 1913
W. B. McCulloch	built in 1899, broken up at Sleightsburg in the 1930s (formerly *P. McCabe Jr.*)
Woodbridge	acquired from Schuyer, never used
Wrestler	ex-Long Island Railroad tug, never used
Havilland	no available information

Sea Gull was the largest tug hull ever owned by Cornell, according to my dad. Like many ocean-going tugs, she was underpowered and far too bulky for river work.

The story of the Cornell Steamboat Company will always be intertwined with the seasonal weather problems at their Rondout Creek headquarters, particularly the freshets of March 1893 and 1936. The following account comes from "Heard on the Fantail" by Captain Bill Benson in the spring 1981 issue of *Steamboat Bill*, the Journal of the Steamship Historical Society of America:

In my own area on the Hudson River on two occasions in particular—March 13, 1893 and March 12, 1936—madcap March weather caused considerable excitement. On both dates, freshet conditions in Rondout Creek, the Hudson's principal navigable tributary, caused the ice covering the creek's surface to go out rush, carrying everything in its path out towards the River.

On both occasions, the conditions were similar. The preceding winters had been severe with heavy ice. During early

John D. Schoonmaker in the New York State Barge Canal between Albany and Buffalo circa 1940s. Note the handmade rope bow bumper. (Captain Dick Sherman's collection)

Cornell #41 with other vessels astern at the Cornell Repair Shops circa 1930s. (Captain Dick Sherman's collection)

March the weather turned warm causing runoffs from melting snow into the upper Rondout Creek. Water and broken ice cascading over a dam at Eddyville, three miles from the creek's mouth, backed up behind the solid creek ice creating considerable pressure. Finally, the solid ice below Eddyville began to crumble. Once the ice started to move, its movement accelerated rapidly, moving down the creek with great force and speed. Anything in its path was swept along downstream, including vessels moored along its banks. In both instances, this was mostly the fleet of the Cornell Steamboat Company.

Those who witnessed the moving ice described it as an awesome sight. Mooring lines were snapped like strings. Vessels in the path of the grinding ice moved like ghosts down the creek and out into the Hudson River where they came to a stop in a jumbled mass against the solid ice of the River. In both instances, despite damage to the vessels involved, surprisingly there was only one reported personnel injury in 1893 and none in 1936.

The freshet of 1893 was probably the more spectacular since more vessels were involved, including at least eight big side-wheel towboats. All told, approximately 50 vessels were swept out of the creek which, in addition to the big side-wheel towboats, included at least 15 Cornell tugboats and two dozen canal boats and barges.

. . .

Warm weather earlier in the month had permitted resumption of ferry service a few days before between Kingston and

Rhinecliff. At the time, the ferryboat *Transport* was coming across the river from Rhinebeck and was just inside the dikes of the creek when she was met by the outgoing ice and army of drifting vessels. She was enveloped by the advancing fleet and swept back into the river. Some of the ferry's passengers were reported to have been panic stricken and to have leaped

New York harbor during that winter and spring, and I have spoken since that time with many Cornell employees who were witnesses to the event. They considered the 1936 freshet to be the more damaging because the Cornell tugs, *William E. Cleary*, *Coe F. Young*, and the Rondout Creek standby, *Rob* were all sunk. This 1936 marine disaster started about 7:30 AM on Thursday, March 12th. There were 12 tugs tied up at the Cornell

J. G. Rose with a small tow of two coal barges and canal boats in New York Harbor circa 1945. Italian Line's *Conte di Savoia* is passing by. (Captain Dick Sherman's collection)

across floating blocks of ice to the solid ice of the Hudson. Apparently, they all successfully made it.

The only reported injury was to Captain Charles Post of the Cornell tugboat *H. T. Caswell*. His right foot was broken when caught between the mooring line and a cleat. A Dr. Smith and a Dr. Stern made their way across the ice in the river to the tugboat where they treated the injured boatman. He was later carried in a blanket across the ice to shore."

Although I was not present at the 1936 freshet, I was active as a Cornell pilot on the lower river and

shops at Rondout. Nine more and a derrick lay at the Sunflower dock. The Sunflower dock was spared, but the 12 tugs at the shops joined the total of 30 tugs that were sent out to the Hudson by this freshet. A fog had developed and many of the drifting vessels disappeared into the mist. When the fog lifted shortly before noon, eight of the tugs were strewn on the Sleightsburg south shore, while the others were jumbled together against the solid river ice off Rondout Lighthouse.

Fortunately, Cornell's large towboat, *J. C. Hartt* was being made ready for the coming season. In short order steam was raised. She got underway and set about her task of corralling the swept away fleet. By March 15th, most of the runaways were back at their berths. The sunken *Rob* and *William E. Cleary* were subsequently raised and put back in service. The *Coe F. Young* was never raised and remained a sunken fixture on the south bank of Rondout Creek for years. And so ended the worst episode of one local springtime peril that was not uncommon to winter-berthed steamboats in Rondout Creek.

This is my story of the world's largest towing company, the Cornell Steamboat Company of Rondout, New York, taken from many records, from conversations with older boatmen, and from my own personal knowledge and memories.

C. Vibbard northbound near Hook Mountain passing shad fishermen in 1885. Hudson River sloop is astern. (Oil painting by William G. Muller)

Hudson River Day Line

The Day Line began as the Hudson River Line in 1863, a joint ownership by Alfred Van Santvoord, born in Schenectady, and John McB Davidson of Albany.

In 1879, Van Santvoord and Davidson perceived that the time had come to incorporate their holdings, so the necessary certificate was filed on June 17th. The directors were Alfred Van Santvoord, John McB Davidson, Charles T. Van Santvoord, Abraham Van Santvoord, and Charles Van Benthuysen. Alfred Van Santvoord was elected president. Of the 1,250 shares Alfred Santvoord and Davidson owned 600 each, Charles Santvoord 40, Abraham 5, and Charles Van Benthuysen 5. When John McB Davidson died in January 1887, Van Santvoord, quickly acquired his holdings and was now in complete control of the company.

Later, Charles Townsend Van Santvoord, son of Alfred, went to work for his father in the Hudson River Line and eventually became general manager. He had been born in Albany in 1854, and graduated from Rutgers in 1873. Young Van Santvoord was a gentleman with charming manners. He attracted a wide range of friends. He loved art and was strongly inclined toward athletics, hunting and yachting.

Alfred Van Santvoord had a wide variety of business interests. The Hudson River Line invested in the Catskill Mountain Railway and the Otis Elevating Railway, which provided passengers easy access from Catskill Landing to mountain resorts, including the famous Catskill Mountain House and its rival Hotel Kaaterskill. Van Santvoord also was connected with other railroads, was the founder of Lincoln National Bank, and belonged to several noted social and yacht clubs. Primarily, however, his life was devoted to steamboating, and like other prominent boat owners, he became known as "Commodore" Van Santvoord.

Charles Townsend Van Santvoord died in July 1895 at age 41 during an operation for appendicitis. He had never married and lived with his father. To succeed his son as general manager of the Hudson River Line, the Commodore chose his daughter Kate's husband, Eben Erskine Olcott.

Born in New York City on March 11, 1854, Olcott's background was unusual for a man about to enter the steamboat business. He had attended City College of New York, and then the School of Mines of Columbia University. After graduation, he worked as a chemist in North Carolina, was associated with the Pennsylvania Lead Company, and later went to Venezuela as superintendent of a gold mine. Thereafter, as a consulting engineer his profession took him on expeditions to investigate gold, silver, and copper deposits in the western United States, Mexico, and many South American countries.

The Hudson River Line turned out to be yet another gold field to be mined by Olcott. Once he had gained both experience and a free hand, he made the most of it. He built the line into something that probably exceeded the wildest dreams of the old Commodore. Olcott was an extremely

Albany southbound in Newburgh Bay in 1906. *M. Martin* of Central Hudson Line is to the left. (Oil painting by William G. Muller)

energetic man. He was popular and gained the trust of his employees, which continued as long as he lived. It was probably he who convinced the Commodore that the line should change its formal name from the Hudson River Line to the Hudson River Day Line. By order of the Supreme Court, the name took effect on October 1, 1899.

While his side-wheel yacht *Clermont* was anchored at Sea Gate, Commodore Van Santvoord died aboard at age 82 on July 20, 1901. Following a wake at his home in New York on July 23rd, the Commodore's body was placed aboard *Clermont* for his last trip up the Hudson for burial at Albany Rural Cemetery. Graveside services were conducted the next morning by his son-in-law, the Reverend Wilton Merle-Smith.

Eben Olcott succeeded Van Santvoord as president. When Captain George A. White, the line's superintendent, died on March 8, 1917, the senior Olcott turned the superintendent job over to his son, Alfred Van Santvoord Olcott, who had been Treasurer since

June 15, 1909. A graduate of Princeton, Alfred was to follow in the footsteps of his grandfather, the Commodore, for whom he was named.

On June 5, 1929, Eben Olcott died. The mining engineer who became a steamboat man had been one of the most successful the Hudson River had ever seen. Building on his father-in-law's firm foundation, he had made the Day Line into the greatest organization of its kind.

Alfred succeeded Eben Erskine Olcott as president. For the younger Olcott, the demands of the office were not easy. The period of post-war prosperity was almost over. Traffic continued to decline in 1931 and 1932. In the latter year, total passengers carried fell to 1,205,908. This total is in sharp contrast to the 1925 peak year when 1,968,744 passengers were carried; 100,732 went all the way through to Albany or the reverse. Operating revenues peaked at $2,517,100.

The Day Line maintained its own coal pockets above Newburgh and Poughkeepsie, ran a chair factory and laundry at Newburgh, an icehouse at Poughkeepsie, and a private park and vegetable and flower farms at Indian Point.

As the number of passengers declined, so did the type of passenger. Many rowdies, who were now attracted to a means of cheap transportation, presented problems. The era when the line catered "the best to the best" had faded. There was still, however, a hard core of Day Line patrons who traveled on the boats because they loved them as much as their crews did and looked forward to a beautiful sail on the river.

During World War Two and in the postwar era, the line ran at a profit, but rumors circulated in the late 1940s that something was going to happen to the Day Line. The rumors came to fruition when on November 8, 1948, the line ceased operations.

The steamboats *Daniel Drew*, built by Thomas Collyer in 1860, and *Armenia*, built in 1847 by Thomas Collyer, were the first boats in service. *Armenia* operated fully in 1863 only. Thereafter, it was used as a spare boat. It was sold in 1883 to operate on the Potomac River, and burned in 1886. *Daniel Drew* operated from 1863 to 1880, until the advent of *Albany*. From then on, it too was used as a spare boat.

The first new vessel after the original two was *Chauncey Vibbard*, built at the shipyard of Lawrence and Foulks, Brooklyn, New York. The name painted on her paddle boxes was *C. Vibbard.* She operated from 1864 to 1887 until the advent of *New York*. The *Chauncey Vibbard* was sold to operate on the Delaware River in 1890.

The *Albany* was the next in line of the fleet of boats used in over 100 years of service. She was built with an iron hull at the Harlan & Hollingsworth shipyard in Wilmington, Delaware. The new vessel presented an exterior different from

Albany leaving the Albany, New York, waterfront on a summer morning in 1900. Night boat *Adirondack* is in background. Side-wheel towboat *Oswego* is passing through the drawbridge on left. (Oil painting by William G. Muller)

its predecessors. The Hudson River Line believed that boilers on the guards were a thing of the past, so the three boilers were installed in the hold. The dining room was located on the main deck aft, completely windowed so passengers could watch the scenery. The hull was launched on January 13, 1880. A reporter for the *National Gazette* was quite carried away and wrote, "The hull was smooth as a kid glove, graceful as a swan, and sits on the water like a cork. She is a thing of beauty."

Potomac. She ran there until relieved by the steamboat *Bear Mountain* in 1949, ending 69 years of steamboat service.

The Hudson River Line had long thought about a new vessel, and I am sure the total loss by fire of the spare boat, *Daniel Drew* at Kingston Point on Sunday, August 29, 1886, helped them to finally come to a decision. The hulk had barely cooled when the Day Line had an estimate, dated September 3, 1886, from Harlan and Hollingsworth

Hendrick Hudson leaving Poughkeepsie Landing in 1909. (Author's collection)

Albany began regular service in July 1880. She had no trouble keeping the tight schedule. In fact, *Albany* rivaled the fleet *Mary Powell* for speed. It is said that *Albany* was faster over the shoal waters of the upper Hudson, which was probably because of her lighter draft. *Albany*, with no stops en route, on October 22, 1880, arrived in Poughkeepsie from New York in 3 hours and 8 minutes. David H. Hitchcock was *Albany's* first captain, but William Van Woert served the longest.

Albany ended her days as an active Day Liner in 1930, and was sold at public auction in New York City on March 6, 1934. B. B. Wills purchased her for service on the Potomac River out of Washington, D. C. and renamed her as the

for a new hull. It was to be the same model as *Albany* but 17 feet longer.

The new vessel was named *New York*. The paddle wheels were to be of the feathering type, which were so little used in the United States as to be considered novel here. In the radial paddle wheel, the paddles were fixed and banged in to the water. The feathering wheels' driving and radius bars changed the angle of the paddles as the wheels revolved. The result was that each paddle sliced into the water, straightened to present a full surface for the catch, then sliced out of the water. This increased the wheels' efficiency and eliminated the constant jarring of the radial wheel.

The finished hull, launched on February 5, 1887, left Wilmington, Delaware, on February 24, 1887, under tow. In New York, W. & A. Fletcher supplied the engine and John E. Hoffmire & Son erected the joiner work. The official trial trip took place on July 13th with Hoffmire's joiner workers still toiling away. The vessel was bedecked with flags and bunting and 500 to 600 guests were aboard strolling the decks, which were littered with sawdust and shavings.

laid up at T. S. Marvel's Shipyard in Newburgh undergoing routine overhaul and steamboat inspection. Her fires were killed and her boilers cleaned. Around midnight, fire broke out in the steward department's crews' quarters. It seems that someone among the men broke the no smoking rule.

The vessel was in a most vulnerable condition. Everything was shut down. There was no steam to operate the pumps. Water was carried from the kitchen and a hand pump on deck was used, with-

Mary Powell northbound off Storm King Mountain in 1905. (Oil painting by William G. Muller)

The instant the vessel got underway, most on board shifted their champagne glasses to their left hands and took out their pocket watches. The official timer was Stephen G. Taylor, a draftsman for W. & A. Fletcher Company. He reported, "She made from 34th Street to Yonkers in just 33 minutes." That's 24 1/2 miles an hour. Later, the engineer said, "*New York* had ten pounds of steam to spare; that's equal to two revolutions." "We have several links yet; he won't let her out," said the engine's builder, Andrew Fletcher.

New York served the New York and Albany route well through the 1908 season. Ferdinand Frost was *New York's* first captain but Alfred H. Harcourt served longest. In October 1908, she was

out success. An alarm was turned in at 12:02 AM. A steamer company, a hose company, a hook and ladder company, and a chemical company of the Newburgh Fire Department rolled to the scene, but saw no fire and there was no one to tell them where it was. The blaze was still confined to the after hold of the *New York* and a new hull (to be the night boat, *Trojan*) was between the firemen and the burning vessel.

At last, the firemen got the word, but no company had sufficient hose to reach the *New York*. A debate developed between the Washington Steamer Company and Columbian Hose Company as to who should man the hydrant. This was finally settled when Washington took the hydrant and

Columbian moved to another one in the area. Columbian had great difficulty getting the hydrant open, but at last they were successful. They found no water. The hydrant was dead. Back at the other hydrant, the Chemical Engine Company was refusing to let the Washington firemen use any of its hose. Later, the waterless Columbians aided in putting enough hose together to reach the fire. These stops and starts had continued for about twenty minutes. When water finally was brought to bear on the fire, the firemen could barely hold their own.

At 12:47 AM, a second alarm went in, and for good reason. Two minutes earlier, in the words of the *Newburgh Daily News*: "The flames burst above the hull for the first time and a great bright glare on deck betokened the doom of the beautiful vessel. Almost immediately, as the flames spread through the wooded house, there came the cry to the men to get ashore. Fanned by a gentle breeze from the southwest, they swept the boat from stern to bow. Then was unfolded the most terrible spectacle Newburgers had ever seen." All that was left of the vessel the following morning was the hull, engine, boilers, and smokestacks.

Hendrick Hudson was built in 1906 at the T. S. Marvel Shipyard at Newburgh. It was decided to use Catskill Mountain water to christen the vessel at launching, contrary to the custom of christening boats with bottles of champagne. Eben Olcott's wife, Kate Van Santvoord Olcott, was a strong advocate of temperance. She is said to have been responsible for the original plans to have a bar on the *Hendrick Hudson* being changed so that there was no bar upon completion. The launching took place promptly at 3:00 PM. Practically simultaneously as Katharine Olcott, daughter of Eben and Kate, smashed a bottle of Catskill Mountain water on the bow with the words "I christen thee, *Hendrick Hudson*," and her father removed his hat and exclaimed "She moves!" and white carrier pigeons were released from the bow, the shipyard owner broke his own bottle of champagne on the hull and performed his own private christening. Following the ceremony, the Cornell Steamboat Company towboat *Hercules*, captained by my dad, brought the hull back to Marvel's Shipyard.

Hendrick Hudson made her trial trip on the Hudson on August 28th, but the vessel was not finished. She still needed considerable work done on her fittings and interior. Her maximum speed on that day was 23 7/8 miles per hour. Her maiden voyage was practically a holiday in the Hudson Valley. Everyone who could get in sight of the river turned out to meet her. Everything on the river saluted the *Hendrick Hudson* that day, including Cornell's side-wheel towboat *Norwich*, the oldest steamboat operating on the river, built in 1836. At Newburgh, where the vessel was built, the crowd was enormous, and at Poughkeepsie it seemed as if the whole city had stopped work for the occasion. Kingston Point was jammed. The mayor of Hudson, the Honorable Henry Hudson joined the cheering crowds at his port city. At Albany, an estimated 4,000 people waved torches, fired skyrockets, and built bonfires. The vessel presented a brave sight with a huge name flag flying from the pole abaft the pilothouse, a line of flags running down either side of the pole, and flags strung between the side poles.

With her steel hull, steel deck beams and trusses, inclined engine, and feathered paddle wheels, the steamer had no need for spars and rods to strengthen her hull. She was the first Day Liner built that way. The vessel was elaborately furnished throughout. The walls were adorned with paintings by Emile Princhart of Paris, F. D. Briscoe of Philadelphia, and Yzquierdo of Madrid. Robert Fulton Ludlow executed a painting of her namesake. Vincent Howe Baily was commissioned to do a number of murals of Hudson River scenes. The vessel had 24 private parlors, two on the hurricane deck and the rest located off the main saloon. Styles included Louis XV, Louis XVI, Art Nouveau, Dutch, Colonial, and Empire, with furnishings of poplar, oak, and mahogany. Also located off the main saloon was the Persian Writing Room, where there were writing paper and souvenir postcards at no charge. Among other facilities were a barbershop with a bath attached, and a photographic dark room. The bandstand was suspended between the main deck and the saloon forward, hence the orchestral concerts could be heard all the way from the hold to the third deck.

Hendrick Hudson operated as a Day Liner from 1906 through 1948, giving 42 years of service to the Hudson Valley patrons. George A. White was the vessel's first captain, but Alonso Sickles served the longest.

The loss of the *New York* in 1908 came at the worst possible time. It was a severe blow to the Day Line. Only three steamers remained—the *Hendrick Hudson*, *Albany*, and *Mary Powell*. A new steamer had to be built, and it had to be built fast. Originally, the plan had been to build a vessel of the same size as the *Hendrick Hudson*, but it was soon found that no shipyard could make delivery of such a vessel in time for the 1909 season. The engine of *New York* and her three, practically new boilers were inspected and found to be serviceable, and by reducing the size of the new vessel, they could build it faster. Frank E. Kirby designed the steamer, with J. W. Millard working with him.

On November 24, 1908, Mr. Olcott went to Camden, New Jersey and signed a contract with the New York Shipbuilding Company for the *Robert Fulton*. The yard had covered ways, so prolonged delays because of adverse winter weather would be obviated. She would be the first Day Liner completed at the shipyard.

The keel was laid on January 11, 1909. No difficulty seems to have been experienced with the boilers of the *New York*, but the engine proved troublesome. As its parts were removed from the wreck at Newburgh, they were sent to the Fletcher works in Hoboken. Whether it was normal wear and tear, or damage from the fire's heat is not clear.

The cost of the major rehabilitation of the old engine was far in excess of what had been anticipated, and higher than the cost of a new engine.

The *Robert Fulton* sailed from Camden on May 18, 1909, bound for New York. On May 29, about four and a half months after the laying of the keel, the vessel sailed for Albany in regular service, with far less attention than had been given *Hendrick Hudson* three years earlier. Alfred H. Harcourt was the first captain. There would be others, and J. Rodney Magee would serve the longest.

Robert Fulton was not a step forward. Her outward appearance was reminiscent of the 1880s. Her three stacks athwart ship were a familiar sight on the Hudson; *C. Vibbard*, *Albany*, and *New York* all had similar stack arrangements. Her interior was very acceptable for the era, however. The main saloon had the light treatment of a formal Italian garden. The colors were largely white, gold, and green, with the effect of a blue sky overhead. There were vines, palms, plants, and caged birds. The garden theme was continued in the private parlors, but there the treatment was domestic. Each parlor was frescoed in Hudson Valley flowers like mountain laurel, pinxter, dogwood, and goldenrod. The dining room was in delft blue. The cafeteria was finished in ship's cabin style. The main entrance staircase had a miniature garden growing in it decorated with entwined roses and fitted with clerestory windows of rich yellow and golden brown stained glass.

Washington Irving, the largest Day Liner with a passenger capacity of 6,000, getting underway from her Albany berth in the early 1920s. (Roger Mabie collection)

Alexander Hamilton northbound through Haverstraw Bay in 1940. (Oil painting by William G. Muller)

Robert Fulton Ludlow's contributions were portraits of noted Americans, including one of Robert Fulton. There were also 14 paintings of Hudson Valley scenes by Vernon Howe Bailey, Frederick C. Glover, and Raphael A. Weed. Samuel Ward Stanton, the marine artist, historian and editor, painted five murals illustrating the development of steam navigation on the Hudson.

One fascinating object that never failed to draw passengers' attention on *Robert Fulton* was the walking beam, which was required by the beam engine. (The side-wheelers *Hendrick Hudson* and *Alexander Hamilton* had inclined engines that did not require the walking beam.) Passengers would be captivated for long periods of time just watching the beam's movement.

With *Robert Fulton* adding her 4,000-passenger capacity, the year 1909 was successful and earnings reached well over $600,000.

In the early fall, the eagerly-awaited Hudson-Fulton Celebration got underway with a great inaugural parade in New York on Saturday,

September 25th. Almost 750 vessels participated, including 100 steamboats and ferryboats, 270 yachts and motor boats, and 300 tugs. The *U. S. S. Gloucester* headed the procession as flagship, commanded by Captain J. W. Miller. Three torpedo boats in the escort squadron were commanded by young lieutenants whose names were destined for fame decades later, J. O. Richardson, H. R. Stark, and W. F. Halsey. The Day Line's assistant general manager, Captain George A. White, was flag officer of the first squadron, which was composed of 12 divisions of steamboats and ferries.

The centerpieces of the celebration were the replicas of Henry Hudson's ship, *Half Moon*, a gift of the people of Holland, and Robert Fulton's first Hudson River steamboat, *North River Steamboat*. The latter replica was built at Staten Island for the celebration and christened *Clermont*, the name eventually given to the *North River Steamboat*. She was entrusted to the Clermont Committee, of which Eben B. Olcott, the Day Line president, was chairman. Both replicas made the lengthy passage upstream to Troy and were greeted en route with a succession of elaborate ceremonies.

Eventually, after moorings at many berths, *Clermont* ended up in 1914 in a tidal lagoon at Kingston Point Park until she was broken up in 1936. *Half Moon* burned in 1931 at a park in Cohoes, New York.

After 29 years of service to Day Line patrons on the Hudson River, *Robert Fulton* had the singular distinction of being the last Day Line steamer to sail out of Albany. On September 13, 1948, under the command of Captain George C. Reitnauer, *Robert Fulton* ended over 100 years of Hudson River Day Line service between New York and Albany.

She was purchased by Owens-Illinois, and left New York under tow to Jacksonville, Florida, on June 28, 1956. There, her engines, including walking beam and 3 smokestacks, were removed with other equipment. In the spring of 1957, she was towed to Riding Point on Grand Island, Bahama, where her new owners were in the pulpwood harvesting business. She became a floating office and hotel for their personnel. After operations at Riding Point ceased, she was moved in 1959 to Great Abaco Island and then to her final resting place, Snake Cay. In 1960, she started to leak from age and saltwater contamination and was getting to the point where the bilge pumps could not keep her afloat. It was decided to allow her to sink to the bottom. She did sink, but only up to her guards. Then, she was landlocked by piling fill completely around her. Thus ended *Robert Fulton's* days as a floating steamboat.

On October 6, 1902, the famous *Mary Powell*, the illustrious "Queen of the Hudson," was purchased rather secretively by Eben Olcott from the Mary Powell Steamboat Company to prevent Charles Wyman Morse, the speculator and promoter who had acquired the Albany and Troy night lines, from doing the same. The Day Line acquired 419 of the 420 shares belonging to Captain A. Eltinge Anderson, Isaac Wicke's 360 shares, and 4 of the 5 shares of Joseph W. Hatch, giving them 52% of all outstanding shares. Later that fall,

Olcott acquired the solitary share still held by Hatch. In 1906, the Day Line acquired the 715 shares of the estate of John H. Brinkerhoff, which had been acquired by Benjamin B. O'Dell, the former state governor. This gave the Day Line full ownership except for a few odd shares owned by individuals.

The sequence of ownership of the *Mary Powell* is quite unusual. Captain Absalom L. Anderson (father of Captain A. Eltinge Anderson) had the vessel built by Michael S. Allison at Jersey City, New Jersey, in 1861. Absalom Anderson was her first master and captained her until he sold the vessel to Thomas Cornell in 1865, who eventually sold her to Alfred Van Santvoord in 1869. Then, Captain Anderson purchased her a second time in 1872 and came out of retirement to return as her master. In 1882, Anderson again sold her to Thomas Cornell and retired again. Cornell soon became tired of his passenger steamboat interests and turned his talents to the towboat field, where eventually he built the largest fleet of towboats in the world. In March of 1884, a group including William H. Cornell and A. Eltinge Anderson purchased the *Mary Powell* from Thomas Cornell and incorporated as the Mary Powell Steamboat Company. Captain Anderson became master of the *Mary Powell* in 1886 and continued in that capacity until relieved by Captain William Albertson in May 1914.

Before opening her regular Day Line Rondout run in 1903, *Mary Powell* spent nine days in May on the round-trip New York-Poughkeepsie route. At the close of the season in October, she went to Shooters Island on the north shore of Staten Island to the yard of Townsend-Downey Shipbuilding Company. Extensive repairs were made, including new smokestacks, reductions in paddlewheel diameter, engine work, and the installation of her 6th and final set of boilers. Alexander Rodie, boss of the boiler shops, said he "installed an excellent set of boilers as his father had done before him." His father had worked on 3 of the 5 previous sets.

In 1904, the schedule called for leaving Rondout at 6:00 AM and making stops at Hyde Park, Poughkeepsie, Milton, New Hamburgh, Newburgh, Cornwall, West Point, Cranstons, and on to New York, arriving at Desbrosses Street Pier at 11:10 AM. The return trip left New York at 3:15 PM, making the same stops en route and arriving in Rondout Creek at 8:30 PM.

Mary Powell was considered a fast steamboat in her time. She was beautifully maintained, but as time went on newer, larger, more powerful steamboats came into being. Yet *Mary Powell's* loyal followers never wavered. They expected her to go on forever.

But old age and time caught up with the proud vessel *Mary Powell* on October 3, 1911. On her northbound return trip, she landed at 129th Street to take on some homeward-bound excursionists.

Anderson never spoke to *Odell's* chief engineer again, even though they were both Rondout area residents.

1912 was the last year *Mary Powell* put in a full season on her route. In 1913, she plied her regular route through July 5th. Then, on Monday, July 7th, *Albany* with Captain William Van Woert in command, replaced *Mary Powell* because she was licensed to carry two-thirds more passengers. *Mary Powell* was relegated to service as a charter vessel and spare boat. On the morning of July 13, 1914, while vacationing with Mrs. Anderson at Greenkill Park Inn near Kingston, Captain

The Day Line's smallest vessel, the yacht-like *Chauncey M. Depew*, was used for charters and daily round trips from Poughkeepsie to New York. (Roger Mabie collection)

After she departed, the northbound *Benjamin B. Odell* landed, then sailed at 4:47 PM, about 17 minutes behind *Mary Powell*. The stern chase lasted for 36 miles. At Iona Island, the Central Hudson night liner finally drew alongside. Through the Highlands, the steamboats sailed side-by-side, then *Benjamin B. Odell* moved into the lead. Captain Anderson denied that there had been a race. He said that *Mary Powell* was too old for racing and he would not have permitted it. Allegedly, Captain

Anderson was stricken with apoplexy and died a few hours later. The funeral was held at 3:00 PM on July 15th. While it was in progress, memorial services were held on both *Mary Powell* and *Albany*. Captain William Albertson, who had been pilot for a number of years, succeeded Anderson as master.

When *Mary Powell* entered service in 1916, Arthur Anderson Warrington was appointed captain. He had joined the vessel 15 years earlier and had served as a bootblack, deck hand, quartermaster, and pilot for 6 years. He served as master till his death on October 12, 1918, at age 31 during the influenza epidemic. He was the vessel's last master.

Mary Powell was sold by bid to Israel Levinson and Ruby Cohen, and later resold to John A. Fisher, who operated a hotel along Rondout Creek. She was towed by the Cornell tug *Rob* to her final resting place on the south bank across from Fisher's hotel.

The Day Line passenger service had increased so substantially by 1910, that in 1911 they were considering plans for a new larger vessel. The liner was to carry 6,000 passengers, 500 more than

Camden, New Jersey, and the engine was to be the product of the W. and A. Fletcher Company.

Washington Irving was a steel side-wheeler. She was the greatest of the Line's "floating art galleries." Originally, Samuel Ward Stanton was commissioned to do a series of Spanish views for the *Washington Irving*. He went to Spain to gather material, but chose to return on the *Titanic* and was lost. Herbert W. Faulkner, who had earlier sketches of Spain, was then commissioned for the work. Raphael A. Weed, a close friend of Stanton, did a series of Hudson River paintings, an old New York series among them. A portrait of Washington Irving

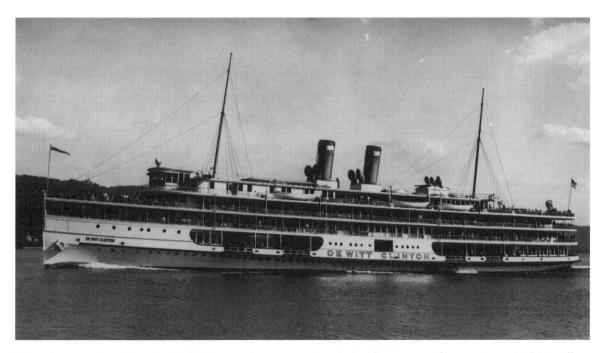

The twin screw Day Liner *De Witt Clinton* on her way upriver during the summer of 1939. (Roger Mabie's collection)

Hendrick Hudson. Washington Irving was the name chosen. I am sure that Washington Irving, who once wrote his thanks to God that his youth had been spent on the banks of the Hudson, would have been pleased with the honor.

Frank E. Kirby and J. W. Millard & Brother were the designers of *Washington Irving*. Louis O. Keil did the interior architecture. The New York Shipbuilding Corp. (originally the New York Shipbuilding Company) was to build the vessel at

was executed by Harper Pennington, while Victor D. Brenner, who designed the Lincoln penny, produced a bronze relief portrait of Irving. The ornate Alhambra writing room added to the beauty of the saloon deck, as did the 19 parlors elaborately furnished and embellished with coats of arms from different states.

The launching was set for December 7, 1912. Captain George White, the Day Line superintendent, was acquainted with William McAndrew, principal of Washington Irving High School for Girls in New York City. The two men thought it would be a fine idea and good publicity to have a delegation of girls from the school attend the launching. Some members of the school's Mascot Club were considered to be most suitable because they were redheads. So 50 redheads went to the launching. With the rest of the launching party, they left New York on a special train that the Pennsylvania Railroad called the "Redheaded Special." The railroad even found a redheaded engineer to handle the throttle. Chief chaperon to the girls was Principal McAndrew, whose hair and beard were still liberally tinged with red.

All the girls wore white sweaters with "WIHS" in white letters on a red sash, and on their heads they wore wreaths of ivy from the vine that was claimed to have been given to Washington Irving by

Sir Walter Scott and planted at Sunnyside by Irving. They won the affection of the large crowd that had gathered.

The launching took place at 1:30 PM. Mrs. Eben E. Olcott, the sponsor, had brought a white-ribboned bottle of water from the well at Sunnyside. As she raised this for the christening, all the redheads stood on tiptoe, swung their arms above their heads, and crossed their fingers. When the hull began to move, Mrs. Olcott, breaking the bottle, said, "I christen thee *Washington Irving*." The girls tossed their ivy wreaths at the vessel. When it was over, Mrs. Olcott breathed a sigh of relief and confessed, "I've had it on my mind and I was so afraid I'd say, 'I name thee *George Washington*.'"

Although the shipyard should have been familiar with the temperance launchings of the Day Line,

William G. Muller, now a widely known marine artist, at the wheel of *Alexander Hamilton* circa 1956-57. (Author's collection, taken from *Day Line Memories*, a publication edited by cadet George V. W. Kelly of Westwood, New Jersey)

Maritime historical artist, William G. Muller, aboard sailing ship *Eagle* in 1998. (Courtesy of William G. Muller)

a bottle of champagne lay ready on the platform. It was ignored by Mrs. Olcott.

On the sunny afternoon of May 1, 1913, the *Irving* made her official trial trip on the Delaware River. Subsequently, she went to New York under her own steam. On May 12th, a celebration dinner was held on board. Two days later, she made an invitation trip upriver on which came the redheads of the launching, dressed in white and with a blue ribbon tied in their hair to supply a red, white, and blue effect for the occasion. On May 16th, the entire student body of Washington Irving High School was invited on board for an afternoon sail upriver to Irving's home at Sunnyside, giving the girls ample time to consume 75 gallons of lemonade.

Washington Irving was what she was intended to be—a larger version of *Hendrick Hudson*. She was the first Day Liner to exceed 400 feet. She was 20 feet longer than her older sister, and 2 feet wider. The obvious differences in the profiles were that *Washington Irving* had her hurricane deck extend to the stern and carried three stacks. The forward one was a dummy. A less noticeable difference was

that *Washington Irving* had a torpedo, or cruiser, stern. *Hendrick Hudson* had a tendency to drag by the stern in shallower waters, while the *Irving* did not. Because the engines of the *Hudson* and *Irving* were identical in size, you would think the *Irving* would be somewhat slower because she was larger. The Day Line considered her faster than the *Hudson* because the shape of her hull created less disturbance in the water.

On May 24, 1913, *Washington Irving*, under the command of a proud Captain David H. Deming, made her first trip to Albany. The day was cloudy and rainy, and the crowd that had met the *Hendrick Hudson* on her inaugural voyage was conspicuous by its absence. The new Hudson River Night Line's new steamer, *Berkshire* which had arrived in Albany that morning, was on display for inspection by the public and that put a further damper on the *Irving's* debut. There was no disputing the fact that *Berkshire* was the larger of the two vessels. That night, an invitation reception was held aboard the *Irving* as the two largest vessels ever built for day and night service on the Hudson lay near each other.

1st Pilot De Forest Rainey on the bridge of the *Peter Stuyvesant* at Kingston Point, New York, in 1944. (Author's collection)

Although the operating season on the New York-Albany route in later years ran from late May to mid-September, in earlier years this run operated somewhat longer. The 1917 season was one in which it was operated the longest—May 12th through November 7th.

Since its beginning in 1863, the Day Line never operated a Sunday schedule, out of respect for the Christian day of rest. Now, facing increasing competition on its lower river excursion runs, the Day Line began Sunday service, (even through to Albany), in 1918. This venture proved financially successful. The number of patrons increased to 1,217,398 in 1919, and 1,460,847 in 1920. In 1925, when Day Line steamers totaled seven vessels, the fleet reached its highest overall capacity of 28,650 passengers. They carried a season total of 1,968,744 patrons, 100,732 all the way to Albany, with thousands upon thousands more to Kingston Point and Catskill Landing, mostly bound for Catskill Mountain vacation spots.

With the start of Sunday service, the Olcott family ordered that the church flag be flown above the national standard on the aft flagpole, and that a nondenominational religious service led by a visiting chaplain, be held on board.

In 1926 the Day Line celebrated its 100th anniversary. It proudly advertised, "And with the 2,000,0000 passengers carried in 1925 alone, there has never been a fatality." The 1926 season was formally opened on May 12th when a granddaughter of Eben E. Olcott ran up the flag on *Washington Irving*. Two days later the vessel began its regular trip to Albany.

Passenger volume on the Tuesday following the Decoration Day, May 29, 1926, holiday weekend was not expected to be heavy, and it wasn't, only 200 on board plus a crew of 112. As *Washington Irving* prepared to get underway at 9:00 AM, Captain Deming was in the pilothouse with Second Pilot Frank Brown and Quartermaster Herbert Hunter, while First Pilot Harry W. Kellerman was overseeing gangway removal, ready to signal the master all clear to sail at the captain's discretion. As the *Irving* began to move, she sounded one long blast on her whistle to indicate to other vessels in the vicinity that she was leaving her berth and getting underway. The weather was hazy and harbor traffic was heavy. A U. S. Army Lighter,

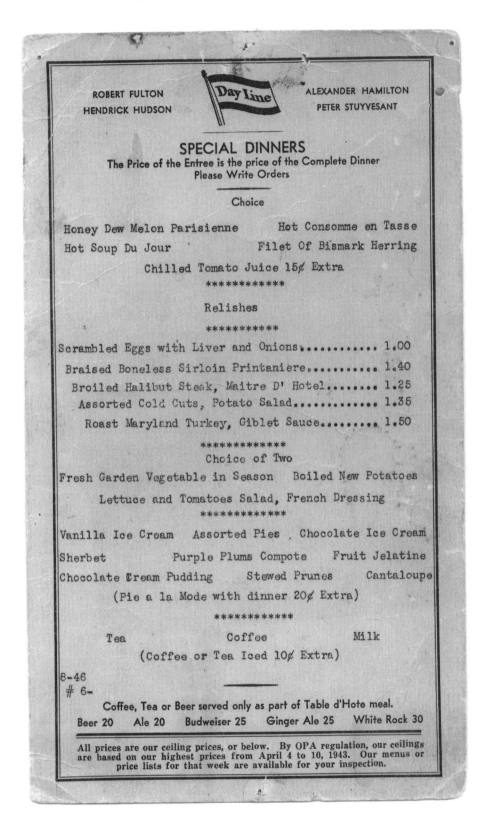

ROBERT FULTON **Day Line** ALEXANDER HAMILTON
HENDRICK HUDSON   PETER STUYVESANT

SPECIAL DINNERS
The Price of the Entree is the price of the Complete Dinner
Please Write Orders

Choice

Honey Dew Melon Parisienne Hot Consomme en Tasse

Hot Soup Du Jour Filet Of Bismark Herring

Chilled Tomato Juice 15¢ Extra

****

Relishes

****

Scrambled Eggs with Liver and Onions............ 1.00

Braised Boneless Sirloin Printaniere............ 1.40

Broiled Halibut Steak, Maitre D' Hotel........ 1.25

Assorted Cold Cuts, Potato Salad.............. 1.35

Roast Maryland Turkey, Giblet Sauce.......... 1.50

****
Choice of Two
Fresh Garden Vegetable in Season Boiled New Potatoes

Lettuce and Tomatoes Salad, French Dressing
****
Vanilla Ice Cream Assorted Pies Chocolate Ice Cream

Sherbet Purple Plums Compote Fruit Jelatine

Chocolate Cream Pudding Stewed Prunes Cantaloupe

(Pie a la Mode with dinner 20¢ Extra)

****

Tea Coffee Milk
(Coffee or Tea Iced 10¢ Extra)

8-46
6-

_____

Coffee, Tea or Beer served only as part of Table d'Hote meal.
Beer 20 Ale 20 Budweiser 25 Ginger Ale 25 White Rock 30

All prices are our ceiling prices, or below. By OPA regulation, our ceilings
are based on our highest prices from April 4 to 10, 1943. Our menus or
price lists for that week are available for your inspection.

Menu from the dining room of the *Peter Stuyvesant*, 1945. (Author's collection)

Day Line alumnus Roger Mabie in summer 2000. Mabie is currently president of the Hudson River Maritime Museum at Kingston and a well known scholar of Hudson River navigation. (Courtesy of Roger Mabie)

carrying troops, and the tugboat *Thomas A. Moran* which had an oil barge on either side of her bound for refueling of a transatlantic liner, were coming upstream.

Captain Deming, after evaluating the situation, promptly blew one blast of the whistle indicating that he intended to cross the bows of both oncoming vessels. The lighter responded and went around the stern of the *Washington Irving*. The tug did not, but eventually set her engines astern. The *Irving* was falling downstream with a strong ebb current. The oil barge on the tug's starboard side cut the port side of the *Irving* behind the paddle box. The barge struck into the Day Liner's number two fire room and on into the kitchen, cutting a gash about 20 feet long. Two of the vessel's six watertight compartments were opened and the water rushed in to flood the hold from the fire room to the kitchen.

After sounding the proper distress signal and informing passengers to don life belts, Captain Deming maneuvered the sinking steamer to Pier 9,

Erie Railroad, Jersey City, so that her forward guard was over some piles. By so doing, the rapidly sinking vessel was held on even keel until the last of the known passengers were safely on the pier. Then, the largest Day Liner ever built sank to the bottom, water reaching her third deck. Beneath her was the unfinished Holland Tunnel.

Later, three persons were found to be missing. A mother with her three-year-old daughter remained on the lower deck, looking for her two older children, ages 5 and 7. She did not know an assisting tug had taken them off. A recently discharged mess boy was also missing.

The Day Line chose to abandon the *Washington Irving* after divers concluded that the hull had been twisted and strained. She was raised by Morris and Cummings Dredging Company in 1927, floated, and put on dry dock. Little remained of her original splendor. She stayed tied up in New York until 1933 when she was towed to the Delaware River for scrap by none other than the *Thomas E. Moran*.

Those who knew Captain Deming always claimed that he was the fourth victim of the sinking. For the man who spent his life with the Day Line, the loss of the *Washington Irving* was a deep and personal one. In 1927, he served as captain on the *Hendrick Hudson*. She was to be his last command. On November 24th of that year, he died at his home in Albany.

After Captain George A. White died on March 8, 1917, Eben Olcott decided to simply become president and turn the general manager duties over to his son, Alfred Van Santvoord Olcott.

Following the First World War, traffic increased substantially and the Day Line felt that expansion of its fleet was clearly indicated. A roomier vessel was needed for the New York-Poughkeepsie round trip run which, with Indian Point Park and Bear Mountain Park, had steadily grown in popularity. The Day Line decided to buy a steamer, an unusual move given its history of building its own vessels. Their selection was a Long Island Sound night boat that had done duty as a troop transport on the English Channel. She was very fast, driven by a twin screw propeller. She had been designed by Frank E. Kirby and J. W. Millard and Brother, known designers at Day Line.

The steamer was originally named *Manhattan*. Harlan and Hollingsworth of Wilmington, Delaware had built her, along with her sister ship *Narragansett*, of steel in 1913. The two vessels were intended to be part of a transportation system that included the Grand Trunk Railroad joined with the Central Vermont Railroad, to be known as the Southern New England Railroad. The rail and steamship network was to be a direct route from New York to Montreal via Providence, Rhode Island. Charles M. Hays, president of the Grand Trunk, however, was lost aboard the *Titanic*, and the project faded away. The boats lay idle in the Delaware River, and later at New London, Connecticut. Finally, during World War One, the United States government acquired them for service as troop transports. The *Manhattan* was renamed *Nopatin*.

The Day Line felt that the *Nopatin's* twin-screw propeller propulsion and deep draft would be no obstacle to service on the Hudson, because the channel to Poughkeepsie had ample depth. The draft did prove troublesome, however, because she caused considerable suction to vessels berthed along the route.

Showboat *Buccaneer* anchored off Dobbs Ferry, New York, in August, 1933. (Author's collection)

The work to alter the vessel from a night boat to a day boat took place at the Tietjen and Lang Shipyard in Hoboken, New Jersey. The main deck was left closed forward and midship, with the dining room aft. The vessel did not rival other Day Liners in interior beauty, but it was most pleasingly furnished. The Day Line operated on the principle that the more it offered to its passengers, the more passengers it would get.

The steamer was re-named *De Witt Clinton* in keeping with the policy of commemorating famous men from the Hudson Valley. *De Witt Clinton*, as rebuilt, had a 5,000-passenger capacity. Her top speed was 23 knots. She had her first official trip on May 12, 1921. Off the 129th Street pier, *De Witt Clinton*, the great-grandson of Governor De Witt Clinton, poured water from Lake Erie into the Hudson, while Eben E. Olcott's daughter Katherine intoned, "I rename this ship *De Witt Clinton*."

De Witt Clinton ran as a Day Liner from 1921 to 1933, then laid up. She was operated again in 1939. Captain J. Rodney Magee was her only master. She was requisitioned in 1942 by the United States War Shipping Administration and re-named *Frederick Johnson*. After World War Two, she was sold to Samuel Derecktor and renamed *Derecktor* for service in the Mediterranean. Later on, as *Galilah* of the Zim Israel Navigation Company of Halifax, she ended her career serving largely as an immigrant ship. Then, she was broken up and sold for scrap in Italy.

In the early 1920s, the Day Line set to work on a plan that would increase its revenue beyond boat tariffs by building a recreational park for one-day excursionists out of New York. They selected and acquired a 320-acre site just south of Peekskill. They built facilities for picnics and dining in a cafeteria, and the site offered visitors swimming, strolling through the woods, or just sitting along the river to enjoy a leisurely day. Two separate piers were built to berth steamers. Because it was said that at one time the site had been a meeting place for Indians, the Day Line named the new park, Indian Point. The park opened for business for the 1923 season and became, like Bear

Mountain, a popular resort. For a touch of old Day Line tradition, the bell from the *Mary Powell* was installed and sounded five minutes before every steamer's arrival. The Day Line also established a farm there to raise fresh vegetables for its steamers.

Prior to the opening of Indian Point, the Day Line was at work on another steamer. Designed by J. W. Millard and Brother, this boat was not intended to be a new giant of the fleet but, rather, similar in size to the 4,000 passenger *Robert Fulton*. The construction contract was awarded to the Bethlehem Shipbuilding Corp. at Sparrows Point, Maryland. Mrs. Alfred Van Santvoord Olcott christened the vessel *Alexander Hamilton* at the launching on October 20, 1923. Hamilton, who had been fatally wounded in a duel with Aaron Burr on the hilltop across from the 42nd Street pier, had a connection with the Hudson River that was less well known than that of Hudson, Fulton, Irving, and Clinton, but he had been married in Albany and was a prominent attorney in New York City before becoming the first Treasurer of the United States.

Hudson River Day Line Treasurer Arthur Ferris with Captain Frank Briggs, 1946. (from *Day Line Memories*)

The *Alexander Hamilton* burned oil as fuel, the first of the Day Line boats built to do so. The *De Witt Clinton* was converted to oil between 1922-1923 and proved so economical to operate that the *Hendrick Hudson*, *Washington Irving*, and *Robert Fulton* were all converted to oil, leaving only the *Albany* as a coal burner.

The *Alexander Hamilton's* interior followed the same tried and true design of the other large side-wheelers, although it was not decorated on as elaborate a scale. Paintings by Herbert W. Faulkner depicted scenes connected with Alexander Hamilton's career.

The new steamer entered service in 1924 and made her first trip to Albany on May 29th. As a boy of 10, I made this trip with my mother as far as Kingston Point. Although the *Alexander Hamilton's* first trip did not create the hoopla of some of her predecessors, the event did create widespread interest in the Hudson Valley. She was the last Hudson River steamboat ever to make what could be called a triumphant first trip to Albany. Walter M. Magee was the vessel's first captain. Ralph Van Woert served the longest in that capacity. With the addition of the 4,050-passenger capacity of the *Alexander Hamilton*, the total passenger capacity of the Day Line fleet reached 27,550. In 1924, the line carried 1,934,822 passengers.

When the Day Line ceased operations in 1948, Mr. Olcott sold the *Alexander Hamilton*, *Robert Fulton*, *Peter Stuyvesant*, and *Hendrick Hudson* to a group headed by George Sanders. Later, purchased by Francis J. Barry's Circle Line, *Alexander Hamilton* ran on the Poughkeepsie-Bear Mountain route through the late 1960s.

Between the seasons of 1924 and 1925, the Day Line purchased another steamer. In comparison with the rest of the fleet, the new acquisition was a minor addition. On her own merit, however, she was a fine little vessel named *Rangeley*, built in 1913 for the Maine Central Railroad. Her primary service had been from the railhead on the mainland to Bar Harbor on Mount Desert Island. She was perfect for charters. The charter business had become increasingly important to the Day Line. Weather

Some of the Day Line alumni aboard *Alexander Hamilton* in 1961. (from *Day Line Memories*)

presented no problem. Once a club, school, or church chartered a vessel, you had to use it. There was no canceling.

The new acquisition was reconditioned by the Day Line and renamed *Chauncey M. Depew*. She had been built of steel at the Bath Iron Works at Bath, Maine. The *Chauncey M. Depew* had a passenger capacity of 1,100. The Day Line, having for so many years stressed the size, speed, and capability of its steamers, dubbed her the "Day Line Yacht." Grant Lezatte was assigned as her first captain and later his son Grant Briggs Lezatte commanded. Between the two of them, they covered most of her 15 years of service as a Day Liner.

The U. S. War Shipping Administration in 1942 chartered the *Chauncey M. Depew*. After World War Two, she was sold to the Government of Bermuda for use as a tender for cruise ships.

On February 2, 1927, the Day Line launched a new vessel that was both the first propeller-driven steamer built for the company and the last vessel it was ever to construct. The *Peter Stuyvesant* was designed by J. W. Millard and Brother with the desire to incorporate features attractive to large organizations interested in chartering her, and with the intent that her general service would be exclusively on the lower river. She was built at the Pusey

and Jones Corp.'s yard at Wilmington, Delaware, and was decidedly different from any other vessel in the fleet.

Peter Stuyvesant, named for the first Dutch governor of the colony of New Amsterdam, had a passenger capacity of 3,750. Eben E. Olcott's daughter Katharine, who previously had christened the *Hendrick Hudson*, did the honors for the Day Line's final vessel. This time, the water came from a Saratoga spring because, it was said, the Dutch settlement farthest north in the Hudson Valley was Saratoga.

The *Stuyvesant's* third deck cabins were built on a trunk deck raised well above the outer promenade deck. The carpeted saloon was located there, and from it the passengers could view the scenery unobstructed by anyone sitting in front of them on an outside deck. There, too, were eight private parlors and a writing room. The 2nd deck was surrounded by plate glass windows and could be used for dining parties or as a spacious dance hall. The dining room was on the main deck aft, and a lunchroom in the hull forward. The vessel's paintings were by Herbert W. Faulkner.

In later years, when through business to Albany decreased with the increased use of the automobile, the *Peter Stuyvesant* was assigned to that route. Upriver folks were more used to the elaborate furnishings and wide decks of the great side-wheelers, so *Stuyvesant* was not readily accepted. The vessel suffered principally by comparison. Taken by herself alone, she was fast, comfortable and proved to be a competent steamboat, well-suited for the work that she had been assigned.

After the Day Line's demise, the *Stuyvesant* operated as an excursion steamer in the New York area, but ended her career as a floating restaurant. While she was being used as an adjunct to Anthony's Pier Restaurant in Boston, she was damaged and sank in a severe nor'easter in February 1978. The hull was completely exposed at low tide, but no attempt was made to raise her. She was ripped apart by a clamshell bucket crane and her scrap sold. So ended the career of the *Peter Stuyvesant*, a steamboat that gave me many happy memories of bygone times.

Two well-known Hudson Valley natives were members of the *Hendrick Hudson* crew in 1937 as cadets: Don Ringwald, as manager of the candy and cigar stand forward on the main deck, and Roger Mabie, as manager of the newsstand on the saloon deck aft. Don Ringwald was the longtime editor in chief of *Steamboat Bill*, the journal of the Steamship Historical Society. He was considered a prime authority in this field and his several books are a fine collection of Hudson River steamboat material. Don died on June 19, 1987.

Roger Mabie, grandson of the 1st Pilot of the *City of Kingston*, served in the U. S. Navy during World War II. He also served as a director of the Kingston Savings Bank, supervisor of the Town of Esopus, and president of the Steamship Historical Society of America. At present, he is president of the Hudson River Maritime Museum at Kingston. His publications and articles are well known to Hudson Valley citizenry.

During the depression years 1932-1935, the Day Line ran "showboat trips" out of New York. These trips included an evening sail on the river, a "gala" revue, dining, and dancing. In 1933, a group headed by James A. Kenyon, an officer of the Day Line, acquired the one-time barkentine *City of Beaumont* and renamed her *Buccaneer*. She was anchored in the river under the Palisades off Dobbs Ferry, where an outstanding, rollicking revue was presented. The down boat from Albany upon arriving in New York became a moonlight cruise vessel, making the trip to *Buccaneer* and return except on Sundays and holidays. The *Buccaneer* shows continued through 1935 and, in lieu thereof, in 1936 moonlight sails were operated, but the Day Line's efforts in the showboat business had ended, although for years moonlight sails on Saturday nights continued out of New York.

After prohibition's end, beer and liquor appeared on Day Line vessels. The need to make money overrode the old anti-liquor feelings. On regular trips, bottled beer could be purchased in the cafeteria, but liquor was served only in the dining room.

The Day Line re-instituted an old favorite of its upriver patrons in the mid-1930s. It was a very popular trip, a special pre and post season round-trip excursion to the capital city. *Alexander Hamilton* was chosen to make the initial trip on Tuesday, August 27, 1935. Some of her more erudite crewmembers who were college students during the rest of the year dubbed the trip "The Farmer's Frolic."

Hamilton's schedule called for her to leave Newburgh at 8:00 AM, Poughkeepsie at 9:00 AM, and Kingston Point at 10:00 AM. She arrived at Albany at 1:30 PM. On the return, departure from Albany was at 5:00 PM with arrival at Kingston Point at 8:30 pm, Poughkeepsie at 9:30 PM, and Newburgh at 10:30 PM. The adult round-trip fare was $1.00. Children under twelve rode for $.50. A full-course "special dinner" consisting of soup, relishes, a choice of two entrees, vegetables, salad, dessert and beverages was served in the dining room for $.65.

The following year, because of the success of the original trip, it was necessary to use *Robert Fulton*, which had a larger passenger capacity. Flushed with the success of the 1935 and 1936 runs, the Day Line placed the still larger (5,500 passenger capacity) *Hendrick Hudson* on the run. The schedule was altered so that the trip originated at Indian Point (Peekskill) and en route Catskill was added. Although the round trip fare remained at $1.00, the dinner price was increased to $.75.

A good time was had by all on these trips. Shortly after leaving Albany on the return trip, dinner was served as the orchestra played for late dancing. Added attractions included the boys from Camp Notre Dame serenading the passengers on the top deck with songs and cheers from their camp. Students from various valley high schools also lent their talents to the occasion.

"The Farmer's Frolic" was carried out by the *Hendrick Hudson* until the first year of World War Two. With the stringent gasoline rationing of the

The Albany upriver excursions became a casualty of the Day Line's regular schedule success. In 1943, as the effect of the gasoline rationing reached its peak, the traveling public used the Day Line steamers in the greatest numbers since the onset of the Great Depression of the 1930s. The Day Liners were so busy carrying scheduled passengers, there was no time or room available for in-season excur-

Hendrick Hudson being towed away to the shipbreakers in 1951. (Oil painting by William G. Muller)

war years beginning to severely limit the use of the family automobile, the number of Day Line passengers increased dramatically. In 1942, it was necessary to have two late-season Albany excursions, one on Tuesday, July 28th, and the other on August 25th. The fare had increased to $1.25, and the dinner in the dining room had gone up to $.85.

sions. Thus ended a pleasant late summer's interlude for both the crews of the steamers and the many passengers who sailed on the excursions.

The Day Line's wartime boom was its last hurrah, however. The increased use of the family automobile after the Second World War finally caused the Day Line to cease operations in 1948.

Ocean liner *Normandie* arriving in the lower Hudson after an Atlantic crossing in the mid or late 1930s. (Oil painting by William G. Muller)

CHAPTER SIX

Deep-Draft Piloting

Geographers tell us that the Hudson River, with its tides and currents, is a fjord-like arm of the sea. Since 1927, when the newly dredged channel was opened to Albany, that reality has become apparent. As the sea stretches its arm up through New York State, large sea-going vessels travel up and down the river between the Atlantic Ocean and the Port of Albany. Some are smart and shipshape, others faded and worn. Some are American tankers from Gulf ports, lumber ships from our northwest Pacific coast, or passenger liners like Grace Line's *Santa Paula*, but most fly foreign flags from far-away ports and bear names that sound strange to our ears. They pass by with their propeller blades chunking their wake, heavy-laden and low in the water, or traveling light and empty bound for Albany's massive grain elevator to load cargo for some far distant land.

Spectators along the river banks must wonder sometimes how such massive vessels, the largest movable objects made by man, can find their way safely and surely up and down through the twisting Hudson Highlands and the narrow, dredged channels of the river between Kingston and Albany's port. The answer lies in a small flag at the top of the signal halyard. It is the international code "H" flag with two vertical divisions, one red and one white, and it says to all, "I have a pilot on board."

Although piloting is one of the world's oldest professions, the particulars of the job are among the least well known among the general population. Pilots are mentioned in the Old Testament, and in

the early Christian era the Arabs were quite active in piloting operations. The first journey of Marco Polo to the Orient was made with the assistance of Arab pilots. Two centuries later, Vasco De Gama used Arab pilots in his first voyage around the Cape of Good Hope.

By the time of Columbus, pilotage had made great strides. The *Santa Maria*, Columbus' flagship, belonged to Juan De La Costa who served Columbus as chief pilot on the first two voyages to

Author and several New York State Pilot Commissioners as observers onboard a ship bound for Albany in 1974. (Author's collection)

the New World. During the post-Columbian era, the loss of the Spanish Armada has been attributed, in part, to the fact that no pilots were aboard. The fleet admiral, therefore, had no local knowledge of the treacherous nature of the English Channel.

Piloting in early times was not the specialized occupation limited to specific areas that it has become today. At first the term "pilot" was used to indicate a mariner on board a vessel who directed the course of the ship throughout her voyage. Gradually, as ships increased in size and draft, it became recognized that expert knowledge of local harbors, with their individual problems, was necessary.

The term "pilot" later became associated with those who conduct ships over bars, shoals in rivers, and other hazards. The first organized pilotage system originated in The Netherlands when Frans Naerebout became the first professional pilot in 1749.

The colonization of America was done with the aid of pilots. Boston seems to have had the first bar pilots. When Boston Lighthouse was built in 1716, George Worthylake, its keeper, was also a bar pilot. Thirteen pilots formed an honor guard from Elizabeth, New Jersey, to the Battery for President George Washington when he came to New York for his second inauguration.

The second Congress of the United States gave each seaboard state the right to regulate pilotage systems in accordance with its needs, and one of the world's finest pilotage systems governing foreign commerce is found in the State of New York. U. S. Navy vessels are not required to employ the services of a state pilot; however, most do.

A Hudson River pilot performs dual functions, unique in his profession. He not only guides vessels on the voyage upstream, but docks and/or undocks ships at various ports that dot the river's banks, sometimes with the assistance of a tugboat, more often without.

It is not by chance that the Hudson River pilotage service exists today as a standard for excellence. In the public interest, and in the interest of shippers desiring to use the Hudson River, New York State has created and maintains one of the safest and most efficient pilotage services in the world. The lawmakers have provided a guiding and

protective hand in the background—the Board of Commissioners of Pilots. The wisdom of the legislatures is evidenced by the fact that three of the pilot commissioners are appointed by the Chamber of Commerce of the City of New York, two by the Board of Marine Insurance Underwriters, and one by the governor of the state from the members of the Albany Port Commission. The board sets the number of pilots necessary for the route, licenses and bonds them, alters or amends existing regulations, and duly promulgates and enforces new rules. The board may take any disciplinary actions that it deems necessary. The state legislature sets the pilotage rates, taking into consideration competition from other ports and the finances necessary to operate and maintain a healthy, efficient pilot service.

The breathtaking views as you approach New York's state capital no longer thrill thousands of steamboat passengers as their stately vessels glide into port. The scene is now enjoyed by the recreational boatman, tugboat crews, and the crews of the deep-sea vessels that now ply the Hudson, and who may or may not be impressed by memories of yesteryear.

Since 1614, when the United New Netherlands Company founded a fur trading post on Westerlo Island, Albany has been an important river port. Fort Orange was the original name given to the area when it was under Dutch rule. In 1652, Governor Peter Stuyvesant re-named it Beverwyck. That name was retained until 1664, when the English Governor Donegan named it Albany in honor of one of the titles of the Duke of York. It was during Donegan's governorship that Albany received its first city charter. Governor Peter Schuyler appointed its first mayor.

Albany's strategic position on the Hudson River as a gateway to the Iroquois nation made it very important in the colonial period. During the American Revolution, the British looked upon Albany as "a capital to be subdued." It was the object of General Burgoyne's expedition that ended in disaster for the British at Saratoga. Political scientists regard Albany as the vortex of policy-mak-

Port of New York, Yonkers Line	PILOTAGE RATES		*Effective June 1, 1969*

All vessels of 100 pilotage units and over shall pay **$2.00** per pilotage unit for Section 1, Lower River; Yonkers, all ports through Peekskill.

The following minimum charges shall prevail to Section 1,

Up to 50 pilotage units	$150.00	More than 50 and up to 100 pilotage units	$200.00

All vessels of 100 pilotage units and over shall pay **$2.75** per pilotage unit for Section 2, Middle River; Yonkers, all ports beyond Peekskill through Kingston.

The following minimum charges shall prevail to Section 2,

Up to 50 pilotage units	$225.00	More than 50 and up to 100 pilotage units	$275.00

All vessels of 100 pilotage units and over shall pay **$3.50** per pilotage unit for Section 3, Upper River; Yonkers to all ports beyond Kingston through Albany or Troy.

The following minimum charges shall prevail to Section 3,

Up to 50 pilotage units	$300.00	More than 50 and up to 100 pilotage units	$350.00

A maximum charge of **$1200.00** shall be applicable to all vessels of 100 Pilotage Units or more.

DOCKING OR UNDOCKING VESSELS

Without Tug	$75
With Tug	$35

Vessels 550 ft. or over shall have an additional charge to those mentioned above as follows:

	Additional Fee
Vessels 550'. - 599', L.O.A.	$10.00
Vessels 600' - 649', L.O.A.	15.00
Vessels 650', - 699', L.O.A.	20.00
Vessels 700' or more L.O.A.	25.00

TRANSPORTING VESSELS BOUND TO OR FROM YONKERS, ONLY $50

SHIFTING VESSELS AT HUDSON RIVER PORTS—
When a Hudson River Pilot is required to shift a vessel from one berth to another he is entitled to $100 for each shift.

DETENTION

3 hours	$ 50
6 to 24 hours	$100

CARGO STOPS

Up to 6 hours	$ 25.00
6 to 12 hours	$ 50.00
12 to 24 hours	$ 75.00
For each 24 hours or in excess thereof	$100.00

ICE CONDITIONS

Vessels bound for any port, detained on account of ice conditions for each day $75.00

In the event ice conditions require 2 pilots on board the fee will be $125 for the second pilot in addition to the regular pilotage fee.

Hudson River State Pilot rates, 1974. (Author's collection)

ing action during and after the rebellion against English rule, and the embryo from which united colony development grew through Benjamin Franklin's "Albany Plan." The source of Albany's economic wealth over the years has been the Hudson River and its main tributary, the Mohawk.

The Port of Albany is approximately 143 miles from Ambrose Tower at the entrance of New York Harbor in the Atlantic Ocean, and 122 miles from the Battery in New York City. While this may seem a great distance inland for a seaport, it is not unusual. Philadelphia is 100 miles from the sea, Baltimore 170 miles, Montreal 180 miles, and Portland, Oregon 113 miles.

For decades, public opinion had been galvanizing for deepening the Hudson River to allow ocean traffic. Then, on December 8, 1913, the Honorable Peter G. Ten Eyck introduced a bill in Congress to provide for a survey and an estimate of the cost of a deep-water channel in the Hudson River to Albany. This bill was included and passed in the Rivers and Harbor Act of March 1915.

With the approval of the U. S. Army Corps of Engineers and the New York State Legislature, among others, a bill was proposed authorizing $11,200,000 to deepen the river to a minimum depth of 27 feet at low water, a sufficient depth at that time to float 85% of all ocean-going ships in the world. The bill passed the U. S. Senate on February 26, 1925, the U. S. House of Representatives on March 2, and on March 3, 1925, it was signed by President Calvin Coolidge.

Within a month, the state legislature created the Albany Port District Commission. Governor

Ship unloading rock salt at the Port of Albany for use on New York State highways during the winter of 1998. (Captain Tom Sullivan's collection)

Alfred E. Smith signed it into law on March 25, 1925. The Port District included all territory on both sides of the river within the cities of Albany and Rensselaer, and all lands and waters in the river contiguous thereto. The commission consisted of four members from Albany and one from Rensselaer, all appointed by the governor.

In my time of pilotage service, there were two port managers—James G. Brennan, Sr. (1932-1952), and Captain Frank W. Dunham, Jr. (from 1952 on). Frank was later appointed by Governor Nelson A. Rockefeller, at the request of Albany City Mayor Erastus Corning II, to the Board of Pilot Commissioners of the State of New York.

The Port Commission purchased 200 acres of land on the river's west bank at Westerlo Island, transforming it into 4,000 feet of dockside. The 100 acres on the east (Rensselaer) side was converted into 600 feet of dockside designed to handle shipments of lumber. The entire port area was raised 18 feet to allow ocean freighters to load and discharge cargoes.

Transit Shed # 1 is 500 feet long and 120 feet wide, while Shed # 2 is 1200 feet long and two stories high with 144,000 square feet of storage space on each floor. Powerful freight elevators connect the two floors. An automatic sprinkler system protects valuable products from fire. An administrative office building contains comfortable private rooms for visiting guests. Railroad tracks encompass the entire port.

The port's most impressive structure breaks the skyline toward its southern end. This is the world's largest single-unit grain elevator. The main building covers 253,000 square feet of an 8-acre site. Its 104 circular bins tower 97 feet into the air. Each measures 28 feet in diameter. These bins, together with 8 storage rooms, constitute a total capacity of 13,000,000 bushels, a greater storage capacity under a single roof than the entire grain facilities at New York Harbor.

Grain arrives by rail car and is unloaded by an ingenious device that lifts the entire car from the tracks and pours its contents into a hopper. It has the capacity to handle ten cars per hour. Telescopic spouts (50,000 bushels an hour capacity) are provided for loading grain into ships. They are fitted with bifurcated ends, which are designed so that ships may be loaded without hand trimming. They are also fitted with sacking horns to facilitate bagging the grain for hatch trimming on ocean vessels. Just after World War II, we pilots sailed one loaded grain ship a day from the Port of Albany.

In addition to the grain elevator, United Fruit (now United Brands) moved their northeast terminal from Weehawken, New Jersey, to Albany in 1971. Gone are the days when bananas were delivered in three-foot-long stalks on top of men's shoulders—stalks that often held spiders, snakes, and other hitchhikers. When the fruit arrives today, it has already been decontaminated. It arrives off the stalk packed in 40-pound boxes. From 1982 until recently, two ships a week arrived carrying some 3,500 tons of bananas, representing the port's second largest business. Distribution was then made by truck or train to New England, Canada, and the mid-western United States. United Brands has recently moved from Albany.

Wood pulp, most of which comes from Scandinavia and Canada, is another big commodity import.

Major oil company docking terminals for tanker ships in the Albany-Rensselaer area included Atlantic Refining, Sears Petroleum, Exxon, Texaco, Sun Oil, Cities Service, Tidewater Oil, Gulf Oil (now British Petroleum), and Mobil.

Other shippers and importers included Barber & Bennett (animal feed), National Molasses Company (Caribbean molasses), Pacific Molasses, Seaboard Allied Milling (baker's flour), Anvil Fence & Supply (fencing materials), Gorman Brothers (wholesale asphalt), Hudson River Construction (paving material), Albany Asphalt & Aggregates, Port Concrete Company, Shields & Company (fasteners, nuts, and bolts), Porte Construction (heavy construction needs), Goodyear Tire & Rubber, Vorelco Inc. (importers of Volkswagen cars), Ashland Chemical Company, and Cibro Petroleum Products (the largest private investor in the port, with a regional refinery capable of producing 2,000,000 gallons of petroleum products every 8 hours).

The Port has 16 acres for use as an automobile distribution center, a 12,000,000-gallon molasses

Heavy derrick ship approaching Castleton Railroad Bridge bound for Albany to load turbines from the General Electric Plant at Schenectady. (Captain Tom Sullivan's collection)

storage and distribution facility, 15 acres for scrap metals and recyclables, and a 60-carload-per-day feed mill. Matton Towing Line tug *Ralph Matton* provided service to ships in the port. Ralph Carpino was still her captain in 1999.

Navigationally speaking, the safest hours in the life of a ship are those she spends at sea, where there are plenty of fathoms under her keel, no channels to follow, and no traffic to evade. Weather is not the

reefs and shoals, and the ever-increasing traffic both large and small, all of which is operated by people, the one unpredictable element in the whole picture. To counteract this element, there are two New York State pilot associations that assure safe navigation of large vessels from the sea to the head of deepwater navigation at Albany: the Sandy Hook pilots, or bar pilots, who bring seagoing vessels from Ambrose Tower into New York Harbor at

Cement transport *M. H. Baker III* turning at Albany, bound for Coeymans cement plant in 1955. Tug assisting. (Captain Tom Sullivan's collection)

major problem it once was, because today's modern vessels are designed and built to survive all kinds of weather. A fully loaded and properly ballasted ship with adequate handling can ride out any storm. Violent storms still do cause anxiety and discomfort, but they can usually be avoided with the use of present-day communications. So, as long as the course is in open water, life is relaxed onboard and the vessel is safe.

The story changes when a ship approaches land. Then, she has to contend with narrowing channels, sharp turns, strong tidal currents, rocks,

the Narrows; and the Hudson River Pilots, who bring vessels bound for Hudson River ports from the Narrows northward through the busy harbor and upriver.

Let us consider how these men reach their lonely positions of command on the navigation bridges of vessels of all nations. A man who can bring vessels of all sizes and handling characteristics through the maze of Upper Bay traffic and the narrow winding channels of the Hudson River must be an expert who has devoted his life to the preparation, observation, and discipline necessary for this job. Today's Hudson River state pilot is a professional, the product of at least seven years of rigorous and dedicated training before he becomes a full-branch Hudson River pilot. At that point, he holds both a state and federal pilot's license allowing him to pilot ships of any weight and draft. He also holds a master's license.

During his training period, he must pass several examinations held by the Board of

eral pilot's license for New York Harbor and the Hudson River for vessels of at least 500 gross tons. This license takes a minimum of three years to obtain. After being interviewed by the association's executive committee, passing a complete physical examination, and receiving the approval of the Board of Commissioners of Pilots, he is then accepted by the Hudson River Pilots for a three-year apprenticeship.

Francis Turecamo assisting the *Georgia S.* to dock at the Port of Albany in 1999. (Captain Tom Sullivan's collection)

Commissioners covering all phases of pilotage. He develops a keen judgment of distance and momentum, as well as the "feel of the ship." He learns about the various types of ships, their machinery and general characteristics. He learns about their capabilities and limitations until they become almost second nature to him, for he must do many things instinctively. This is what enables the pilot to make quick and accurate judgments in an emergency. He must train his mind and eyes to be ever alert to danger and learn to react appropriately.

To be considered for a Hudson River pilot apprenticeship, the applicant must first hold a fed-

During this apprenticeship, he must accompany full-branch Hudson River pilots on at least 100 trips aboard deep draft vessels over the full route. Upon completion of his apprenticeship, and when he has raised his federal pilot's license to unlimited gross tonnage, he is given an oral and written examination before the Board of Commissioners of Pilots. If he qualifies, he is granted a license as a state deputy pilot, fourth grade, licensing him for vessels of 8,500 gross tons and up to 22 feet of draft. At intervals of one year, he appears before the Pilot Commissioners for a review of his record and a re-examination. If he shows satisfactory progress, he is gradually raised to deputy pilot, third grade, and then the following year to second grade, allowing him to pilot successively larger ships. Finally, at the end of seven years of successful progress and examinations, the Pilot Commissioners may issue a full-branch Hudson River state license, unlimited as to tonnage and draft. In order to maintain the highest standards, every licensed pilot is re-examined every year until his retirement.

Loaded molasses tanker passing New Baltimore, New York, bound for the Port of Albany circa 1952. (Photograph by Captain Mel Hamilton)

Requirements to become a state-licensed pilot today are far more rigorous and time consuming than when I entered the service. One is now required to be a college graduate, and an active state pilot must put one on the apprentice list. Then, if called and approved by the pilot association members and the New York State Board of Pilot Commissioners, one is appointed as an apprentice pilot. As an apprentice, one must serve a minimum of three years riding with an experienced pilot. During this time, one receives no income, only travel expenses. Next, with the same previously-mentioned approvals, one is appointed a fourth grade deputy pilot, limited as to size and draft of ships. At this time, one is entitled to one-fourth of a full pilot's pay. After serving a minimum of four years as a deputy, with increasing responsibility as to ship's size and draft, and appropriate increases in income, one rises in grade until one is ready to be approved as a full-branch state pilot.

The full-branch state pilot is not under the command of any ship's captain. He is independent. He must answer for his own decisions on navigational matters. As he is not the employee of any private company, he is thereby relieved of any company pressures that may be brought to bear to try to influence his judgment. From his apprenticeship throughout his career, however, it is instilled in him that he is there because a pilot service exists and such a service will continue only if a port is attractive to shippers. Consequently, it is his duty to his port to accommodate skippers within the boundaries of safety to life, limb, and property.

In 1932, with the completion of dredging operations from New York to Albany, sea-going traffic on the Hudson increased accordingly. New Pilotage Laws required all foreign-registered ships over 250 gross tons and 6 feet of draft, as well as all American vessels, to have a pilot on board. Carl Barnes, Marty Woods, and William Buckley were among the first active pilots. There were several years of increasing competition among individual pilots. Then, a loosely knit group of individual pilots formed an association. Bill Myers was elected first president.

During World War II, ship traffic on the river decreased substantially, so many Hudson River pilots served as East River Hell Gate pilots and temporary Sandy Hook bar pilots. It was finally realized that the pilot service could be made more effective by the organization of a true pilots' association. In 1942, a set of by-laws and working rules was drafted, thus forming the Hudson River Pilots Association. The association elected its own officers and committees on a yearly basis and was, therefore, self-governing. Through the main office on State Street in New York City, ship owners and agents order their pilots as needed. They are available at any time of the day or night, observe no holidays, and charge no overtime fees. The schedule of pilotage rates is fixed by the state legislature.

After serving aboard many vessels—tugs, tow boats, trailer ships, ferry boats, night boats, Day

Liners, etc.—for 25 years, I was chosen by the members of the Pilot Association to take the examination for a Hudson River ship pilot. I took the required examination, passed, and was accepted. Because of my experience, after my examinations I entered the Hudson River Pilots Association as a

accounts with various steamship lines and hesitated to give those accounts up. They were uncomfortable with the control that both the association and the state would have over them. In time, with the help of a few of the older pilots, we accomplished our goal for the betterment of the pilot system and

Francis Turecamo, helper tug for the Port of Albany, winter 1995. (Captain Tom Sullivan's collection)

deputy pilot. After one year of active service, I was promoted to a full-branch pilot.

The members of the Hudson River Pilots Association Executive Committee and I were influential in having a bill that formed the present State Pilot Association passed in 1959 in the New York State Legislature and signed by Governor Nelson Rockefeller. This was not an easy task, because many of the older pilots at that time had individual

all that used its service. The pilots shared equally in the income and expenses according to their grade. Later, I was able to establish an unusually fair pension system for all. A retired pilot with a minimum of 20 years service would receive a one-half share of what an active full-branch pilot received. This pension plan continues to this day.

I served as a state pilot for 26 years. I was elected to serve on the executive committee, and I was

U. S. Coast Guard cutter #685 performing icebreaking duty south of the Port of Albany in the winter of 1999. (Captain Tom Sullivan's collection)

elected the first president of the association, a position I remained in for 12 years. As president, with the executive committee, I was in charge of all business matters, pilot discipline, apprenticeships, and pilot boat maintenance. I retired on October 1, 1976. James Maloney, Tom Sullivan, Edward Ireland, and Frank Cowan have served as presidents after me.

A pilot association is not any easy group of men to govern. Each pilot is individually licensed and fully responsible for his own actions aboard ship. Each full-branch pilot has one full vote at association meetings and the right to express his personal opinion for as long a period as he wishes. I recall many meetings, especially annual meetings, that lasted well into the early morning hours. Although elected officers ran the business, it

appeared at times that everyone was a chief and there were no Indians present. It was democracy in the raw, but everything always ended well for the vast majority, and good fellowship among equals remained happily in place.

The pilots contribute time, money, and knowledge to recommend improvements to the channels where they serve. Continuing improvements are necessary to meet the needs of the larger and deeper drafted vessels that are continually entering the trade. A recommendation may deal with a major project for the entire area. This requires an appearance before Congress or the state legislature, or it may address the needs of an individual local terminal operator.

There is a pilot working board—a list of available pilots—in the main office of the association.

Assignments are made in accordance with the license each pilot currently holds. When a man finishes an assignment, his name goes to the bottom of this list and gradually rises to the top as new tasks are given out to the men at the top of the list.

When a pilot is requested for a vessel leaving a pier or anchorage within New York Harbor, he is taken on board at that point. For vessels coming directly from sea, he relieves the Sandy Hook pilot off Quarantine Station on Staten Island. Boardings are made from the open bay pilot launch in all sorts of weather. The pilot, often at the risk of his life, must climb up the side of the vessel on a rope ladder to a special boarding port or to the weather deck from the pilot boat moored alongside. He goes directly to the bridge, where his job begins. In the case of a Hudson River pilot, he assumes the conn to insure the safety of the vessel and her precious cargo of lives and goods on the voyage upstream.

Pilots call no ship their own, yet they have command of many. They are deepwater sailors who rarely go to sea. They have no foreign port of call, yet, through the years, tens of thousands of foreign-flag ships come under their command.

The pilot never fully supercedes the complete authority of the master on the ship. He is aboard in the capacity of a trained advisor, required by law and responsible for the safe navigation of the vessel throughout her trip through these inland waters. These professionals, dressed in business suits and known internationally as "Sailors in Civvies," are responsible every year for the safe transport on the Hudson River of billions of dollars worth of products and many human lives. Their knowledge of the river, its tides, currents, wind funnels, and the crooked, narrow deepwater channel, ensures the safe travel of heavily-laden vessels often with the keels only inches from the bottom.

Once on the bridge, the pilot never leaves it while the vessel is underway in his area. He also serves as docking pilot, with or without the aid of tugs. Should the ship be inbound to Albany, he must be alert for sixteen hours of continuous service. Only for large, deep-draft vessels in the area from Hudson to Albany is night-time navigation suspended. Otherwise, the trip either way is made without stopping. In the future, however, certain major improvements in this part of the channel's width, and additional aids to navigation, could permit twenty-four-hour sailing for the entire length of the trip. On a typical run, there may be recorded an average of 100 reduced speed bells for other vessels, tows, docks, and small boat anchorages. The run from Kingston to Albany is made almost entirely under reduced speed.

Peter Stuyvesant passing Mobil oil tanker at Port of Albany in 1946. (Author's collection)

In the old days, when the magnetic compass was in use and courses were timed, night boat pilots listened to whistle echoes from ashore to determine their position. Today, most vessels have radar for conditions of reduced visibility or darkness. Consequently, the pilot must be thoroughly experienced in the interpretation of the radar screen.

Radar is an invaluable asset to modern navigation. Many times, however, when I boarded a ship and asked the captain if his radar was operating properly, his response was "Yes, pilot, it is," but when he turned it on, I found this not to be the case. Radar at sea need not be exact to the foot, but when navigating a large ship in the narrow, dredged channels of the Hudson River, especially with two vessels passing in the fog, it is of the utmost importance.

When I was an active pilot, as an additional aid to safety all pilots carried VHF walkie-talkie sets using a frequency of 156.65, which is limited to pilots by the Federal Communications Commission. When passing other ships or in times of reduced visibility, bridge-to-bridge conversations could be carried on to clarify the exact intent of the pilots involved. Fog may prevail at any place

most important talents is the ability to instill confidence in the master of the vessel that he is boarding. The concern of the master for his vessel cannot be overstated. Without exaggeration, it is comparable to the love a husband has for his wife and children. The tenderness and affection that a master holds for his ship is a beautiful phenomenon to behold. When a master surrenders his control of the vessel

Author talking to (then apprentices) Captains Russell Syvertson III and Dominic Cassano on the pilot launch *John E. Flynn* at the Yonkers Pilot Station circa 1959. (Author's collection)

along the Hudson, but in the freshwater stretch from Poughkeepsie to Albany it is particularly common in spring and autumn, and is particularly dense at the water's surface. Under these conditions, the pilot must use all the tools at his command to stay in the channel and to avoid other shipping.

Besides the actual piloting of a ship, the pilot has many other, varied responsibilities. One of his

to the pilot for its transit up through inland waters with dangerous rock cuts and winding narrow areas, he must do so with full confidence, entrusting his ship, without reservation, to a man he has just met for the first time. This transfer of control is made less uneasy by the worldwide respect for the competence of the men of the state pilotage system. Nevertheless, a stranger suddenly being placed in a position of authority, one who might conn the ship just a little differently from the master, can create momentary tensions on the bridge.

On foreign vessels, there is always the language barrier to surmount. Either the pilot or some member of the ship's force must be bilingual or they must find some means of communication. Food service varies with the vessel's nationality, and the pilot must acclimate himself to a variety of dishes and a diversity of quality. Even the old standby, naval coffee, is never the same twice.

During my days as a pilot, the United States Coast Guard had four large icebreakers named after the four winds. These ships had a propeller forward in a cylinder, as well as the usual propellers aft. They were built to break ice in the Arctic Ocean. One severe winter, I received an assignment to pilot the *West Wind* up the Hudson and break a track in the heavy ice so that some oil tankers could reach Albany. Fuel supplies were getting low and the Albany city fathers feared they would have to close the schools.

I boarded the vessel at Staten Island. A full-fledged Coast Guard captain was the skipper. We proceeded upstream through the salt-water ice as far as Poughkeepsie with no problems. However, as we got into the solid freshwater ice, the *West Wind's* performance decreased rapidly. Saltwater ice is soft somewhat like a honeycomb. Three or four-foot-thick freshwater ice is solid. It is like hitting a rock.

When *West Wind's* forward progress stopped, it was necessary to back her up three or four lengths and then plow ahead at full speed and run the vessel's bow up on the ice, thereby breaking the ice

Author disembarking via pilot's ladder from tanker *Gulfpride* to pilot launch during "Operation Sail" in 1976. (Photograph courtesy of Barbara Maloney, wife of Captain Jim Maloney)

under the ship's weight. I continued this maneuver several times, much to the dissatisfaction of the captain. He seemed very concerned (I suppose, with promotion in mind) that his vessel might be damaged and it would be held against him. He finally got so annoying that, for the first and only time in my career, I told a master off. I told him it was my understanding that his vessel was sent to the Hudson River to break a track in the ice so that we could get the needed fuel to Albany. This method was the only way his vessel could break through the heavy ice when her headway was stopped. He could relieve me of my piloting duties, or I would, at his request, pilot his vessel back to New York, leaving his assignment unfinished.

With that, he calmed down and did not bother me any more. The *West Wind* continued on toward Albany, and whenever she got stuck in the ice, I used the same tried and true method to free her. We finally arrived in Albany with the oil tankers, I must say I was more than happy to leave the *West Wind* and her captain.

There is another problem which, in its season, increases all the other worries of the river pilot. The Hudson is to be used with equal facility by both commercial and pleasure craft. Therefore, the responsibilities for safe navigation must be held equally by the professional pilot and the small boat operator. There are only a few standards of precaution for handling large, deep draft vessels in constricted waters to protect life and property, and these standards are observed rigidly by the professional pilots. Many small boats, however, are operated in a most careless, if not reckless manner, and are berthed along the shore with complete disregard of the possibility of personal injury or damage to the craft.

Most small boat operators adhere to the rules of safety and common sense, but incidents involving irresponsible pleasure boating are increasing to such a degree as to cause pilots grave concern during the boating season.

Every vessel, large or small, has its own handling characteristics. These variations are set by many factors, including the number of propellers, location of the rudder, hull form, and conditions of loading. Consider that the average large vessel in open water may need upwards of a mile in which to stop due to the inertia of its large mass and the fact that its propellers are designed to move it ahead and are, thus, quite inefficient when reversing. When a ship starts a turn in one direction, the whole vessel could move almost three times the width of its beam in the opposite direction before the desired turning motion is finally established. Then, too, ship response in shallow water is much more sluggish than in deeper water. All these factors make it almost impossible for a large vessel to maneuver to avoid small boats in restricted channels without running a chance of grounding. The small boat, on the other hand, is much more maneuverable and manageable and can use the areas beyond the channels where the depth of water is still ample for its lesser draft. The larger vessels should be given undisputed use of the dredged channels, when sufficient depth for smaller boats can be found elsewhere.

With the height and wide bows of the larger ships and the location of the navigating bridge, there is an area forward of the bow that is a blind spot for the pilot. This is particularly true of tankers and cargo vessels that are designed with the bridge located on the stern house. Some small boats take up a position just forward of the large vessel, in many cases just out of sight of the pilot on the bridge. No matter how much the pilot shears the vessel, blasts alarm whistles, or reduces speed, some boats remain in this chosen, dangerous position. A sudden engine failure in the small boat would surely mean that it would be run down. A similar fate could befall the foolhardy operator who races back and forth across the larger vessel's bow. In recent

Former New York State Governor Malcolm Wilson and former State Senator John E. Flynn with Hudson River State Pilots at a 1962 dinner dance. Front Row (left to right): Joseph Budinich, Hudson River Pilots' agent, Dominick Cassano, Hudson River Pilot. Second Row: Edward Ireland, Hudson River Pilot, New York State Senator John E. Flynn, New York State Governor Malcolm Wilson. Third Row: Hudson River Pilots Thomas Sullivan, Joseph McKay, Melvin Hamilton, and Richard Sherman, Pilot Association President John G. Hamilton, and Roy Cohn. (Photograph courtesy of Patricia Budnick)

years, more and more water skiers with complete disregard for personal safety take pleasure in going round and round large ships underway. When a large hull slides past a small boat, there is suction as the water rushes back to fill the void left by the passing hull. It would not take too many blows for those thrashing propeller blades to demolish a small boat and its occupants.

This suction is felt not only close to a passing ship, but along the shore as well, especially in narrow stretches of the river with fairly shallow water between the channel and the shore. Water is a noncompressible liquid and when a ship with a length of 700 feet and a beam of nearly 100 feet, displacing thousands of tons of water, moves along the Hudson, this displaced water has to go somewhere. As a large vessel passes, there is first an upward surge of water along the shore, followed by a shoaling caused by the water rushing back into the ship's wake. Then, the turbulence caused by the wave train comes. All this happens no matter how slowly the vessel is traveling. Small children left swimming alone could be pulled out into deeper water by this suction. The safest mooring for small boats is behind a breakwater. In the absence of a breakwater, deepwater moorings are preferred to prevent a passing vessel from sucking the water out from under a small craft and causing it to ground. A float is safer than a pier, unless proper lines are used to allow for tidal and suction ranges in the area. A trip to the fuel dock just as turbulence strikes may cause serious consequences. A few minutes wait until things quiet down would be prudent. Operations with outboards at launching ramps should be postponed until surge, suction, and wake have subsided.

Small craft under sail should invoke their right of way privileges sympathetically, and not persist in sticking to the channels and forcing the larger vessels to maneuver to clear them. Finally, a small boat anchoring near a channel should choose a point where a change in wind or current would not cause the boat to swing close to or into the fairway. Once

the warning whistle sounds, it may take too long to power up and scurry out of the way of one of those unstoppable big fellows.

Weather has always been a major consideration in navigation of the Hudson. Tidal constants for a river like the Hudson do not have the same significance as when applied to coastal waters. Hudson River tides vary greatly because of prevailing meteorological conditions. Wind and freshwater discharge are probably the most important disturbing factors. At the times of the larger freshets, the tide may be completely masked in the upper portions of the river for a period of several days without any tidal oscillation.

The highest tide recorded at Albany was 23.5 feet above the Sandy Hook Sea Level Datum on May 28, 1913. This was due to a freshet that followed heavy rains and the rapid melting of snow in the Adirondack Mountains. The height below the dam at Troy was 29.5 feet above sea level datum, or eight feet higher than Albany, making a slope of a little more than one foot per mile. The maximum

John E. Flynn pilot launch approaching ship underway off Yonkers pilot station to board a Hudson River State Pilot and disembark a Sandy Hook Pilot in 1967. (Author's collection)

Norrie Point Pilot Station in fall of 1998. South end of Esopus Island is in the foreground. (Captain Tom Sullivan's collection)

downstream current was eight knots. The downtown areas of both Troy and Albany were under a substantial amount of water. The lowest tide recorded at Albany was 2.2 feet below low water on December 8, 1931. When the Great Sacandaga Lake was dammed to catch the waters from the Adirondack Mountains' streams, it helped to control major flooding and freshets in the Mohawk and Hudson River Valleys. In my lifetime, however, I have seen downtown Albany several feet under water, and six to eight knot currents in the river.

When turning a vessel for the return trip to New York from Albany on a normal flood or ebb tide current, the pilot turns the ship's bow into the Rensselaer Turning Basin, then backs the ship until the bow clears the Tidewater Terminal while a tugboat pushes on the port bow. In a spring freshet, it is necessary to pass close to and above the turning basin, then with the help of a tug on the port quarter the pilot must drop the ship stern in the slack water of the turning basin while the swift water current of the freshet swings the bow rapidly downstream. When there are ships tied up at the Albany Port docks and the Rensselaer Tidewater dock, there is little or no room for pilot error. A properly trained and experienced Hudson River pilot completes this maneuver successfully year after year, much to the amazement of many nervous shipmasters.

For many years, during the Memorial, Independence, and Labor Day holidays, the United States Navy sent a destroyer or submarine on a public relations visit to West Point, Poughkeepsie, Kingston, and the Port of Albany. Residents of the surrounding areas could make inspection tours of the craft, and the various cities played host to the ship's officers at special events on shore.

On one occasion when I was assigned to pilot a destroyer from the Brooklyn Navy Yard to the Port of Albany, we had onboard members of the Navy League and their wives. On another occasion, we stopped at the Day Line dock at Newburgh to pick up local dignitaries, and further upriver at Saugerties and Catskill we stopped in mid-stream to pick up more guests from launches.

Destroyers were piloted from the bridge in the usual manner. On a submarine, however, you stood in the open conning tower and directed the wheelsman below through an open hatch. This was not pleasant duty if the weather was windy or rainy.

I remember one severe winter being stuck in heavy ice off the Greenhorn dock in lower Port Ewen aboard an Italian vessel just after World War Two. The ship was bound for the Cargil grain elevator in Albany to load grain for Genoa, Italy. The ship's captain was Jewish, which seemed strange to me. I guess I thought all Italians were Catholics.

Because the vessel had no cargo or ballast, the propeller was half out of the water. Consequently, there was not enough power to propel the ship through the ice. The captain had been warned of this before attempting the voyage, but his countrymen in Italy were so short of food that he wanted to get the grain at any cost. She remained ice-bound for eleven days before she finally arrived at Albany with the aid of an icebreaker and a tug. Association regulations required the pilot to stay aboard for 96 hours (four days) before being relieved by another pilot.

My time aboard this vessel before I was relieved was not unpleasant. The captain and offi-cers were good hosts. Every evening at 6:00 PM, we climbed down the pilot ladder onto the ice and walked the quarter mile to shore. We had befriended an Italian family at the beach area, the Costellos, who came from the same area in Italy as the captain, and they had asked the captain, first mate, and me to have dinner with them every night that we were lodged in the ice. They also invited us to use their telephone. In turn, we brought them provisions from their homeland ashore with us.

Special knowledge of ice conditions is necessary to walk safely ashore on ice in a tidal stream like the Hudson River. If ice is covered by snow, and it usually is, you must carry a stick to prod the area in front of you before you step so as not to step in an air hole. Once a track is made, the prodding stick is no longer needed. You must also carry a plank several feet long, because at the shoreline the rise and fall of the tide break up the ice. The plank is used to walk over this area between the solid ice and the shore.

John E. Flynn at Norrie Point (Staatsburg) during the winter of 1998. (Captain Tom Sullivan's collection)

Author dining on the bridge aboard the tanker *Gulf Tiger* while proceeding up the Hudson in 1955. (Author's collection)

One severe winter in late November, I was piloting the loaded molasses tanker *British Atlas* through heavy ice bound for the port of Albany. My wife and I had planned a family dinner for Thanksgiving Day, a few days hence. When I received my assignment, I had hoped with good luck to be back home for the affair.

We had an uneventful voyage until we reached freshwater ice at Hyde Park. From that point on, the ship's water-cooling intake was being constantly blocked by crushed ice, causing the diesel engine to overheat and requiring the motor to be stopped. The ship would then lie dead in the water for some time until the engineer cleaned out the line. I advised the captain that if this problem continued, we might not get the ship underway again when we got upriver into even heavier ice. The ship's draft was twenty-eight feet, well below any ice problem, but the lower water intake was not in working order. Finally, abreast of Cruger's Island near Tivoli, New York, the *British Atlas* had to stop again, and this time, try as we might, we could not free the vessel. We were icebound.

I did not want to use the ship's wireless for a personal matter, and there was no radio telephone aboard ships in those days. However, I learned that the chief mate had a ham radio aboard, so I asked him if he would help me get a message to my wife. He said, "Sure, let's try." We reached a ham operator on the island of Jamaica in the West Indies. He, in turn, relayed the message to a ham operator in Blowing Rock, North Carolina, in the Great Smokey Mountains. She graciously used a regular long distance phone to contact Norma at our home in Woodcliff Lake, New Jersey. During the conversation with Norma, she said that she was sorry that I was stuck in the ice and would miss Thanksgiving at home.

Fortunately, that did not happen. The next day the larger and more powerful *Esso Raleigh*, also bound for Albany, came by and freed us. Her beam was wider than the *Atlas* so we had no trouble following her track through the ice to our destination. I was home that year to have Thanksgiving dinner with my family. During my fifty-one years of service on the Hudson, however, that was not always the case.

One unusual close call will always be remembered. I was passing Stuyvesant, New York, northbound for Albany on the Finnish cargo ship *Finn Star*, which was loaded with wood pulp for the paper mills in Glens Falls, New York. It was a beautiful sunny afternoon, and I stood on the starboard wing of the open bridge talking to the mate. Our conversation was broken by the crack of a gunshot and a bullet hitting the side of the bridge about three feet from where I stood. The bullet fell to the deck of the bridge, leaving a big dent in the heavy steel of the bridge house. Was it a stray shot from a deer hunter? Why would a hunter aim so that a bullet would end up as high as a ship's bridge? On arrival in Albany, I reported the matter to the New York State Police, who took photographs and confiscated the bullet, but I never heard any more about the incident.

On February 4, 1950, I received an order to pilot the Finnish ship *Finntraveler* to the Port of Albany. I boarded the vessel in mid-stream off Stapleton, Staten Island, and relieved the Sandy Hook pilot who had brought the ship in from *Ambrose Lightship* at the entrance to New York Harbor. (Before the stationary structure known as Ambrose Tower was built, a vessel called *Ambrose Lightship* equipped with navigational aids was anchored at seas signifying the entrance to New York Harbor. A Sandy Hook bar pilot boarded an incoming ship here to direct her into the harbor.) After climbing aboard via the pilot ladder from the launch and making my way to the ship's bridge, I was welcomed by Captain E. Luireboy and we began the long voyage that soon would encounter navigation through heavy Hudson River freshwater ice. The vessel was diesel powered, 455 ft. in length, showing 24 ft. 9 in. draft, loaded with wood pulp for the paper mills at Glen Falls, New York.

We arrived at the anchorage off Port Ewen about 6:30 PM, where we stopped for the night. Prior to the ice season, all navigational aids north of this area are removed from the river. Consequently, deep-draft vessels in these narrow dredged channels and rock cuts carry out no night navigation in winter. Daytime navigation continues with the use of personal landmarks and ranges.

When stopping a ship for the night in heavy ice, it is not necessary to drop an anchor because there is no way a ship can venture out of the track made in the ice. It is necessary, however, before settling in for the night to back up the ship several lengths in order to get some headway in the morning before encountering solid ice ahead. Once the vessel was secure, with a mate and seaman left on the bridge-chartroom area as lookouts, the captain and I left for our quarters to wash for dinner.

Upon completion of a fine dinner, as I always found aboard ships from Scandinavia, Captain Luireboy asked me if I would extend to him the honor of having a sauna with him. I answered "Yes." He asked, " Did you bring a robe and slippers with you?" I replied, "Skipper, I can have a nightcap just as I am." I thought he was offering me some special Finnish drink. The captain laughed heartily and said, "Pilot, it is not a drink. A sauna is a Finnish bath." I was truly embarrassed. Being a Hudson Valley sailor, the word "sauna" was foreign to me at that time.

I carried a small leather bag in which I packed a change of underwear, clean socks, a shirt, toiletries, etc, but I did not come prepared for an extended period of time aboard any vessel. A robe and slippers were not included. Captain Luireboy said that he had an extra robe and slippers, and that he would

The author standing next to a model of the U. S. Coast Guard cutter *West Wind* in the Smithsonian Institution in Washington, DC circa 1960s. The author piloted the *West Wind* on Hudson River icebreaking missions. (Author's collection)

have one of the stewardesses bring them to my cabin. He asked me to meet him in his quarters after I had changed. This I did. Then, we both left his cabin, went three decks below and entered a room.

The wood-paneled room had a large stove-like fixture in the center on which drops of water fell. Three tiered, stadium-style benches lined two of the side walls. We removed our robes and slippers. The captain sat on one side and I sat on the other. Captain Luireboy then pushed a nearby button and a stewardess appeared and handed us each a bottle of beer. It was extremely hot in the room, and we perspired profusely while we carried on an animated conversation.

After a period of time, we walked through a door to an adjoining room that had several showers. The captain immediately got completely under his, but the water was so cold that I was just sticking my toes under the spray. (It was ice water being pumped out of the river.) The Captain said, "Pilot, don't be chicken. It is necessary to get fully under to reap the healthy benefits." Reluctantly, I finally did, but the shock was terrific.

We repeated the procedure in the first two rooms, then went into a third room where there were several tables. The captain jumped up on a table and reclined, and advised me to do the same on the adjoining table. He pressed a button and two stewardesses entered the room. Each carried frozen birch branches in her hands. One stewardess began swatting the captain gently with the branches, and the other one me. After a time, we were flipped over on our stomachs and the swatting took place on our backs. This was my introduction to the Finnish sauna.

Captain Luireboy told me that whole villages take part in this ritual in Finland. A large hole is cut in the ice of a lake, and they all jump into the icy water. We returned to the captain's quarters, had a glass of *aquavit*, a strong Finnish liquor, and socialized until around 10:00 PM.

We arrived in Albany about 12:00 noon the next day. I returned home on a Greyhound bus, and Norma picked me up at the bus terminal on Route 17 in Paramus, New Jersey. The next day, I woke up with a severe cold that my physician later diagnosed as pneumonia.

I boarded the old British tramp ship *Wandby* that was anchored off Quarantine Station, Staten

Ship at Buchanan Terminal near Peekskill, New York, unloading gypsum rock in 1998. (Captain Tom Sullivan's collection)

Island, on October 15, 1959, at 5:00 PM, and the skipper, F. D. Lloyd, greeted me. We got underway just as darkness set in.

As we were passing the Statue of Liberty, Captain Lloyd informed me that he was very tired because they had encountered bad weather at sea for a couple of days, then fog as they approached Ambrose pilot station, so he said he was going to turn in for the night. He said he would have dinner sent to me on the bridge. That was the last time I saw the captain until after docking at the Cargill grain elevator in Albany the next morning when he signed my pilot ticket.

As we sailed by Stevens Institute, Hoboken, New Jersey, a steward appeared on the bridge carrying my dinner on a tray. He lifted up a table supported by a folding arm that was attached to the forward bulkhead under a window, and laid the tray on top. As he left, he said "Pilot, sir, your dinner. Enjoy." The mate on watch moved a tall chair to the table facing the window and invited me to sit down so that I could dine while continuing my piloting duties.

It was an exceptionally dark night, with only a crescent moon in the sky. I removed my small pen flashlight from my pocket and let the beam fall on the plate to see what I was to enjoy for dinner. A large cockroach was partaking of my meal. I quickly turned the flashlight off and made no attempt to eat the food.

The mate noticed that I was not eating and commented several times about it. Finally, I said I was not hungry. He said that I could have told the captain not to send a meal up. I said, "Mr. Mate, come here and I'll show you why." Sure enough, our visitor was still there when I beamed my little

Author on ship's bridge while underway on the Hudson River in 1961. (Author's collection)

flashlight on the plate. The mate said, "Brush him off. That's what we do." I replied, "Sorry mate, I haven't come to that practice yet."

It turned out to be a long night without food. I had a couple cups of warm British tea and two O'Henry chocolate bars, which I always carried with me.

This was the only incident of this type that I recall. Some of the most enjoyable dinners I've had in my life were served while I was sailing on the Hudson River's waters. Eating on several thousand ships of all nations and partaking of a variety of foods prepared in many different styles requires a strong stomach and a willingness to try new things. Obviously, the fare never hurt me. At age 87, I still enjoy a good meal.

Every spring, shad came into the Hudson River to spawn. From Weehawken to Haverstraw Bay, fishermen drove wooden stakes into the river bottom and attached their nets. Many times, the nets measured hundreds of feet long. These nets were not a hazard to steamers or ships because they were in 20-25 feet of water out of the main channel. In the area of Weehawken and Edgewater, however, when the towboats had to round up and land a large flotilla tow at 30th Street, New York City, they were in the way.

It was more of a problem in the upper reaches of the river because the fishermen used large drift nets that, at times, reached across the entire navigable channel. We had no other recourse but to cut right through the nets. I always stopped the vessel's

The coal ship *Thor Hild* discharging at Central Hudson Power Plant at Roseton, New York, in 1998. (Captain Tom Sullivan's collection)

propeller, when I was forced into this situation and I also remained inside the bridge. On occasion, we would hear a gunshot ring out. I hope it was meant as a warning not an attempt at murder. I never heard of anyone aboard a vessel being hit by gunfire, although I did have that one close call as a state pilot, which I mentioned earlier.

When we built a new pilot launch for our Yonkers station, the pilots wanted to honor me for my accomplishments by naming the vessel *Captain Jack Hamilton*. Although I felt deeply honored, I suggested that we should name it for someone outside of our membership. We then unanimously chose *John E. Flynn* after the long-time state senator from Yonkers.

Any number of mechanical failures can pop up aboard a ship while you are underway, and I have had several. Thankfully, it was always in an area where I had the opportunity to drop an anchor or

two, and stop the vessel from grounding or hitting a dock or another vessel. I recall one situation when I was piloting the Holland America Line's *Westerdam* (not the present cruise ship). It was a combination passenger and freighter bound from Albany to their Hoboken terminal with a load of grain. I was proceeding downstream with an ebb tide in the upper Hudson when her motor failed. I could not drop the bow anchor. There was insufficient room for the vessel's length to swing around in the narrow channel. She would have caught up on the banks and laid crossways, blocking the channel. Luckily, *Westerdam* had a stern anchor, which few vessels have. When the vessel lost steerage, we dropped the stern anchor, and the vessel lay safely at anchor until the engine was repaired an hour later. Then, we raised anchor and proceeded to Hoboken, where she picked up passengers bound for The Netherlands.

A pilot must know the "feel" of scores of ships and how they react under various conditions. One day, he may handle a small light-draft freighter, a large high automobile carrier, or someone's million-dollar yacht. Another day, his talents are aboard a deep-laden grain ship or a massive super tanker in

174

foul weather. He must handle each ship differently, yet guide each safely to its destination.

One year, while attending the American Pilots Association's (a state pilot lobbying group stationed in Washington, DC) biannual convention in New Orleans, I learned that the Delaware River pilots were using a portable two-way radio communication system. They were hand radios, which each pilot carried aboard ship. The units were one-watt transistor transceivers weighing 52 ounces, with nickel cadmium rechargeable batteries. This radio system, which had a range of ten miles, per-

Albany was being dredged to 32 feet deep and 400 feet wide. This channel included several rock cuts. While the channel was being deepened, there was to be 200-foot clearance for ships to pass the dredges or drills. Two ships of perhaps 90 feet of beam would present a very big problem should they accidentally meet at these points.

As Association president, I reported my findings to the pilot membership, the State Board of Pilot Commissioners, American Merchant Marine Institute, U. S. Army Corp. of Engineers, U. S. Coast Guard, Port of Albany

Two Esso tugs prepare to undock the tanker *Esso Norfolk* and get her squared away for a trip up the Hudson in October 1950. (Courtesy of SeaRiver Maritime, Inc.)

mitted the pilot to radio ahead when approaching sharp bends. The ship proceeding against the current would slow down and allow the ship with the fair current to proceed.

I immediately realized what an asset this was to Hudson River pilots, because we had several sharp blind turns on the river. In addition, our 27-foot-deep, 300-foot-wide channel between Kingston and

Commission, New York State Legislature, and all major tanker operators. It was approved by all. We rented the equipment, $700 a set, from General Electric Company of Lynchburg, Virginia. A pilot rate adjustment was made to cover the expense.

This was the first time (1962) such equipment was used anywhere in the State of New York. In fact, the Hudson River pilots were the second in the whole American pilotage system to have this equipment. As time went by, ships installed built-in equipment of the same type on their bridges and the handsets became outdated; however, for many years our portables proved to be an essential aid to safe, deep-draft navigation on the waters of the Hudson.

Another major change that I was successful in promoting was shortening the distance of the pilot route. Originally, the northbound route began at the Narrows (Verrazano Bridge) and continued to Albany. It was a very long and hazardous journey, with pilots sometimes spending as many as 16 grueling hours on the bridge. Subsequently, our pilotage responsibilities were from Yonkers to Albany, and vice versa. This was accomplished on March 1, 1967, after several months of negotiations with the New York State Board of Commissioners of Pilots and our brother New York and New Jersey United Sandy Hook Pilots Association. In the winter months, however, when ice conditions would not allow our pilot launch to operate safely at Yonkers, we continued to pilot ships from and to the Narrows.

Motorists traveling high atop the Palisades along the Palisades Interstate Parkway can pull into the parking area at the overlook opposite the Yonkers Pilot station and observe the changing of the pilots in midstream via the Hudson River launch. One can view the Sandy Hook pilot (known as the bar pilot) being relieved of his duties by the river pilot, who then pilots the vessel to its Hudson River destination.

On June 12, 1963, I received an order to pilot the New York State Maritime School ship *Empire State* from its berth at Kings Point, New York, down the East River and up the Hudson to the Port of Albany. The vessel was originally a C3 troop transport with a 26-ft. draft. Her usual officers manned her, with Robert Olivet as her master. The crew consisted of hundreds of cadets in various stages of their education. We left Kings Point about 6:45 AM, and entered the Hudson River off the Battery at 7:50 AM.

The voyage navigating upriver to Hudson was uneventful. Then, in the narrow reaches from Hudson to Albany, the wheelman, no matter which cadet was assigned as helmsman, could not keep the ship straight on course, and wandered from side to side. The *Empire State* nevertheless arrived at its namesake's capital about 7:30 PM, and after turning around to berth head downstream, we were safely secured to the dock at 8:15 PM.

I suspect many of those cadets aboard went on to be captain or engineer on their own ships.

On a Sunday in late May 1965, I had our agent, Joseph Budnick, arrange with the Swedish Transatlantic Line for my daughter Patricia and her fiancé, Joseph Esposito, to be guests on their motorship *Arizona*, which was sailing out of their Brooklyn pier at 7:00 AM for the Port of Albany with myself as pilot. *Arizona* was a beautiful combination passenger and freight carrier 472 ft. long, 65 ft. wide, drawing 23 ft. 10 in. of water, with a speed of 20 knots. Because the vessel was leaving from a dock and would be berthing at the Port of Albany, my daughter and her fiancé would be able to embark by the gangway and not have to climb aboard by the pilot ladder.

Captain Kai J. Palm treated them royally. They enjoyed both breakfast and the mid-day meal, as his table guests. With the vessel underway, I ate my meals on the ship's bridge. The soon-to-be-married couple had a great time viewing river scenes from the bridge and inspecting the engine room and galley. They presented Captain Palm with an appreciation gift for his hospitality and even invited him to the wedding. Patty and Joe now have three daughters, all married, and one son who is a sophomore at Loyola College at Baltimore, Maryland.

Over the years I received many gifts from shipmasters after completing my pilotage duties aboard their vessels. It was usually a bottle of a favorite wine or liquor, but on occasion I received some item that would represent their country's talents. One such gift was a Japanese doll elegantly gowned and holding a beautiful parasol. This doll was 2 1/2 feet tall, and the workmanship was outstanding.

Pilots and guests at the 1973 Hudson River Pilots Association dinner dance at the Hilton Hotel in Tarrytown, New York. (Author's collection)

I received the doll from Captain K. Yah after completing pilotage of the large Japanese bulk carrier *Hiei Maru* to the Port of Albany on July 8, 1973. He presented me with a bottle of sake, then he gave me a large box for my wife that turned out to contain this beautiful doll. Although I did not pilot a large number of ships flying the flag of Japan, I found each one to be exceptionally clean and well equipped, and the captains and officers were universally extremely courteous.

Early on the evening of October 10, 1974, I boarded the United Fruit Line ship *Musa*, registered under British flag and met Captain J. Cruickshanks, her master. She had just completed unloading her cargo of bananas and was bound for Honduras to reload. *Musa* was a trim, modern, diesel vessel, 474 feet 1 inch long, 6,510 gross tons, with a speed of 18 knots. We sailed from Albany at 6:45 PM. The trip downriver was uneventful until the watch change at midnight, when the second mate relieved the chief mate on the bridge.

As always, conversations with the mate took place, and I learned that my bridge partner was Goefrey Marr, ex-skipper of Cunard Line's *Queen Elizabeth*. Naturally, I was surprised to find Captain Marr as second mate on

this ship. (Seamen referred to these as "banana boats.")

So, I took the liberty of asking him why. His explanation was that when Cunard took the two Queens, *Mary* and *Elizabeth*, off the transatlantic run, both skippers were pensioned off. *Queen Mary* went to Los Angeles as a floating hotel, and *Queen Elizabeth* ended up in the Orient as a floating university, where she caught fire and sank. He explained that Cunard's pension was insufficient to keep him in the lifestyle that he was used to, so he took this second mate's job to supplement his income. He was still young enough to spend a few more years at sea.

It was common practice aboard ships of northern European nations not to have heat on the bridge. The theory seemed to be that the officers on watch should not be too comfortable. If you kept them cool, or even cold, they would be more alert. During a winter trip through ice up the cold Hudson River Valley, occupancy of the bridge was usually limited to the pilot and a wheelman. The others enjoyed the comfort of the heated chartroom and only occasionally ventured onto the bridge.

When I received a pilot assignment for a Norwegian, Swedish, Danish, Finnish, or Russian vessel, experience told me how to prepare. I wore a full-length, down-lined overcoat, a pair of down-lined flight boots, down-lined gloves, and a down-lined cap with earflaps. The boots especially served me well. Your feet can get very cold, even numb, standing on a cold steel deck for a period of time.

After World War Two, we had numerous broken down, worn out, old Italian ships carrying grain to war-torn Italy. Most of these vessels had no heat anywhere aboard ship. Food was also scarce. Many times I saw the crew have just diluted wine and bread for meals. I learned to travel prepared for anything. Many nights when I had to sleep on board, my down-lined clothes did double duty as bedclothes. When I arrived home after piloting this type of vessel, I had to empty my bag outside before entering and have everything fumigated before it went into the washing machine.

During my entire career, however, I never caught any infectious disease from any of the several thousand ships that I piloted. The U. S. Department of Health Quarantine Station examines health conditions on vessels entering our waters from foreign countries. They must give a vessel a clean bill of health before they allow it into New York Harbor.

During my years of service as a Hudson River pilot, many outstanding professionals wore the title of Hudson River state pilot with me: Carl Barnes, William Buckley, Martin Wood, Roy Coan, Harold Dederick, John Dearstyne, Jr., William Warner, John Aitken, Raymond Buckley, Grant Bullen, Clarence Plank, Charles Holliday, Edward Ireland, Melvin F. Hamilton, my brother, Colin McCluney, Richard Sherman, James Maloney, Thomas Sullivan, Joseph McKay, Russell Syvertson III, Dominic Cassano, and Frank Cowan.

Piloting is a profession that requires calmness and a strong steady nerve, mixed with the Lord's blessings and good luck. You can have an excellent career for many years, and then have one mishap that may be the only thing for which you are remembered. With God's grace and good luck, I had 26 perfect years of deep-draft Hudson River piloting.

Author and wife, Norma, at the 1974 Hudson River State Pilots Association dinner dance. (Author's collection)

BOAT SPECIFICATIONS

HUDSON RIVER NIGHT BOATS

Adirondack—388 ft. 2 in. long, 50 ft. beam, 12 ft. 1 in. draft, vertical beam engine, cylinder 81 in. by 12 ft., 4 boilers.

C. W. Morse—steel hull, 411 ft. 1 in. long, 50 ft. 8 in. beam, 12 ft. 8 in. draft, vertical beam engine, cylinder 81 in. by 12 ft., 4 boilers.

Rensselaer and *Trojan*—twin steamboats built at T. S. Marvel's Newburgh shipyard in 1909. Steel hull, 317 ft. 2 in. long, 42 ft. 5 in. beam, 12 ft. 5 in. draft, vertical beam engine, cylinder 70 in. by 12 ft. 5 in., 2 boilers.

Berkshire—422 ft. 4 in. long (440 overall), 50 ft. 6 in. beam (88 ft. at the guards), 12 ft. 9 in. draft, vertical beam side-wheeler engine, cylinder 84 in. by 12 ft., 4 boilers.

James A. Baldwin (later the *Central Hudson*)—wooden hull, 240 ft. 10 in. long (later lengthened to 273 ft. 5 in.), vertical beam engine by Fletcher Harrison and Company with a cylinder 60 in. by 11 ft, and 2 boilers on the guard.

Mason L. Weems—221 ft. 7 in. long, 52 ft. 9 in. beam, 12 ft. 3 in. draft, vertical beam engine, cylinder 56 in. by 11 ft., 1 rectangular tubular boiler. Renamed *William F. Romer*.

Daniel S. Miller—wooden hull, 182 ft. 6 in. long, 34 ft. 6 in. beam, 10 ft. 4 in. draft, vertical beam engine built by Fletcher Harrison and Company, cylinder 44 in. by 6 ft., 1 boiler.

John L. Hasbrouck (later the *Marlborough*)—192 ft. 9 in., 34 ft. 1 in. beam, 11 ft. draft, vertical beam engine built by Fletcher Harrison and Company, cylinder 44 in. by 6 ft., rectangular tubular boiler.

Newburgh—iron, 200 ft. long, 32 ft. beam, 11 ft. draft, compound engine, cylinders 26 in. by 45 in. by 36 in. Originally had 2 boilers, but later in life was equipped with 4 Scotch boilers.

Homer Ramsdell—iron, 200 ft. long (later lengthened to 225 ft.), 32 ft. 1 in. beam, 11 ft. 9 in. draft, compound engine by William Wright, cylinders 28 in. by 52 in. by 36 in. Originally had 2 lobster back boilers, but also added 4 Scotch boilers later.

James T. Brett—wood, 184 ft. 5 in. long, 28 ft. 5 in. beam, 8 ft. 3 in. draft, 1 rectangular tubular boiler, vertical beam engine from *Chingarora* with a 40 in. by 12 ft. cylinder.

M. Martin—wood, 191 ft. long, 29 ft. 3 in. beam, 8 ft. 1 in. draft, vertical beam engine by Fletcher Harrison and Company with a cylinder 44 in. by 9 ft., 1 rectangular tubular boiler.

Jacob H. Tremper—wood, 180 ft. long, 30 ft. 2 in. beam, 8 ft. 7 in. draft, vertical beam engine by Fletcher, Harrison and Company with a cylinder 44 in. by 10 ft., 1 rectangular tubular boiler.

Benjamin B. Odell—solid steel hull, 263 ft. 6 in. long, 48 ft. 8-in. beam, 17 ft. 3 in. draft, triple expansion engine, cylinder 26 in. by 41 in. by 68 in. by 36 in., 4 single-ended Scotch boilers, single raked smokestack.

Hudson Taylor—64 ft. 8 in. long (lengthened to 87 ft. in 1885), 13 ft. beam, 4 ft. 4 in. draft.

Poughkeepsie—reinforced steel, single-screw propeller, 206 ft. 8 in. long, 47 ft. beam, 14 ft. 2 in. draft, triple expansion engine, cylinder 18 in. by 29 in. by 37 in. by 30 in., 3 Scotch boilers.

Ansonia—wood, 190 ft. 1 in. long (202 ft. overall), 28 ft. beam, 8 ft. 7 in. of draft, vertical beam engine, cylinder 36 in. by 11 ft. (a larger, 44 in. cylinder was installed later).

Shenandoah—wooden hull, 200 ft. long, 33 ft. beam, 10 ft. 6 in. draft, vertical beam engine, cylinder 36 in. by 10 ft. by McKay and Aldus for the *Nathaniel P. Banks* of 1863, (refitted by John A. Carnie). Renamed *Saugerties*.

Ida—iron hull, 190 ft. long (overall, 200 ft.), 30 ft. 5 in. beam (50 ft. 6 in. overall), 9 ft. 8 in. draft, vertical beam engine, cylinder 40 in. by 10 ft.

City of Catskill—250 ft. long, 35 ft. 8 in. beam, wooden hull, beam engine by Fletcher.

Kaaterskill—265 ft. long, wooden hull with large hog frames and an extensive paddle housing.

Onteora—steel hull, 236 ft. 7 in. long, 35 ft. 2 in. beam, 10 ft. 1 in. draft, vertical beam engine, cylinder 55 in. by 10 ft., 2 boilers.

Clermont—steel hull, 271 ft. 5 in. long, 39 ft. 2 in. beam, 11 ft. 2 in. draft, vertical beam engine, cylinder 55 in. by 11 ft., 2 boilers.

Iroquois—265 ft. long, 37 ft. 6 in. beam, 12 ft. draft, beam engine, cylinder 60 in. by 11 ft.

Mohawk—255 ft. long, 38 ft. beam, 12 ft. draft, beam engine, cylinder 58 in. by 12 ft.

CORNELL STEAMBOAT COMPANY

Telegraph—147 ft. 8 in. long, 21 ft. 8 in. beam, 7 ft. 11 in. draft, vertical beam engine, 30 in. cylinder, stroke 7 ft. 11-in.

Norwich—160 ft. long, 25 ft. 3 in. beam, 9 ft. draft, vertical engine, crosshead by Cunningham & Hall, 2 boilers.

North America—222 ft. long, 25 ft. 6 in. beam, 9 ft. draft, vertical beam engine by James Cunningham, 48 in. cylinder, 11 ft. stroke, 2 boilers.

Manhattan—256 ft. 9 in. long (subsequently lengthened twice), 26 ft. 6 in. beam, 8 ft. 8 in. draft, vertical beam engine, 50-in. cylinder, 11 ft. stroke, 2 boilers.

Thomas Cornell—286 ft. 6 in. long, 38 ft. beam, 10 ft. draft, vertical beam engine from Morgan Boat Works of Buffalo, New York, designed for the lake Erie steamer *Southern Michigan* but never used, rebuilt and installed in Jersey City, 72 in. cylinder, 12 ft. stroke, 2 boilers.

City of Kingston—246 ft. long, 33 ft. 5 in. beam, 10 ft. 5 in. loaded draft, compound engine with cylinders of 30 in. and 56 in., stroke 36 in., 2 Scotch boilers supplied steam at 90 psi, Neafie & Levy propeller turned at 100 rendering an IHP of 1,400.

Cornell—steel hull, 149 ft. 7 in. long, 28 ft. beam, 15 ft. 2 in. of draft, gross tonnage of 435, 2 smokestacks.

John H. Cordts—wooden hull, 114 ft. 6 in. long, 25 ft. beam, 12 ft. draft, compound engine, cylinders 28 in. and 52 in., stroke 40 in., 2 boilers.

J. C. Hartt—wooden hull, 115 ft. 7 in. long, 27 ft. beam, 15 ft. draft, compound engine, cylinders 24 in. and 22 in., stroke 38 in.

Edwin H. Mead—steel hull, propeller driven, 122 ft. 4 in. long, 26 ft. beam, 11 ft. 4 in. draft.

Geo. W. Washburn—iron hull, 123 ft. long, 26 ft. beam, 10 ft. 6 in. draft, compound engine, cylinders 24 in. and 48 in., stroke 36 in., 2 smokestacks.

Osceola—wooden hull, 118 ft. long, 26 ft. 4 in. beam, 9 ft. 3 in. draft, compound engine, cylinders 24 in. and 42 in., stroke 34 in.

Perseverance—155 ft. long, 31 ft. 6 in. beam, 18 ft. 5 in. draft, triple expansion engine, cylinders 17 in., 25 in., and 43 in., stroke 30 in., 2 boilers.

E. L. Levy—steel hull, 104 ft. 5 in. long, 21 ft. 5 in. beam, 9 ft. draft, 550 horsepower.

E. C. Baker—steel hull, 102 ft. long, 21 ft. 6 in. beam, 9 ft. draft, 550 horsepower.

S. L. Crosby—98 ft. long, 22 ft. 5 in. beam, 11 ft. draft, 450 horsepower.

Bear—wooden hull, 95 ft. 5 in. long, 24 ft. 7 in. beam, 14 ft. draft, compound engine, cylinders 18 in. and 38 in., stroke 26 in., 550 horsepower.

Burro—identical dimensions to *Bear*.

Senator Rice—wooden hull, propeller, 90 ft. 1 in. long, 20 ft. 2 in. beam, 10 ft. draft, compound engine, cylinders 15 in. and 34 in., stroke 36 in.

R. G. Townsend—81 ft. 6 in. long, 20 ft. 5 in. beam, 8 ft. 8 in. draft.

G. C. Adams—wooden hull, propeller, 83 ft. 6 in. long, 20 ft. beam, 9 ft. draft.

George W. Pratt—76 ft. 5 in. long, 17 ft. 5 in. beam, 8 ft. draft, high pressure engine, 300 horsepower.

W. N. Bavier—steel hull, propeller, 82 ft. 4 in. long, 21 ft. 5 in. beam, 11 ft. 4 in. draft; engine, house, and joiner work installed at the Rondout shops, 300 horsepower.

Victoria—wooden hull, propeller, 82 ft. long, 17 ft. beam, 8 ft. 8 in. draft.

Edwin Terry—iron hull, propeller, 84 ft. 5 in. long, 19 ft. 2 in. beam, 10 ft. 2 in. draft.

Ellen M. Ronan—wooden hull, propeller, 79 ft. 4 in. long, 18 ft. 6 in. beam, 7 ft. 6 in. draft.

John D. Schoonmaker—wooden hull, propeller, 82 ft. 5 in. long, 17 ft. 9 in. beam, 7 ft. draft.

Rob—74 ft. 8 in. long, 18 ft. 2 in. beam, 7 ft. 5 in. draft.

Wm. S. Earl—55 ft. long, 14 ft. 8 in. beam, 5 ft. 8 in. draft, 150 horsepower.

Cornell #41 (originally the *Eli B. Conine*)—diesel powered, propeller, 85 ft. 7 in. long, 21 ft. beam, 11 ft. 4-in. draft, 450 horsepower.

Cornell (originally the steamer *Charlie Lawrence*, built in Philadelphia in 1874 for the Knickerbocker Ice Company)—diesel, 74 ft. long, 17 ft. 3 in. beam, 7 ft. 2 in. draft, 350 horsepower.

Cornell #21 (originally the *J. H. Williams*, built in Newburgh in 1904)—steel hull, propeller, 75 ft. 6 in. long, 19 ft. 5 in. beam, 11 ft. draft.

Coe F. Young—wooden hull, propeller, 74 ft. 3 in. long, 19 ft. beam, 8 ft. 6 in. draft, 250 horsepower.

Saranac—wooden hull, propeller, 69 ft. long, 18 ft. 8 in. beam, 7 ft. 4 in. draft.

Geo. N. Southwick—69 ft. long, 17 ft. 6 in. beam, 7 ft. draft.

George Field—55 ft. 8 in. long, 15 ft. beam, 6 ft. 2 in. draf.t

G. W. Decker—68 ft. 1 in. long, 19 ft. 6 in. beam, 8 ft. 3 in. draft, compound engine, cylinders 13 in. and 29 in., stroke 18 in., 271 horsepower.

J. G. Rose—68 ft.1 in. long, 19 ft. 6 in. beam, 8 ft. draft.

H. D. Mould—propeller, 67 ft. long, 18 ft. beam, 7 ft. draft.

Eugenia—propeller, 43 ft. long, 12 ft. beam, 5 ft. draft.

Wilson P. Foss—64 ft. 2 in. long, 18 ft. beam, 8 ft. 1-in. draft.

C. W. Morse—154 ft. 4 in. long, 30 ft. beam, 17 ft. 6-inch draft, 1,050 horsepower.

Dr. David Kennedy—46 ft. 1 in. long, 13 ft. 1 in. beam, 5 ft. 6 in. draft.

Imperial—107 ft. 5 in. long, 21 ft. 6 in. beam, 11 ft. draft.

Princess—107 ft. long, 22 ft. 2 in. beam, 10 ft. 7 in. draft.

Ira M. Hedges—76 ft. 6 in. long, 18 ft. beam, 9 ft. 8 in. draft.

Stirling Tomkins (built as *Artisan* in 1919)—126 ft. long, 29 ft. 9 in. beam, 13 ft. 7 in. draft, 1000 horsepower.

HUDSON RIVER DAY LINE

Daniel Drew—length of 224 ft., beam 30 ft. 6 in., vertical beam engine by Neptune Iron Works, cylinder 60 in. by 10 ft.

Armenia—length 181 ft. 9 in., beam 27 ft. 6 in.; twice lengthened.

Chauncey Vibbard—267 ft. long, 34 ft. 9 in. beam, vertical beam engine by Fletcher Harrison and Company, cylinder 55 in. by 12 ft. with 2 boilers on guards. These measurements were altered twice during the life of the vessel as a Day Liner.

Albany—iron hull, length 284 ft. (lengthened in 1893 to 325 ft. 6 in.), beam 73 ft. 3 in., draft 4 ft., a Fletcher and Harrison vertical beam engine, cylinder 73 in. by 12 ft., 3 boilers.

New York—steel hull, original length 301 ft. (lengthened in 1898 to 335 ft.), beam 40 ft. 2 in., 11 ft. draft, engine cylinder 75 in. by 12 ft., 3 boilers forward of the engine.

Hendrick Hudson—length 390 ft., beam 82 ft., draft 10 ft. 4 1/2 in., inclined compound engine by W. & A. Fletcher, cylinders 45 in., 70 in., and 70 in. by 7 ft., 6 boilers, 6,200 horsepower, passenger capacity 5,500.

Mary Powell—wooden hull, 267 ft. by 34 ft. 6 in (lengthened in 1862-1863 to 288 ft.), draft 9 ft. 2 in. Fletcher Harrison and Company built her vertical beam engine. The original 62 in. by 12 ft. cylinder was replaced in 1874-75 by one 72 in. by 12 ft. She had 2 boilers on guards.

Robert Fulton—346 ft. long, beam 76 ft. 2 in., 8 ft. 2 1/2 in. loaded draft, vertical beam engine, cylinder 75 in. by 12 ft., 3 boilers, 3850 horsepower.

Washington Irving—414 ft. 5 in. long, 86 ft. beam, 10 ft. 1 in. loaded draft, inclined engine, cylinders 45 in., 70 in., and 70 in. by 7 ft., with 6 boilers, 6,200 horsepower.

De Witt Clinton, as rebuilt (formerly the *Manhattan*)—332 ft. long, 48 ft. 1 in. beam, 16 ft. 1 in. draft, two triple expansion engines by Harlan and Hollingsworth, cylinders 23 1/2 in., 37 1/2 in., 42 in., and 42 in. by 3 ft., 6 boilers.

Alexander Hamilton—349 ft. long, 77 ft. beam, 8 ft. 4 in. loaded draft, triple expansion inclined engine, cylinders 36 1/2 in., 56 in., and 85 in. by 6 ft., 4 boilers, 3,900 horse power.

Chauncey M. Depew—194 ft. 11 in. long, 35 ft. 6 in. wide, 11 ft. 7 in. loaded draft, triple expansion engine, cylinders 16 in., 26 in., 30 in., and 30 in. by 2 ft., 1 boiler, single screw.

Peter Stuyvesant—269 ft. 6 in. long, 60 ft. beam, 13 ft. 5-1/2 in. loaded draft, single screw with a triple expansion engine, cylinders 25 in., 40 in., 47 in., and 47 in. by 3 ft., 4 boilers, 2,700 horsepower.

OTHERS

South America—252 ft. 6 in. long, 27 ft. beam, 9 ft. 6 in. draft, vertical beam engine by James Cunningham, 54 in. cylinder, 11 ft. stroke, 2 boilers.

Knickerbocker—291 ft. 6 in. long, 31 ft. 6 in. beam, 9 ft. 6 in. draft, vertical beam engine built for *De Witt Clinton* in 1828, rebuilt by Hogg & Delamater, 65 in. cylinder, 10 ft. stroke.